THE
HISTORY OF
ITALY

THE HISTORY OF ITALY

Charles L. Killinger

The Greenwood Histories of the Modern Nations
Frank W. Thackeray and John E. Findling, Series Editors

Greenwood Press
Westport, Connecticut • London

Library of Congress Cataloging-in-Publication Data

Killinger, Charles L.
   The history of Italy / Charles L. Killinger.
     p. cm.—(The Greenwood histories of the modern nations, ISSN 1096–2905)
   Includes bibliographical references and index.
   ISBN 0–313–31483–7 (alk. paper)
   1. Italy—History. I. Title. II. Series.
  DG467.K55 2002
  945—dc21   2002016620

British Library Cataloguing in Publication Data is available.

Library of Congress Catalog Card Number: 2002016620
ISBN: 0–313–31483–7
ISSN: 1096–2905

First published in 2002

Greenwood Press, 88 Post Road West, Westport, CT 06881
An imprint of Greenwood Publishing Group, Inc.
www.greenwood.com

Printed in the United States of America

The paper used in this book complies with the
Permanent Paper Standard issued by the National
Information Standards Organization (Z39.48–1984).

10 9 8 7 6 5 4 3 2 1

To Pam
whose inspiration planted the seeds for this book,
whose love and support sustained it through the difficulties,
and whose spirit always lifts;
and to Valentina and Marco,
fuzzy friends, faithful companions, sources of endless comfort.

Contents

Series Foreword

The Greenwood Histories of the Modern Nations series is intended to provide students and interested laypeople with up-to-date, concise and analytical histories of many of the nations of the contemporary world. Not since the 1960s has there been a systematic attempt to publish a series of national histories, and, as series editors, we believe that this series will prove to be a valuable contribution to our understanding of other countries in our increasingly interdependent world.

Over thirty years ago, at the end of the 1960s, the Cold War was an accepted reality of global politics, the process of decolonization was still in progress, the idea of a unified Europe with a single currency was unheard of, the United States was mired in a war in Vietnam, and the economic boom of Asia was still years in the future. Richard Nixon was president of the United States, Mao Tse-tung (not yet Mao Zedong) ruled China, Leonid Brezhnev guided the Soviet Union, and Harold Wilson was prime minister of the United Kingdom. Authoritarian dictators still ruled most of Latin America, the Middle East was reeling in the wake of the Six-Day War, and Shah Reza Pahlavi was at the height of his power in Iran. Clearly, the past thirty years have been witness to a great deal of historical change, and it is to this change that this series is primarily addressed.

With the help of a distinguished advisory board, we have selected nations whose political, economic, and social affairs mark them as among the most important in the waning years of the twentieth century, and for each nation we have found an author who is recognized as a specialist in the history of that nation. These authors have worked most cooperatively with us and with Greenwood Press to produce volumes that reflect current research on their nation and that are interesting and informative to their prospective readers.

The importance of a series such as this cannot be underestimated. As a superpower whose influence is felt all over the world, the United States can claim a "special" relationship with almost every other nation. Yet many Americans know very little about the histories of the nations with which the United States relates. How did they get to be the way they are? What kind of political systems have evolved there? What kind of influence do they have in their own region? What are the dominant political, religious, and cultural forces that move their leaders? These and many other questions are answered in the volumes of this series.

The authors who have contributed to this series have written comprehensive histories of their nations, dating back to prehistoric time in some cases. Each of them, however, has devoted a significant portion of the book to events of the past thirty years, because the modern era has contributed the most to contemporary issues that have an impact on U.S. policy. Authors have made an effort to be as up-to-date as possible so that readers can benefit from the most recent scholarship and a narrative that includes very recent events.

In addition to the historical narrative, each volume in this series contains an introductory overview of the country's geography, political institutions, economic structure, and cultural attributes. This is designed to give readers a picture of the nation as it exists in the contemporary world. Each volume also contains additional chapters that add interesting and useful detail to the historical narrative. One chapter is a thorough chronology of important historical events, making it easy for readers to follow the flow of a particular nation's history. Another chapter features biographical sketches of the nation's most important figures in order to humanize some of the individuals who have contributed to the historical development of their nation. Each volume also contains a comprehensive bibliography, so that those readers whose interest has been sparked may find out more about the nation and its history. Finally, there is a carefully prepared topic and person index.

Readers of these volumes will find them fascinating to read and useful in understanding the contemporary world and the nations that comprise it.

As series editors, it is our hope that this series will contribute to a heightened sense of global understanding as we embark on a new century.

Frank W. Thackeray and John E. Findling
Indiana University Southeast

Preface

Some twenty-five years ago I began my serious study of Italian history under the tutelage of Philip V. Cannistraro at the Florida State University center in Florence. From the day Phil took me to the Italian state archives in Rome and let me hold Mussolini's handwritten order for the June 1940 invasion of France, I somehow understood the excitement that Italian historical research could provide. From Phil's inspiration and unselfish counsel eventually flowed a number of articles and presentations on various aspects of modern Italian history, several books, and boundless ideas for new projects. At the same time, my loving wife, even more enamored of Italy, has insisted on frequent return trips, so that we have come to regard Italy as a kind of second home. However, in spite of our travels and study, the task of writing a comprehensive history of Italy seemed overwhelming. Comfort came only when my colleagues in Italian history confessed a similar sense of inadequacy. In part, the hesitation to accept a project of this magnitude is a product of professional training; many, if not most historians, rely heavily on documentation provided by original sources and shy away from painting with the broad strokes that this book requires. In the process of writing, I have developed a renewed respect for the historical narrative.

Deciding ultimately to take the challenge, against the advice of some trusted friends, I made the leap into the abyss. Is it possible to write an account of the totality of Italian history in fewer than three hundred pages? Readers will ultimately make that judgment. I only hope that some readers find a measure of the enjoyment in reading the book that the writing process has afforded me. What became immediately obvious in writing was the indispensability of experts and meticulous readers. Thus my gratitude for the assistance rendered extends well beyond the normal debts.

At the risk of omitting a valued contribution, I will extend a gesture of thanks to the many who have helped. Alexander De Grand, Richard Crepeau, and Frank Thackeray directed me to this project and provided expertise. Barbara Rader, Kevin Ohe, and David Palmer contributed careful editorial guidance. Throughout the project, I have been exceptionally fortunate to benefit from the generosity of numerous friends and colleagues. Judi Delisle and Paulette Smith provided imaginative and untiring bibliographical support. Pamela Killinger, Glenn Hayden, Sherry Graber, and Brad Camp patiently read the entire manuscript and offered invaluable advice. Philip Cannistraro, John J. Reich, Roland Sarti, David D. Roberts, H. James Burgwyn, James E. Miller, Cheryl Sowder, Bruce F. Pauley, Jared S. Graber, Robert Flick, and J. Scott Perry added invaluable, expert criticism. The book would have been impossible without their help. Nonetheless, in spite of the support of legions of generous professionals, I take full responsibility for any errors of fact or judgment found herein.

Timeline of Historical Events

THE CLASSICAL PERIOD

753 B.C.	Traditional founding of Rome
509	Romans expel King Tarquin the Proud
499	Romans defeat Latin League at Battle of Lake Regillus
494	Plebeians challenge patricians in First Secession
493	Cassian Treaty pledges "peace between Romans and all Latin cities"
450	Twelve Tables codify Roman law
390	Gauls defeat Roman army at River Allia
295	Romans defeat Samnites at Battle of Sentinum
264–241	Romans defeat Carthaginians in First Punic War
218–201	Romans defeat Carthaginians in Second Punic War despite Hannibal's successes
149–146	Rome wins Third Punic War, severely punishing Carthaginians
118	Romans add province of southern Gaul
91–88	Roman "Social Wars"
60	First Triumvirate is formed: Pompey, Julius Caesar, Crassus

49	Julius Caesar crosses Rubicon from Gaul to Rome to confront Pompey
46	Roman Senate makes Caesar dictator for ten years
44	Conspirators murder Caesar
43	Second Triumvirate: Octavian, Antony, Lepidus
31	Octavian defeats Antony and Cleopatra at Battle of Actium
27 B.C.–A.D. 14	Augustus reigns
A.D. 41–68	Julio-Claudian dynasty
68–96	Flavian dynasty
96–192	Antonine dynasty
284–305	Diocletian reigns as emperor
306–337	Constantine the Great rules as emperor
313	Constantine issues Edict of Milan, legalizing Christianity
410	Visigoths under Alaric take Rome

THE MIDDLE AGES

489	Ostrogoth Theodoric invades peninsula
535	Byzantine emperor Justinian invades
773	Charlemagne leads Frankish armies into peninsula
800	Pope Leo III crowns Charlemagne Emperor in St. Peter's Basilica
827	Arabs invade Sicily
1025–1091	Normans invade Sicily
1176	Lombard League defeats Frederick Barbarossa at Battle of Legnano
1183	Peace of Constance acknowledges autonomy of Italian cities
1266	Charles of Anjou defeats Germans at Battle of Benevento and becomes king of Naples and Sicily
1282	Sicilians expel Angevins in Sicilian Vespers

RENAISSANCE ITALY

1305–1377	Papacy moves to Avignon
c. 1306	Giotto paints frescoes in Arena Chapel, Padua
c. 1320	Dante publishes *Divine Comedy*
1348–1353	Boccaccio publishes *Decameron*
	Petrarch publishes *Canzoniere*
1347	"Black Death" ravages Italy

1378	Ciompi uprising in Florence
1413–1417	Donatello sculpts *St. Mark* and *St. George*
1418	Brunelleschi is chosen to construct *duomo* in Florence
1430	Turkish fleet defeats Venetians
1434	Medici family of bankers seizes power in Florence
1454	Italian League is formed at Peace of Lodi
1469–1492	"Lorenzo the Magnificent" rules Florence
1475	Botticelli paints *Adoration of the Magi*
1478	Pazzi Conspiracy against Florence
c. 1478–1482	Botticelli paints *Primavera* and *Birth of Venus*
1494	French invade Italy, initiating two centuries of foreign occupation of peninsula
	Savanarola begins moral crusade in Florence
1495–1506	Leonardo da Vinci paints *The Last Supper* and *Mona Lisa*
1504	Michelangelo completes *David*
1505–1509	Michelangelo paints Sistine Chapel ceiling
1509–1511	Raphael paints *School of Athens*
1513	Machiavelli publishes *The Prince*

EARLY MODERN ITALY

1525	French lose Battle of Pavia
1527	Spanish sack Rome and capture pope
1559	First Index of Forbidden Books marks Counter-Reformation
	Treaty of Cateau-Cambresis affirms Spanish dominance of peninsula
1564	Guicciardini publishes *History of Italy*
1599–1602	Caravaggio paints life of St. Matthew, *Conversion of St. Paul*, and *Crucifixion of St. Peter*
	Bernini sculpts *Fountain of the Four Rivers*, Rome
1720	Piedmont acquires island of Sardinia
1723	Giannone publishes history of Naples
1725	Vico publishes *Principles of a New Science Concerning the Common Nature of Nations*
1764	Beccaria publishes *Of Crimes and Punishments*
1765–1790	Grand Duke Peter Leopold governs Tuscany
1773	Jesuit order is expelled

THE FRENCH REVOLUTION, NAPOLEONIC ERA, AND RESTORATION

1796	Napoleon Bonaparte invades Italy
1797	Napoleon signs Treaty of Campo Formio, validating control of Italian territory
1798	Napoleon divides Italy into Cisalpine, Ligurian, and Roman republics
1799	Sanfedista army captures Naples from French and restores King Ferdinand
1800	Napoleon wins Battle of Marengo
1801	France acquires Italian territory from Austria in Treaty of Lunéville
1806	Napoleon's army occupies Naples, driving Ferdinand IV into exile
1815	Metternich convenes Congress of Vienna
1818	Leopardi publishes "All'Italia"
1827	Manzoni publishes I promessi sposi
	Mazzini joins carbonari
1829	Rossini composes William Tell
1831	Revolutions erupt throughout peninsula
	Mazzini founds Young Italy
1832	Pellico publishes Le Mie Prigioni
1833	Mazzini flees to Switzerland
1835	Bellini composes I Puritani
1843	Gioberti publishes Il Primato
1844	Balbo publishes Le speranze d'Italia
1846	D'Azeglio publishes Degli ultimi casi di Romagna
	Pius IX (Pio Nono) is elected pope
1848	Revolutions sweep through peninsula
	King Carlo Alberto issues Il Statuto, Piedmontese constitution
	Austrians defeat Carlo Alberto's armies at Custoza

THE RISORGIMENTO AND THE CREATION OF ITALY

1849	Austrians defeat Piedmontese at Battle of Novara; Carlo Alberto abdicates in favor of his son, Vittorio Emanuele II
	Mazzini organizes government of Roman Republic
	Tuscans drive Grand Duke Leopold II into refuge in Gaeta

	Austrians restore power in Tuscany, Parma, Modena, and Venetia
	French forces crush Roman Republic
	Bourbons retake Naples and Sicily
1850	French restore Pope Pius IX to Vatican
	Cavour joins Piedmontese cabinet
1854	Cavour leads Piedmont into Crimean War against Russia
1857	Manin and Pallavicino organize National Society
1859–1860	Second War for Independence
1860	Garibaldi's "Thousand" volunteers invade Sicily
	Garibaldi accompanies Vittorio Emanuele II on triumphal march through Naples
1861	Italian Parliament declares Kingdom of Italy
1866	Austria cedes Venetia to Italy at Peace of Prague
1868	Vatican decrees *Non Expedit*, prohibiting Catholics from participating in Italian politics
1870	Italian troops occupy Rome, completing Risorgimento
1871	Parliament passes Law of Papal Guarantees; Pius IX refuses, declaring himself a "prisoner in the Vatican"
	Verdi composes *Aida*
1876	Depretis comes to power in "parliamentary revolution"
1882	Costa founds Workers' Party and wins seat in Parliament
	Italy signs Triple Alliance
1887	Crispi comes to power
	Verdi composes *Otello*
1890	Mascagni composes *Cavalleria Rusticana*
1891	Pope Leo XIII issues encyclical *Rerum novarum*
1892	Italian Socialist Party is founded
	Leoncavallo's *Pagliacci* is premiered
	Giolitti serves first term as prime minister
1896	Ethiopians defeat Italians in Battle of Adua
1898	*Fatti di Maggio* occurs in Milan
1899	Agnelli organizes Fiat
1896–1900	Puccini composes *La Boheme* and *Tosca*

THE ERA OF GIOLITTI AND WORLD WAR I

1900	King Umberto is assassinated
1903	Corradini, Papini, and Prezzolini found the magazine *Il Regno*

1904	Puccini composes *Madame Butterfly*
1906	Carducci becomes first Italian to win Nobel Prize for literature
1909	Marconi wins share of Nobel Prize
	Futurist Manifesto is issued
1910	Corradini and Federzoni establish Italian Nationalist Association
1911	Giolitti expands franchise
	Italy declares war on Ottoman Empire, annexes Libya
1912	Left-wing Socialists prevail at PSI Congress, name Mussolini editor of *Avanti!*
	Italy renews Triple Alliance
1913	Giolitti makes "Gentiloni Pact"
1914	Italy maintains neutrality in World War I
	Mussolini, expelled from PSI, launches *Il Popolo d'Italia*
1915	"Radiant May"
	Italy signs Pact of London; declares war against Austria
1917	Italian army is routed at Caporetto
1918	Italian army drives Austrians into retreat at Vittorio Veneto

THE FASCIST ERA AND WORLD WAR II

1919	Italian delegation leaves Paris Peace Conference
	D'Annunzio occupies Fiume
	PPI and PSI win sweeping support in national elections
	Mussolini forms Fascio di Combattimento at Piazza San Sepolcro (Milan)
1919–1920	"Red Biennium"
1920	"Occupation of the factories"
1921	Fascist "punitive raids" on peasant leagues, Socialist, labor, and newspaper offices
	Mussolini is one of thirty-six Fascists elected to Chamber of Deputies
	Pirandello publishes *Six Characters in Search of an Author*
1922	Bonomi resigns as prime minister, is replaced by Facta
	Fascist March on Rome
	Mussolini establishes Fascist Grand Council
1923	Acerbo Law and Palazzo Chigi Accords
1924	Mussolini's national list wins decisive victory in national elections

	Matteotti crisis
	Italy acquires Fiume
1925	Mussolini deliveres defiant speech to parliament
	Mussolini makes himself "Head of Government"
1926	"Law for the Defense of the State" establishes OVRA (secret police)
	Mussolini removes managers of *Il Corriere della Sera* and *La Stampa*, shuts down opposition newspapers
	Mussolini establishes Ministry of Corporations
1928	Decree requires journalists to join Fascist Journalists' Association
1929	Lateran Accords
1931	Fascist oath of university professors
1933	Mussolini creates IRI (Institute for Industrial Reconstruction)
1935	Italy invades Ethiopia
1936	Mussolini declares Italian Empire
	Italy forms "Axis" with Germany, sends troops into Spanish Civil War
1937	Mussolini reorganizes propaganda agencies under Ministry of Popular Culture
	Italy withdraws from League of Nations
1938	Mussolini replaces Chamber of Deputies with Chamber of Fasces and Corporations
	Manifesto of Fascist Racism
	Mussolini outlaws American movies
1939	Italy and Germany agree to "Pact of Steel"
1940	Mussolini declares war on France and Britain, invades France and Greece
1943	Allied forces invade Sicily
	Fascist Grand Council votes to remove Mussolini from power
	King appoints General Badoglio head of military government
	Italian government announces armistice with Allies
	German commandos rescue Mussolini, transport him to Lake Garda to establish Salò Republic
	Allied forces land south of Rome
1944	Allied troops liberate Rome
1945	Mussolini and mistress are captured and executed by partisans

THE ITALIAN REPUBLIC

1946	Italians vote to replace kingdom with republic
1945–1948	Neo-realist films directed by De Sica, Visconti, Rossellini, and others
1947	Publication of Gramsci's prison letters and notebooks
1948	Christian Democrats win first parliamentary elections
	Italy joins Organization for European Economic Cooperation
1948–1952	U.S. Marshall Plan assistance
1949	Italy joins NATO
c. 1950–1958	Italy's "Economic Miracle"
1951	Italy joins European Coal and Steel Community
1953–1957	Fellini's *I vitelloni, La Strada, Nights of Cabiria*
1957	Italy joins European Economic Community
1962	Pope John XXIII calls Second Vatican Council
1963–1968	DC-PSI Center-Left coalition
1961–1964	Pasolini's *Accatone, Mamma Roma, The Gospel According to St. Matthew*
1964–1971	Bertolucci's *Before the Revolution, The Conformist*
1968	Student movement spreads through Italy
1969	"Hot Autumn": militant strikes among northern workers
1970	Divorce is legalized
c. 1970–1979	Terrorism of "years of lead"
1973	PCI leader Berlinguer announces "historic compromise" with progressive political groups
1975	Family Law of 1975 establishes gender equality
1977	Workplace anti-discrimination law
1978	Polish-born Karol Wojtyla is elected Pope John-Paul II, first non-Italian in 455 years
	Red Brigades kidnap former prime minister Moro
	Comprehensive national health service is established
	Abortion is legalized
1979	PCI secedes from coalition of "national solidarity"
1981	Republican Spadolini becomes first non-DC prime minister in thirty-five years
1982	*Mafia* murders General Dalla Chiesa
1983–1987	Socialist Craxi governs
1987	Maxi-trial of nearly 500 alleged *mafiosi* in Palermo

1991, 1993	Referenda radically modify proportional system of elections
1992	*Mafia* murders Falcone and Borsellino
1992–1994	DC, PCI, and PSI are dissolved
1993	*Tangentopoli* scandal spreads
1994	Center-Left Progressisti and Center-Right Polo delle Libertà coalitions emerge
1996	Prodi and D'Alema lead Center-Left Ulivo coalition to victory
1997	Fo is named Nobel Laureate in Literature
1998	Italy meets Maastricht standards, gains admission to European Monetary Union
2001	Berlusconi and Center-Right Casa delle Libertà coalition is elected to power

1

An Introduction to Modern Italy

The modern Italian state traces its origins to early 1861 when the first Parliament proclaimed the Kingdom of Italy. The significance of the movement for Italian unification, known as the Risorgimento, cannot be fully appreciated without understanding that Italy had remained disunited since the decline of the Roman Empire some fourteen centuries earlier. Subjugated in various geographical regions by wave after wave of outside powers—Muslims, Normans, Germans, French, Spanish, and Austrians among them—Italians had repeatedly and unsuccessfully challenged foreign rule. Finally, in the second half of the nineteenth century, they began to make progress toward liberating the peninsula by driving out the Austrians and the Spanish Bourbons in a succession of military and diplomatic victories. The armies of the king of Piedmont-Sardinia and the bold maneuvers of the gallant patriot Giuseppe Garibaldi contributed to the military success. All the while, the international diplomacy and astute leadership of Count Camillo di Cavour, the prime minister of Piedmont, proved instrumental. Italians did not complete unification until the acquisition of Venetia in 1866 and Rome in 1870, and even then they had to overcome centuries of lingering fragmentation in building a nation. At the time of the declaration of the kingdom, former Piedmontese prime minister Massimo d'Azeglio declared: "We have made Italy; now we must make Italians."

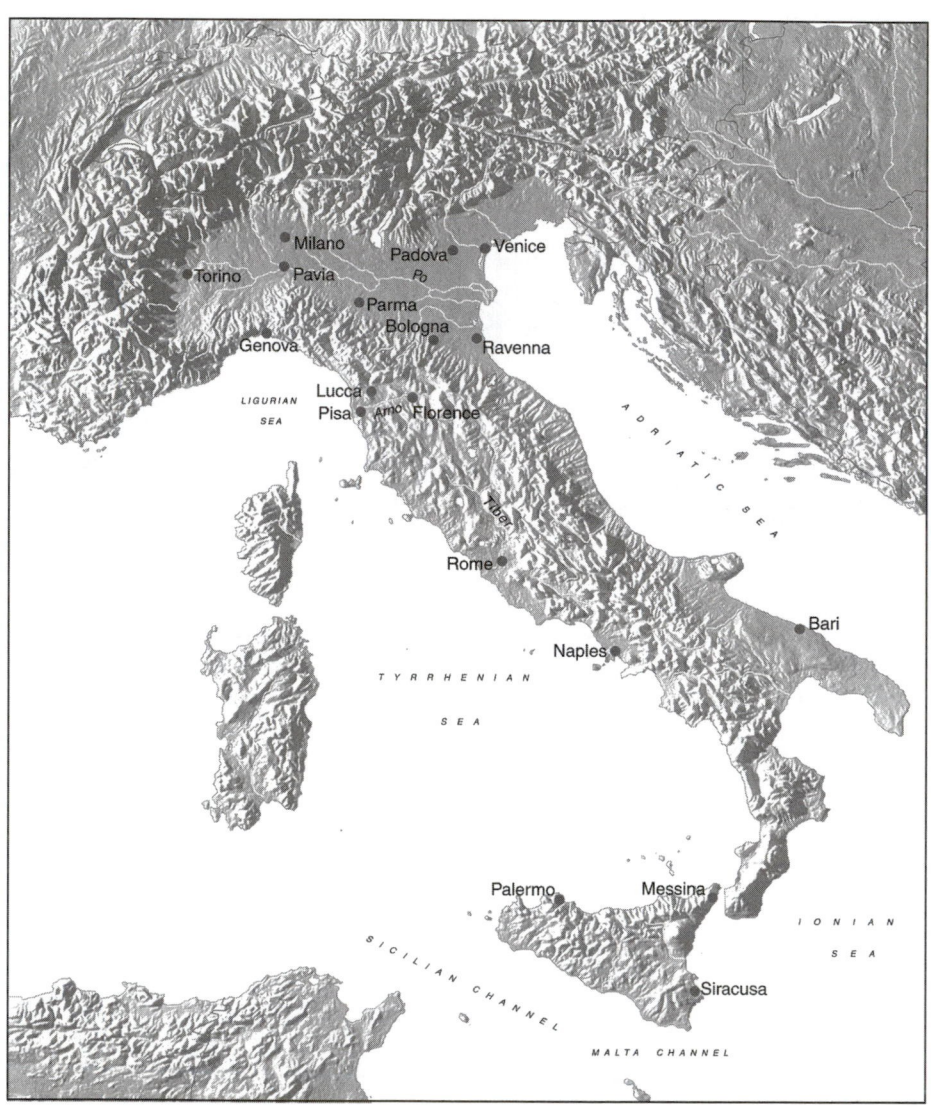

The topography of the Italian peninsula. Digital Wisdom®, Inc.

D'Azeglio's statement has resonated over the years because it captures an essential quality of the Italian peninsula, its people, and its culture. Divided by geography and tradition, Italians have remained fiercely loyal to family, town, and region—and distrustful of central authority. Even though this tendency toward local identity has added great cultural variety, it has at the same time impeded political unity and economic modernization. Similarly, the emphasis on family, kinship, and church, deeply embedded in traditional Italian culture, has retarded the process of nation building in this relatively young state. Even today, as Italy moves toward full integration into the emerging European Union—after a period of unprecedented modernization and standardization of life and culture—it retains historical influences as strong as any in the Western world. Consequently, Italy cannot be understood without an appreciation of its history and geography.

Italy occupies a long, narrow peninsula that juts into the Mediterranean Sea, carving a profile that many have likened to a boot. Roughly the combined size of the U.S. states of Florida and Georgia, about 116,000 square miles, Italy is now subdivided into twenty regions and ninety-four provinces. Its rugged mountain ranges highlight the peninsula in the shape of an oblique T, the Alps "crossing the T" and acting as a partial barrier to northern Europe, the Apennine range dividing east from west.

The population of roughly sixty million is remarkably stable and homogeneous in religion and language, although strong regional dialects persist. Its rate of population growth, 0.2 percent per year, is among the lowest in the world. The Italian government requires fourteen years of formal education and reports a 98 percent literacy rate. All Italians are eligible to vote upon reaching age eighteen. Italians are predominantly Roman Catholic, although the attitudes of the general population toward the Vatican have long been considered skeptical. In fact, this is only one of a number of paradoxes that observers have found in Italian culture. There seem to persist in Italy ironic tensions not only between the religious and the secular, but between the local and the national, between individualism and conformity, between change and stability, and between the ancient and the modern.

After the end of World War II, Italians voted in 1946 to replace the traditional kingdom with the Republic of Italy. Two years later, a new constitution vested the chief of state function in the President of the Republic and placed the powers of head of government in a prime minister called the President of the Council of Ministers. Legislative power is given to a 630-member lower house called the Chamber of Deputies and a 325-member upper house, the Senate. A constitutional court holds the ultimate judicial power.

Since its wreckage in World War II, the Italian economy has enjoyed remarkable growth, a phenomenon of the 1950s and 1960s known as the Economic Miracle. Then, after enduring serious problems of inflation and stagnation, the economy recovered in the mid-1980s and continues to develop. In claiming to surpass the economy of Britain (an assertion many economists challenge), Italy gave dramatic notice of its overall vitality. Its 1999 gross domestic product (GDP) measured $1.18 trillion, with 1999 growth estimated at 1 percent. Per capita income for Italians was reported in 1999 at $20,699, placing it about midway among the European countries. Although Italy was traditionally agricultural, farmers now constitute a mere 7 percent of the work force, producing primarily wheat, rice, grapes, olives, and citrus. The service sector is the fastest growing and now accounts for more than six of every ten Italian jobs. The remaining third of the work force are employed in commerce and industry, the main products being automobiles, machinery, chemicals, fertilizers, textiles, and footwear.

Italy's balance of trade remains healthy. In 1998, Italy exported $242 billion worth of industrial and agricultural products, primarily to European Union (EU) states (55%) and to the United States (7%). Its imports, totaling $215 billion, came primarily from EU countries in the form of industrial equipment, food, and raw materials (OPEC counted for 6%). Certain Italian industries enjoyed great success, particularly such designers as Armani, Benetton, Fendi, Gucci, Krizia, and Valentino; the firms of Olivetti in office machinery and Pirelli in automobile tires; AGIP in petrochemicals; and, once it began to exploit the market for small and inexpensive cars, the automaker Fiat.

However, in spite of remarkable growth and a favorable balance of trade, a number of economic problems persist. With a huge public sector and chronic budget deficits throughout most of the postwar period, Italy jeopardized its acceptance into the EU and weakened the value of its currency, the lira. The banking system remains largely noncompetitive and has failed to keep pace with the industrial sector. In spite of the government's efforts to force greater accountability from retailers, a major portion of the Italian economy is conducted "underground." Consequently, tax evasion is pervasive and economic growth does not produce as much revenue as it might, compounding the deficit problem.

Furthermore, many Italians did not share in the spreading affluence during this period of impressive postwar growth. The agricultural sector lagged markedly behind industry in its rate of development. And even within the urban middle-class work force, the increasing number of parttime workers, often unprotected by social insurance and pension benefits, left many Italians exposed as never before. Also increasingly vulnerable were young Italians, particularly in small towns and in the South; the elderly; and the growing number of immigrant workers, especially from the Balkans and North Africa.

Retarded agricultural development and high regional unemployment reinforced what has been perhaps Italy's greatest problem of the modern era: the vast gap between the economies of the more urbanized North and the agrarian South. The North, oriented toward western Europe, benefited from technological exchanges, demand for industrial goods, accessible trade routes, and some infusion of investment capital from Paris, London, Brussels, Bonn, and Zurich. Northern cities, particularly Milan, Turin, Bologna, and Venice, maintained a lively commercial identity driven by a robust middle class and consequently built their own supply of capital. Northern farmers achieved relative prosperity. Particularly in the Po River Valley and the plains of Lombardy, farmers have developed a system of canals and aqueducts and have modernized technology. Consequently, northern Italian farmers attained levels of productivity comparable to those of northern Europe.

The South, on the other hand, maintained its traditional connections in the less developed world of the Mediterranean Sea and North Africa (a mere three hours distant by boat) and relied primarily on the export of olive oil and wine. Ravaged by unpredictable earthquakes, drought, flood, and malaria, Southerners traditionally lived a precarious existence and sustained themselves agriculturally only with great effort. Compounding nature's ordeals have been problems imposed by oppressors, especially the Spanish Bourbons in the modern period. Out of neglect and an effort to reinforce dependency, the Bourbons intentionally kept Naples and Sicily isolated, with marginal trade, minimal contact with western Europe, few roads, and little hope for modernization. Consequently, the South remains to this day largely devoid of industrial development and trails the rest of the peninsula by most measures of modern development.

GEOGRAPHICAL INFLUENCES ON ITALIAN HISTORY

The great divide between North and South is just one of many geographical factors that have shaped Italian history and culture. The position of the Italian peninsula protruding, as it does, into the Mediterranean Sea has contributed to its essential character and, on the whole, has provided great advantages. Although the vast coastline has rendered Italy vulnerable to invasion, its location has endowed it with strategic importance and opened it to the economics and culture of the world at large.

The Alps, as formidable as they appear, have provided a barrier more apparent than real to invaders from northern Europe. From Hannibal to Charlemagne, and from Napoleon Bonaparte to Adolf Hitler, hostile forces have marched through the passes to descend on the Italian people, just as navies have repeatedly found Italy's shores penetrable. That same position in the Mediterranean world has historically led Italians, their adversaries, and their allies to inflate Italy's importance beyond its actual military strength, based primarily on strategic location. Furthermore, its 4,100 miles of coastline provide abundant natural harbors. In particular, Genoa and Naples on the west (Tyrrhenian Sea) coast have accommodated maritime activity and provided Italians the historical opportunity to connect easily with the outside world. The Adriatic port of Venice has remained for centuries a hub of commercial activity along both east-west and north-south lines. The Adriatic also connects Italy to the Balkans, only fifty miles removed at the nearest point.

Rather than the Alps, it is the Apennine range that has imposed the greater influence on Italian history. Not only have the Apennines divided Italy internally, but the mountains and their foothills have severely limited the acreage of plains essential for growing grains and grazing livestock. With the exception of the highly productive Po River Valley in the North and certain parts of Sicily, the mountains have limited Italians largely to cultivating grapes and olives, and have kept Italian farms small and relatively unproductive and its farmers poor. In addition, the marshland that extended through much of the center of the peninsula required draining and irrigation, an enormous engineering challenge, in order to be productive.

Furthermore, the geography of the peninsula has retarded the development of an extensive transportation and communication network. Of Italy's rivers, only the Po provides a navigation artery of any substantial value. And although the Romans maintained a system of roads, throughout most of the subsequent history of the peninsula a high percentage of villages has remained unconnected by roads, inhibiting commerce and reinforcing the tradition of local self-sufficiency. Only in the twentieth century did the development of a comprehensive infrastructure accommodate the development of a national market.

Italy's physical geography, particularly the isolation of many towns, explains in part the historic pride its people take in their local traditions. The strength of local cultures remains particularly apparent in the many dialects spoken by Italians, from Sicily to Sardinia, and from Naples to Turin. Some linguists actually believe they have found in Italy pockets of separate languages of ancient origin. Italians take pride not only in local cathedrals (a phenomenon known as *campanilismo*, or pride in one's local bell tower) but in local soccer teams, festivals, and saints.

The reluctance of Italians to embrace a common national identity presented difficulties, particularly in the period following the Risorgimento. In the North, where at the time of unification the king and his prime minister spoke French, the area to the south of Rome was viewed as an alien place where the prime minister never traveled and only reluctantly accepted as part of the kingdom. Meanwhile, many Southerners, regarding the Piedmontese dynasty as merely the most recent in a succession of outside conquerors, continued to identify themselves in terms of their town or region.

World War I in a sense completed the process of unification and continued the nationalization of the peninsula, particularly as the Italian government called young men from rural southern villages to go North to put on a military uniform, train, and fight for the Italian kingdom. At the same time, an Italian nationalist movement that had rallied opinion in support of the war effort in Libya portrayed World War I as an opportunity for Italy to gain the "unredeemed" territory along the Austrian border and the Adriatic Sea of which it had been deprived at the time of independence. Benito Mussolini, after taking power in 1922 and invoking a strong theme of hyper-nationalism, continued the process of centralizing government and raising the banner of Italian patriotism by saturating the educational system with a comprehensive program of Fascist propaganda infused with nationalist rhetoric. And although major disagreements exist as to the effectiveness of Fascist propaganda in penetrating civil society, there is little doubt that the government's modernization of the infrastructure and the use of such modern technology as radio and film did heighten Italian national consciousness. The 1935 military invasion of Ethiopia, successfully avenging the embarrassing loss in 1896 (Italy was the first colonial power to be defeated by indigenous peoples), and Mussolini's proclamation of the Italian Empire, marked the pinnacle of national pride in the first half of the twentieth century. In sharp contrast, Mussolini's disastrous decision to follow Hitler into World War II by ordering the Italian army to invade France in June 1940 led to enormous suffering and calamitous defeat. As a result, Italy's quest to become a "Great Power" has both aided and diminished the process of nation building.

In the post–World War II era, the spread of television and movies, the greater ease and frequency of travel, the migration of rural Italians to cities, and the blossoming of prosperity accompanied by a common consumer capitalism have contributed to a profound standardization of Italian language and popular culture, something that the combined forces of the modern age had previously failed to do. However, in spite of this greater uniformity, a residue of localism persists and continues to act as a restraint on the nationalization of culture and the strength of the national state.

Italy's quest for "Great Power" status has been inhibited not only by the lack of military and industrial power, but even more significantly by the absence of basic mineral deposits necessary for heavy industrialization. With the exception of the islands of Sardinia and Sicily, Italians have found only the most limited deposits of iron and coal. Consequently, Italian industrial development has lagged behind that of much of Europe and the United States and has come at the heavy cost of importing essential minerals.

HISTORICAL THEMES

The discrepancy between North and South has been called the Southern Problem. Like many of the features of contemporary Italy, the Southern Problem has deep historical roots, anchored in centuries of exploitation by outside forces and, in the view of many, by a Piedmontese government that essentially "colonized" the South after the proclamation of the kingdom in 1861. As a result of the unique history of the South, the region has struggled with pervasive poverty, a dominant and abusive class of landlords, political conflict, a tradition of defiance to official authority (sometimes in the form of "banditry," sometimes in the guise of the Sicilian *mafia*, the *camorra* of Naples, or the *'ndrangheta* of Calabria), and enormous emigration. In the years between 1880 and World War I, some 25 million people left Italy, the overwhelming majority from the South. More recently, rural Southerners have moved to cities in northern Italy and northern Europe. In fact, the contrast between North and South is just one—if the most dramatic—of many apparent historical contradictions that have impressed travelers to Italy and Italians themselves.

Perhaps even more troubling than the Southern Problem has been a more fundamental issue: What is Italy? In 1814, Austrian Chancellor Metternich dismissed Italy as a mere "geographical expression." Metternich could make such a self-serving denial of Italian statehood, not only because the Austrian Empire controlled most of northern Italy but also because political control of the peninsula had for centuries been divided among self-governing cities, possessions of foreign dynasties, and the Vatican. There had been few exceptions. Italian cities had formed various defensive leagues to protect themselves from recurring invasions, but those shifting associations had proven short-lived. For more extended periods, Italian maritime cities such as Venice and Genoa had established commercial and political hegemony, or dominance, over adjacent areas. But the prevailing pattern had been political disunity. Napoleon Bonaparte had broken that pattern to serve his own imperial agenda by consolidating parts of the peninsula. And although aspects of his modernization program left a permanent residue, Napoleon's political consolidation was reversed by Metternich's program of restoring authority to the traditional, "legitimate" dynasties.

In the face of this fragmentation, writers ranging from Dante Alighieri and Niccolò Machiavelli to Alessandro Manzoni and Vincenzo Gioberti had throughout the centuries portrayed their own visions of a united Italy. And although no such union ever materialized, the vision lived a life of its own, strengthened at least by the contributions of Dante and Manzoni to the standardization of an Italian language. Nevertheless, when Mazzini and the conspiratorial secret societies took up the nationalist cause against Metternich's alliance system in the 1820s, Italy remained a collection of regions, many under outside control. Either directly or indirectly, the Austrian (Hapsburg) dynasty had, since 1815, regained control of much of the North and Center, including Venetia, Lombardy, and the duchies of Modena, Parma, Lucca, and Tuscany. Sweeping across the center of the peninsula, from the Venetian border in the northeast to the Tyrrhenian coast south of Rome, the Papal States had fallen firmly under the temporal authority of the Church. And in the South, headquartered in Naples, Spanish Bourbons had retaken control of the Kingdom of the Two Sicilies. In all of Italy, only the northwestern Kingdom of Piedmont-Sardinia, with its capital in Turin, remained under the control of a native Italian dynasty, the House of Savoy. When Italy unified in 1861, strong sentiment existed to give recognition to the regions by forming a federal state, much as Germans would do in 1871. However, the Piedmontese prevailed in establishing a unified monarchy, at least as a formal system. Nonetheless, in spite of nearly a century-and-a-half of unification, the traditional regions have retained a strong identity, as if to remind us of the doubts expressed by both Metternich and d'Azeglio.

In the modern era, a dominant class of Italian leaders has defined and successively redefined Italy in response to the major political events of its historical experience. Thus, during the Risorgimento some northern liberal leaders defined Italy in the image of English politics. As they prevailed over more radical visions of Italy as a democratic republic, Cavour and his successors shaped a new Italian monarchy in which political power would be limited to the upper and middle ranks of society. They built a consensus around laissez-faire policies of free trade and secular modernization, and they developed a tradition of trading favors and sharing power, forming a political coalition between northern businessmen and southern landlords.

By the early twentieth century, five-time prime minister Giovanni Giolitti seemed to have perfected the politics of *trasformismo* ("transformism"), the system by which the major political parties evidenced little contrast, instead compromising on principle and policy in order to maintain power. From 1861 to 1922, Italy retained the identity of this "Liberal State."

The trauma and great disillusionment experienced by Italians in World War I created conditions under which Mussolini and his Fascist Party, after consolidating political power, redefined Italy. Without ever clearly explaining Fascism, Mussolini seized the opportunity to offer Italians a heroic alternative to the mundane and unprincipled corruption that had dominated much of the public life of the Liberal State. Appealing vaguely to alienated and disenchanted Italians and to fears of a class revolt, Mussolini and his blackshirts (armed Fascist squads) invoked images that recalled the grandeur of the Roman Empire while at the same time challenging Italians to move boldly toward a new Italy. Historians still debate the success of the Fascist state, particularly in terms of its cultural impact: Did Mussolini create a new social model, a "third way" between Bolshevism and the unrestrained capitalism of the Liberal State? Did Fascist culture actually complete the Risorgimento by "making Italians" through its many programs of strident nationalism? Did Fascist imperialism finally elevate Italy to "Great Power" status? Successful or not, Fascism destroyed itself by taking an underprepared Italian military into World War II and to devastating defeat.

As Italians suffered first through German, then Allied occupation, engulfing much of the peninsula in fierce fighting, Italian resistance fighters boldly redefined Italy once again. The heroism of the anti-Fascist resistance, dominated by Communist insurgents who liberated town after town ahead of Allied forces, set the tone for the new Italian Republic. Out of the rubble left by the war, Italians built a set of constitutional institutions and, with U.S. assistance through the Marshall Plan, rebuilt the economy to impressive new levels.

As it emerged, the new Italian Republic seemed to many in the outside world to be filled with paradox. As a pivotal point in Cold War Europe, Italy developed a political system in which its two major parties, Christian Democrats (DC) and Communists (PCI), were supported respectively (both openly and secretly) by the United States and the Soviet Union. At the same time, because of the system of proportional elections, the maneuvers of numerous small parties forced government after government to fall, giving the impression of inherent instability. In the first fifty-five years after World War II—from the government of Ferruccio Parri in 1945 to the second government of Massimo D'Alema in 2000—Italians changed governments fifty-eight times.

Ironically, in spite of the dizzying frequency of changes and bitter partisan rhetoric, Italians managed to find a kind of internal equilibrium. The DC, with a majority for only about five years, orchestrated a shifting sequence of coalitions that preserved its governing power for an uninterrupted period of nearly forty years, never losing to its stalwart challenger, the PCI. All the while, the Socialists (PSI) remained the third largest party and participated regularly as junior partners in the DC hegemony, which managed to provide, for better or worse, one of the most extended periods of political stability in the modern history of Europe.

At the same time, particularly during the height of U.S.-Soviet tensions, many Westerners feared what they viewed as the peril of Communism in Italy. And the left-wing terrorism carried out by the Red Brigades in the 1970s and 1980s reinforced the same impression. The PCI remained poised, or so it seemed, only an election away from governing. Marxist intellectuals dominated much of postwar Italian culture. All the while, the PCI leadership rejected the orthodoxy of Soviet Communism in favor of a European model and disavowed interest in governing. Ironically, at the very time when some NATO nations fretted about left-wing influences that dominated the news, a moderate political consensus prevailed through virtually the entire period.

At the same time, postwar Italian society underwent sweeping change. Millions of Italians, instead of migrating to northern Europe or the Americas in search of employment, now migrated to Italian cities, contributing to a standardization, urbanization, and modernization of Italian culture. The expanding wealth and prosperity of the Economic Miracle spread to all classes and generated a new social mobility and unprecedented numbers of two-income families. Businesses expanded, computerized, and modernized; unions produced generous cost-of-living adjustments for the blue-collar work force; and Italians at all levels of society enjoyed greater leisure time and the fruits of modern consumer technology. The popularity of television contributed to both a new consumerism and a greater uniformity of national language.

Material prosperity also was accompanied by a secularization of society that can be appreciated only against the backdrop of the traditional influence of the Vatican on Italian life. Since the Emperor Constantine in 313 decreed that Christians be tolerated, the Church has played a prominent role in Italy. In the modern era, the Church derived power largely from its influence over the Italian population and from its international prestige. In maintaining a separate power center in the Vatican, the Church thus inhibited the nation-building process. Finally, after almost sixty years of boycotting Italian politics, the Church lifted its ban against political participation in 1919 and, ten years later, signed the Lateran Accords with Mussolini, normalizing its relations with the Italian government. The Republican Constitution of 1948, incorporating provisions from the Lateran Accords, provided that the State and the Church were, each in its own sphere, "independent and sovereign."

However, by the 1970s, church attendance fell and the Church's widespread temporal influence showed signs of waning, in spite of some persistent regional strengths. The birth rate dropped dramatically and the smaller nuclear family, intent on acquiring its own material prosperity, began to replace the extended family as a focus in Italian life. These private changes manifested themselves in public policy as well. In direct contradiction of Church doctrine, the Parliament legalized divorce in 1970, affirmed in a 1974 referendum, and proceeded to legalize both birth control and abortion. A major force in forging these changes was a growing feminist movement. Granted equality and the right to vote in the 1948 Constitution of the Republic, Italian women by 1980 had won a number of legal concessions granting them equality in the workplace in hiring, promotions, salaries, and social security. And, although enforcement of these laws has been uneven, there is no question that Italian social values and public practices have undergone major transformation in the postwar period.

Then in 1992, the most severe political scandals in their history led Italians to define the state for a fourth time. Unfolding first in Milan, which was labeled "kickback city," the scandals quickly spread through accusation, indictment, and trial to envelop much of the country. Thus, it was the DC's governing consensus and the dynamics of traditional power sharing with the Socialists—rather than chronic instability or left-wing radicalism—that fundamentally altered the Italian Republic in a way that the Red Brigades and the PCI had not been able to do.

The roar of public outcry built support for fundamental changes in the constitutional structure that have led some to term the subsequent government the "second republic." The two parties that dominated the previous half-century, DC and PCI, have been dissolved, and a northern separatist party has emerged to challenge fundamental national assumptions. Although few who were charged with participation in the scandal have served prison sentences, the movement for thorough constitutional revision has produced changes in the election laws and demands for new referenda. Regardless, the outlines of this new structure are still too blurred to merit conclusions.

Many observers remain skeptical that the "second republic" will produce a profoundly new political system. Even those who hold the highest hopes for a new beginning acknowledge the great weight of tradition that must be overcome before the movement succeeds in transforming Italian public life. That awareness reinforces the need to understand history and serves as a prelude to the exploration of Italy through its various historical phases, from the Roman Republic into the twenty-first century.

2

Italy in the Ancient and Classical Ages

The history of Italy begins in the long, shadowy period preceding the establishment of the Roman Republic. As early as the second millennium B.C., when Italy was in the Bronze Age, a long series of prehistoric migrations began to populate the peninsula. A number of the earliest inhabitants, including Mycenaeans, Phoenicians, and Greeks, migrated west by ship via the Mediterranean Sea. In that same distant era, the Latins migrated through the passes in the Alps to settle in primitive farming villages. Their language, like most of the languages spoken in pre-Roman Italy, belongs to the Indo-European language family. The most important exception was Etruscan, spoken and written by the mysterious people who would establish a prominent position in the hill towns of central Italy.

In Bronze Age Italy, a cultural pattern had already emerged that persists in some form even today. For thousands of years before the Romans unified the peoples of the peninsula, Italian life remained fragmented into localized geographical regions in which the village was the normal point of identity for the inhabitants. A rich variety of different languages and cultures could be found scattered among the villages from the Po River Valley in the North; along the Tyrrhenian Sea from the Gulf of Genoa past the Bay of Naples to the toe of the Italian boot; on the Adriatic coast from Venice to Brindisi; and on the nearby islands, including Sicily and Sardinia. The

Roman Italy. Digital Wisdom®, Inc.

Apennine mountain range limited east-west contact, reinforcing this early pattern of separation.

Archaeologists tell us that Italians experienced their greatest prehistoric transformation in passing from the Bronze Age to the Iron Age, probably around the beginning of the first millennium B.C. Bronze Age Italian culture, sometimes called "Apennine Culture" because of the many discoveries in the central mountain range, included both pastoral nomads and settled agricultural villages. Sparsely populated in this era, but isolated from the larger Mediterranean world, Italy initially featured a greater degree of cultural uniformity than would later develop. In fact, one sign of change that occurred toward the end of the Bronze Age, around 1200 B.C., was the breakdown of this primitive culture into various components that began to reflect regional differences.

By the beginning of the Iron Age, distinctive cultures emerged that are given such geographical labels as "Villanovan," "Adriatic," and "Apulian." Meanwhile, as the population began to grow, regional differences sharpened. By studying such evidence as burial rites and pottery, archaeologists have developed a picture of a culturally diverse Iron Age Italy. This view is reinforced by the great variety of languages spoken in the first millennium B.C., many of them imported by migrating peoples, such as the Greeks who settled on the Adriatic coast and in eastern Sicily by the eighth century B.C. and the Celts who crossed the Alps into northern Italy in the sixth century B.C.

ETRUSCAN INFLUENCE

Of the non–Indo European speaking peoples, one group stands out because of its great influence: the Etruscans. A people of obscure origin, the Etruscans had developed an advanced civilization that by the eighth century B.C. began to dominate the hill towns of central Italy between the present-day cities of Florence and Rome. Although they never unified the region politically, the Etruscans did introduce a degree of cultural unity in their art work, aristocratic social structure, language, technology, customs, and economic systems. Etruscan culture displays Eastern influences, particularly in its religious and artistic themes. The Etruscan language, still not fully understood in spite of thousands of surviving inscriptions, introduced to Rome the alphabet that remains in use in the Western world today. Moreover, the Etruscans passed on to the Romans a number of aspects of their popular culture, key among them gladiatorial combat and chariot races, the ceremony of military triumph, and the toga, the distinctive dress of the Romans. By affording elevated social and legal status to women, particularly in their ability to own property, Etruscan culture most markedly departed from existing Greek and Latin norms. Thus, in a number of ways, the Etruscans transformed the existing Latin culture.

Italian history reached another watershed when the Etruscans extended their influence to the eventual site of Rome. Ideally located amid the hills next to an island in the Tiber River, along the natural "salt route" that crossed the region of Latium, the site had been inhabited since before 1000 B.C., as the Bronze Age was giving way to the Iron Age. According to the ancient myth of sibling rivalry, the envious brother Romulus overtook his twin, Remus, to found Rome in 753 B.C. Although little stock is to be put in the accuracy of this tale, it is revealing that the Roman historical tradition perpetuated the ideas that the city was founded early and was developed over a long period by an assortment of peoples who imported an array of foreign influences.

Most historians now agree that the Etruscans did not conquer Rome in a military sense. However, Etruscan culture so influenced Rome that some have argued that Rome was, in the seventh and sixth centuries B.C., an Etruscan city. Because Roman culture reflected Greek elements as well, particularly in religion, politics, and warfare, that claim may be overstated. In any event, the Etruscans made a number of important early contributions, two of which shaped the city and its ultimate dominion over Italy. By draining the marshes in and around Rome, they set off an explosion of agricultural activity; and by introducing building techniques, they brought on a surge in construction. These improvements readily provided Rome an economic base and an urban presence, especially when the Etruscans laid flagstone pavement in what would become the city's forum.

Consequently, by around 650 B.C., Rome had begun to change from a primitive collection of scattered hillside huts to a more organized urban center. The Roman city-state now featured temples to revered deities, clusters of houses, and an aristocratic social structure. There is also evidence of an emerging Roman political system of tribes, perhaps ethnic in origin but reorganized for administrative convenience into four geographically based units. Early Romans attended an assembly at which they cast their votes, according to tribe, for such purposes as bestowing the power to command the military and authenticating legal transactions such as wills and adoptions.

It is also clear that archaic Rome was ruled by a series of kings. Details about the reigns of these various kings—said to be four Etruscans followed by three Romans—are obscure. We do know, however, about the legacies left by several. Servius Tullius (ruled 578–534 B.C.), having built a political base of popular support, introduced a program of reforms, including a census and a reorganization of society into classes based on wealth. This social reorganization produced a hereditary nobility, the "patrician order," that was destined to dominate Roman politics. We also know that Servius's successor, Tarquin the Proud (ruled 534–509 B.C.), expanded Rome's prosperity and influence so that the city of perhaps thirty thousand inhabitants was by the end of the sixth century B.C. the largest and most important city in Latium. Nevertheless, Tarquin so abused his power that a group of Roman aristocrats overthrew him, banished him from the city, and founded the Roman Republic.

FORMATION OF THE ROMAN REPUBLIC

Historians generally agree that Roman history begins with the expulsion of the Etruscan king Tarquin the Proud in 509 B.C. In his place, the Roman patricians vested political authority in two consuls and began to develop the political institutions for which the Roman Republic is known. From the start, the consuls and other civic magistrates were required to share power and to limit their terms in office to one year. The only exception was a dictator, who could, only in a declared emergency, act as head of state and military commander for up to six months.

Yet the evolution of the Roman Republic was anything but smooth, as Romans dealt throughout the first century of the Republic's existence with both foreign hostilities and domestic turbulence. A class conflict known as the "struggle of the orders" ensued, as the plebeians, the lower order or class, challenged the dominant patrician aristocracy to relinquish some of its traditional privileges and to share political power. From the start, the patricians had exercised political power through the Senate, a bastion of conservative Roman values. Finally, in 494 B.C., the plebeians challenged the patricians in what is called the First Secession by marching out of the city to protest poverty, debt, and mistreatment. Convening on a nearby hill, the *plebs* formed their own alternative institutions, featuring an assembly, tribunes, and other officials. By depriving the patricians of their labor force and threatening to ally with Rome's enemies, the *plebs* forced concessions. The tribunes, whose responsibility it was to protect the *plebs* who elected them, soon gained the power to veto senatorial legislation.

The plebeians won another major concession around 450 B.C. when they forced the patricians to replace unwritten legal traditions with a written legal code. The Twelve Tables, as the code is called, introduced a greater measure of equality, provided some protection of individual rights, confirmed the right of appeal, limited the use of capital punishment, and, in general, organized Roman law into a more systematic form in which it could more readily survive. Furthermore, the Twelve Tables reaffirmed the traditional power of the father, *pater familias* ("father of the family"), who controlled all the property and persons in the Roman family. Under the law, the father literally "owned" his wife and children. Ultimately, the father could sell a family member into bondage or order death, a prerogative seldom invoked except on the occasion of the birth of a malformed child. As Roman law evolved over the centuries, the status of women would improve somewhat, and the concept of equity (fairness) would serve as the guiding principle.

Most important, the code provides a kind of snapshot of the legal actions and daily transactions of the early Republic. Romans farmed, traded produce and crafts, paid with bronze weighed on scales, and lived in a family-centered, two-class system based on traditional values. They worshipped spirits that they associated with nature and the cycle of farming. Many Romans owned private property, but the patrician elite continued to dominate Roman society. As the plebeians gained some measure of political power, the leading patrician families, in order to maintain control, took *plebs* as clients. Nonetheless, plebeians gained the right to marry patricians and, as a prosperous group of *plebs* emerged, some integration of the classes occurred. Eventually, the 300s B.C. witnessed the emergence of a new ruling class that blended patricians and *plebs* while accommodating additional reforms.

The fourth century B.C. featured further attempts by the *plebs* to acquire land and to overcome the economic hardships imposed by debt and bondage. When the Roman armies began to import prisoners as slave labor, the *plebs* largely succeeded in freeing themselves from servitude and began to enter military service as the drive for empire expanded.

WARS OF THE EARLY REPUBLIC

The Roman overthrow of King Tarquin the Proud was only one aspect of the general instability that dominated central Italy in the years before and after 500 B.C. On all sides, tyrants and private armies threatened. Consequently, at the very time the *plebs* were gaining concessions within Rome, the Romans were busy fighting to maintain some degree of order in the surrounding area. As the Romans fought, they found themselves drawn progressively into conflict in an ever-widening circle until they had managed to extend their power throughout much of the South and Center of the peninsula.

In the first of these conflicts, the Romans engaged a coalition of neighboring Latin cities. The wars of the Latin League featured the great Roman victory in the Battle of Lake Regillus (499 B.C.) and culminated in the

Cassian Treaty of 493 in which the parties agreed to a military alliance and to "peace between the Romans and all the Latin cities so long as heaven and earth are still in the same place." The Romans, now having attained diplomatic parity with the Latins for the first time, began to incorporate many towns on the borders of Latium as colonies in order to provide an expanded zone of security.

The newly found stability was quickly upset by a series of movements of other early Iron Age peoples within Italy that shook most of the peninsula, devastating the Greek settlements along the south Adriatic coast. Among the migrating groups, the Volscians, the Aequians, the Samnites, and the Sabines were most disruptive, the latter threatening Rome itself. In response, the Romans fought regularly throughout the first half of the fifth century B.C., raiding their adversaries annually while probably losing as many engagements as they won.

In contrast, the wars between Rome and the Etruscan city of Veii present a fundamentally different concept. They featured two established city-states fighting more conventional warfare over control of trade, as Rome became more aggressive and more successful. After an extended siege, the Romans destroyed Veii so completely that its remains were not discovered by archaeologists until 1916. In the late fifth century, Romans introduced new taxes to support military campaigns and began to levy reparations on the vanquished and to pay Roman soldiers.

At the beginning of the fourth century B.C., a new threat appeared. A band of Gauls swept down from the Po Valley through Etruria, Umbria, and Latium and, at the River Allia in the summer of 390, delivered the first major defeat to a Roman army. Moving on to the undefended city, they took whatever they could carry away. However, as devastating as the Gallic raid may have been, Rome soon recovered. The military resumed its campaigns, winning victories, annexing territory, establishing alliances, and extending citizenship to some of the newly acquired colonies.

ROMAN EXPANSION AND THE CREATION OF "ITALIA"

During the fourth century B.C., Rome launched a new series of campaigns by which it took control of most of the peninsula. The Roman army now began to distinguish itself. It was a citizen army, with military service considered an obligation of citizenship. It used no mercenaries, and not until the end of the third century did it begin to incorporate units from the allied territories. Adversaries and allies alike regarded Roman soldiers as well trained and courageous and were impressed by the army's organization. It was divided into four legions, each counting about 4,500 soldiers.

Most fought in the heavily armed infantry, while others specialized as light infantry or cavalry. Roman commanders normally divided their legions into two large armies but later began to develop smaller, more versatile units. Each soldier typically carried a javelin and a shield.

The attack on Tusculum in 381 provides a good example of the new Roman militancy. After the victory, the Romans added Tusculum to the Roman state as a self-governing city, granting its residents Roman citizenship and thereby requiring them to pay tribute money and to serve in the Roman army. The Romans resumed this new aggressive foreign policy in the 360s, winning a string of military engagements and establishing greater military prowess in the decades that followed. After weathering another Gallic invasion, the Romans in the 340s launched a successful campaign of expansion in five years of warfare against a nearby federation of hill tribes known as the Samnites.

The Samnite Wars were part of a wider revolt by Latin tribes protesting the new Roman expansion. When the Roman legions prevailed, they imposed a series of settlements that established a Roman commonwealth and created the process that would guide Roman development for several centuries. Dealing with each territory separately, the Romans offered various combinations of terms: Some were fully assimilated into the Roman state, their inhabitants granted full citizenship; others were made allies; some territories were granted partial citizenship without political rights; and still others were made Latin colonies. These terms of settlement enabled the Romans to maintain their republican institutions while expanding throughout the peninsula and beyond.

Conflict in the northern Tiber Valley in 311 B.C. led the Roman legions northward on a campaign that resulted in the conquest of central and north central Italy, culminating in the great Roman victory at the Battle of Sentinum in 295 that eventually reduced the Samnites to allied status. Shortly thereafter, the Romans were drawn south to attend to rivalries among the Greek cities, particularly in Tarentum. In 284, Tarentum's rival requested Roman assistance. When the Romans declared war in 281, the Tarentine assembly invited the ambitious, young King Pyrrhus of Epirus to protect them with his army. He arrived in the spring of 280 with a force of 25,000 soldiers, accompanied by elephants. After several costly ("Pyrrhic") victories, Pyrrhus withdrew to Sicily and ultimately back to Greece, enabling the Romans to take control of Tarentum and the other Greek cities in the 270s and 260s. When the Samnites and other subjects took advantage of Rome's preoccupation with the Greek cities, Rome retaliated, suppressing the rebellions. Consequently, by 260, Rome controlled virtually the entire Italian peninsula, which the Romans began to refer to, for the first time, as

"Italia." The process of domination of Italia had taken them only about seventy years.

EMERGING ROMAN GOVERNMENT

The era of warfare that spanned the fourth and third centuries proved a significant period in the development of Roman government, both within the Republic and throughout the Italian peninsula. The Romans' ability to develop a formula for maintaining stability among their allies enabled them to control the peninsula for two centuries, all the while weathering only one serious challenge. Historians believe that this success can be attributed to several features of Roman government. First, the Romans cemented their various arrangements with subjugated peoples in a series of generous treaties that extended them the benefits of Roman prosperity and military alliance. Each of the agreements required the allies to supply military assistance to Rome, thus greatly augmenting Rome's military resources. Second, the treaties allowed the allies to retain part of the spoils of war, including portions of land in conquered territories. Consequently, the Romans elicited lasting loyalty from their Italian allies, which, in turn, made Roman Italy secure.

At the same time Rome was establishing treaties with its Italian allies, the Roman Republic began to take its classical form. All the while, patricians and plebeians continued to compete for power. By the mid-fourth century, the plebeians extracted from the Senate economic concessions, including a moratorium on debt and a guarantee that one of the two consuls had to be plebeian.

The people's assemblies voted on the magistrates, and the magistrates in turn managed the day-to-day administration of the government. Among the more important magistracies were the two consuls (heads of state), the censors (who, on the basis of the census, parceled out political rights and military obligations), the praetors (judges), and the tribunes (who exercised the veto on behalf of the people).

However, it was not the magistrates but the Senate that, by means of its command of political power, governed Rome. Its members were all former magistrates chosen from the censors' list of the three hundred "best" Romans, revised at five-year intervals. Because its members served for life, the Senate provided exceptional stability. Senate votes, taken after exhaustive debate, became decrees, essentially requiring the magistrates to take action unless vetoed by the tribunes.

By the third century B.C., a senatorial oligarchy, now incorporating ambitious members of the middle and plebeian classes, had consolidated their control of the Republic. The Senate supervised the magistracy, expanded it, and laid claim to the new positions, only to open some to the *plebs* in response to pressure. Senators took power from the consuls, who had originally governed in collaboration with the popular assemblies. They controlled public finances, made diplomatic, military, and judicial policy, and in an emergency could appoint a military dictator.

The senatorial oligarchy maintained its power in spite of various challenges, including the passage of a law in the early third century that appeared to establish democracy through the popular assemblies. However, the power of the popular assemblies was limited by their inability either to meet, unless summoned by the magistrates, or to initiate policy. Furthermore, the assemblies acted collectively and generally were dominated by property-owning classes. Thus, the poorest Romans had few points of access into the political process, very little power, and limited individual rights.

ECONOMIC PROSPERITY AND SOCIAL TRANSFORMATION

Roman military conquests fueled a period of economic expansion and social change in the fourth and third centuries. Although the Roman state remained primarily agricultural, its economic growth generated a boom in public building that eventually provided the city of Rome its classical, monumental appearance. The city's population burgeoned to near 100,000 by the middle of the third century, expanded by immigration and economic growth. Territorial expansion inevitably altered the composition of Roman society, not only by introducing new members of the prosperous commercial class into the senatorial oligarchy, but by assimilating such ethnic groups as the Etruscans, Sabines, Umbrians, and Campanians. Consequently, Roman society diversified and developed as new ideas and energies reshaped its culture. Traditional religious practices now were incorporated into state ceremony, and some nontraditional Eastern religions were given official approval, as was the Cybele cult in 204 B.C.

At the same time, Rome thrived as an important commercial center, producing a variety of pottery and sculpture for export while the acquisition of territory further expanded the economy. Individual Romans took advantage of new opportunities to contract with the government to provide such public services as building roads and aqueducts, collecting taxes, and supplying the military. Consequently, the middle class expanded, disturbing the traditional social balance.

Furthermore, the growth in slave labor proved fateful. Originally an area characterized by small farms, Rome now saw its first large estates appear, as aristocrats applied slave labor to the production of crops. The importation of slaves into both the cities and the countryside greatly expanded the number of *plebs*, particularly as the slaves acquired freedom. At the same time, the government began to resettle the poor into the newly won territories, often replacing populations that had been enslaved.

By the third century, the Roman government took a major step to accelerate further economic development by minting coins—first bronze, then, in 269 B.C., silver. By the end of the century, it had established a system to allow standard monetary exchanges, both domestic and international.

THE PUNIC WARS AND THE BUILDING OF THE ROMAN EMPIRE

In 264 B.C., Rome went to war with Carthage in the first of three Punic (Phoenician) Wars that changed not only the Roman Republic but much of the Mediterranean world. The conflict began as a power struggle between the two, as Carthage (a prosperous former Phoenician colony in North Africa) attempted to protect its vast commercial and maritime empire against Roman expansion.

The First Punic War began in Sicily, when the Romans dispatched forces to Messina. As the fighting continued in a series of indecisive campaigns, the Romans determined to build a navy to confront the renowned Carthaginian fleet; in turn, the Carthaginians employed mercenaries to match the Roman infantry. The war dragged on for twenty-three years until the Romans won a decisive naval battle in 241 and forced a peace settlement by which Rome acquired control of Sicily and the Lipari Islands. In the aftermath, as the Carthaginians struggled in domestic turmoil, Rome seized the island of Sardinia.

The Carthaginians eventually recovered, however, and took Spain, where in 219 their general Hannibal laid siege to a Roman ally as part of a strategy for retaliating against Rome. Rome's response touched off seventeen years of brutal campaigning in which Hannibal took the action into Italy. Crossing first the Pyrenees and then the Alps with elephants he had acquired from Pyrrhus, Hannibal defeated Roman legions in a number of battles while ravaging the land. The worst Roman defeats came at Lake Trasimene in 217, where Hannibal decimated two Roman legions, and in the following year at Cannae in Apulia, where the Romans lost 40,000 troops. However, Hannibal's plan to turn Roman allies and subjects against Rome met strong resistence, especially in central Italy.

Beginning in 211, Roman armies began to reverse the course of the conflict, taking back much of southern Italy, Sicily, and Sardinia and then sweeping north, punishing defectors in the process. But it was the Roman counter-attack on the Carthaginian homeland that marked the strategic turning point. In 204, the Roman general P. Cornelius Scipio invaded North Africa with 35,000 troops. After successful campaigning that forced the Carthaginians to call home their armies, Scipio won the monumental victory at Zama, ending this second war. In the aftermath, the Romans forced a severe peace settlement that required Carthage to relinquish most of its navy, its elephants, a huge sum of money, and its right to make war without permission.

The final Punic War was waged between 149 and 146 B.C., as Rome's forces broadened the conflict with Carthage into a series of campaigns of expansion that would ultimately produce the Roman Empire. Roman legions had moved east into the Balkans, defeating and annexing Macedonia and Greece. In the process they had shown a more aggressive and expansive form of empire building. After destroying Carthage in 146, Rome acquired its first North African province. Then, in a series of victorious battles, Roman troops took Pergamum and Ephesus and added a province in Asia in 126. Having expanded rapidly into two new continents, the army next turned its attention to the difficult task of "mopping up" operations in the Asian province, soon extending imperial control into Syria.

To the north, the armies answered a call for help from Roman citizens in Marseilles and, in the wake of success, added the province of southern Gaul in 118. A half-century later Julius Caesar extended Roman control throughout Gaul in a brilliant series of conquests. By winning the Battle of Actium, Octavian added Egypt as a province in 31 B.C., thus virtually completing (Britain and Dacia were important later additions) the empire that would endure as the largest and longest-lasting territorial empire in history.

DOMESTIC CONSEQUENCES OF EMPIRE BUILDING

Rome's great military conquests of the second and first centuries B.C. signaled sweeping changes, not only in the larger Mediterranean world but in Rome itself, as Roman citizens adjusted to new ideas, newly found wealth, and the great prestige afforded the generals and the Senate. The legions brought back to Rome such plentiful loot as to overwhelm the rather primitive Roman economy. A great abundance of gold drove up the cost of living, while several hundred thousand slaves, taken as prisoners-of-war, drove down wages. Meanwhile, imported grain undercut the market for Italian grains. Consequently, many Roman peasants gave up their land and moved to the cities in search of employment, and wealthy landlords consolidated their estates—which they now farmed with slave labor. At the same time, newly established international commercial contacts expanded the opportunities for the growing Roman middle class of businessmen, merchants, and bankers who developed their political identity and interests. A parallel middle class emerged in the provincial cities, where Romans began to encounter complaints of abusive taxation and misgovernment.

Among the influences brought to Rome by expansion and immigration were forms of philosophy and literature from Greek and Hellenistic (Greek-like, or Mediterranean) sources. The most influential Hellenistic philosophical belief was Stoicism, which appealed to many Romans because of its emphasis on the power of reason, its values of civic virtue, and its seriousness and serenity, which reminded Romans of the culture of the earlier Republic. Roman poets such as Ennius ("father of Roman poetry") and the comic playwrights Plautus and Terence utilized Greek sources in writing for Roman audiences.

Amid the economic, social, and cultural changes of the late Republic, Roman women, particularly of the upper class, enjoyed some improvement in status. Some of the earlier restrictions that subjugated women to the control of a male guardian were ignored, and eventually the laws were modified. Customs of marriage and divorce varied by class, with the rising middle class and the upper class often taking political and economic factors into consideration. By the time of the late Republic, young women began to enjoy greater educational opportunities, and despite being deprived of the right to vote, some Roman women became well known in literary, social, and political circles.

The economic transformations of the late Republic directly changed Roman politics. As the urban population grew, augmented by displaced farmers, emancipated slaves, and the newly unemployed, an alienated and discontented lower class materialized. Various members of the Roman political and social elite now recruited "clienteles," or loyal constituencies among the poor, and Roman politics began to reflect a growing division between conservatives and reformers. This polarization led to growing political conflict and, ultimately, to a century of civil war.

As the client-patron system organized around these factions, the issue of land reform moved to the forefront. In 133 B.C. a young aristocrat with a large clientele won election as tribune and took up the cause of the poor. Tiberius Gracchus immediately introduced a proposal to limit the size of landholdings to about 625 acres for a family of four and to redistribute the excess land permanently among the poor at about 19 acres per person. When his appointment of a reform commission to implement the plan was blocked by another tribune, Tiberius forced the tribune out of office. Tiberius Gracchus then had himself, his brother, and his father-in-law elected to the land commission and announced his candidacy for a second tribuneship.

The senatorial conservative party regarded several of these actions as unconstitutional and Tiberius Gracchus as a dangerously ambitious radical. As Roman political factions took their campaigns to the streets, riots ensued. In the summer of 133, a mob killed Tiberius and threw his body in the River Tiber. But the factionalism did not die out, nor did the reform issue. Ten years later, Tiberius's brother Gaius Gracchus won election as tribune and took up his brother's cause.

Gaius modified the land reform plan in an attempt to build political support. However, his program to distribute free grain to the poor solidified opposition, as did his attempts to integrate the middle class into the political system and to found a colony in Carthage. Frustrated, Gaius attempted to use force and thereby provoked the Senate to issue a decree against him. In April 121, a senatorial mob murdered Gaius Gracchus and three thousand of his supporters.

The brothers Gracchus left a powerful legacy. Their attempted reforms were not wholly abandoned, and the violence they provoked proved only the first chapter in an extended era of civil war that put the Roman Republic to a severe test. To complicate matters, slave revolts spread throughout Italy shortly after the demise of Gaius Gracchus, forcing the Roman government to take drastic action. It is estimated that slaves made up well over 50 percent of the population in some rural areas and only somewhat less than half of the population in Italy as a whole. Abuse of slave labor was widespread, including subjecting them to combat as gladiators (professional fighters). After suppressing slave revolts in Sicily and Campania, Romans mobilized a major force in 72 B.C. to subdue the most threatening uprising led by Spartacus (the Roman slave and gladiator). After laying waste to large areas of southern Italy, Spartacus recruited support in the Apennines and headed north. Eventually, the following winter, the legions of Crassus and Pompey defeated the insurgents, killing Spartacus and six thousand of his followers.

While Roman forces were battling slave revolts, an even more threatening insurgency materialized in the "Social Wars" of 91–88 B.C. Exasperated by the Romans' refusal to extend citizenship throughout the peninsula, non-Roman citizens demanded full rights. When the Senate defeated a proposal to make all Italians citizens, rebellion spread throughout central and southern Italy. The Roman government responded by assembling a military force under Marius and Sulla, while at the same time offering citizenship to all except those who persisted in armed rebellion.

In the wake of the Social Wars, political factions continued to struggle with questions of assimilation of the new citizens into the Roman social and political body. Within about twenty years the ranks of Roman citizenship had doubled in number, and the new citizens had become politically active. Eventually many moved into the ruling elite and into the hall of the Senate itself, permanently altering the Roman power structure.

FINAL CENTURY OF THE ROMAN REPUBLIC: CIVIL WAR AND THE RISE OF CAESAR

The upheavals of the second and early first centuries set the stage for the entrance into the political arena of a series of ambitious generals, culminating in the dictatorship of Julius Caesar and the end of the Roman Republic. As a result of changes in the military, Caesar and other generals built armies of volunteers from the ranks of the poor, paid them, rewarded them with loot and land, and thus commanded spirited personal loyalty in the ranks. Among Caesar's predecessors, Marius, Sulla, and Pompey built similar armed forces and began in the first century to employ them as a resource in their respective campaigns for power. This trend threatened the republican system.

Based on his military reputation, Gaius Marius was recruited to politics by an aspiring Roman family of the *populares* ("people's") faction and was eventually dragged into the partisan conflict. After a stint in the magistracy, Marius served as consul for an unprecedented seven terms while continuing to lead his armies against outside threats. Banished by the Senate and Sulla's *optimates* ("the best") party, Marius returned when Sulla took his legions into Asia. After bloody retaliation against the *optimates*, Marius died in early 86 B.C. of natural causes.

The aristocratic and conservative Lucius Sulla returned with his army in 83 B.C. to seize power and to turn the tables on the *populares*. Already an accomplished general, diplomat, and public figure, Sulla fought his way back to Rome in a series of clashes that produced more than fifty thousand deaths. Once in control of the city, Sulla struck back at the *populares* by posting dreaded "proscription" lists, specifying names of hundreds of public enemies with rewards for their murder and punishment for any who protected them. In the process, he purged the Senate of *populares* and doubled its size to six hundred, further fortifying his personal authority. With opposition virtually eliminated, Sulla moved to consolidate his power in Rome's first extended dictatorship. The Senate moved to legalize Sulla's actions, and he in turn expanded the Senate's powers while weakening other republican institutions. After invoking the gods on his behalf, he launched a campaign of municipal development. Assuming that he had restored the Republic to its former stability and greatness, Sulla retired from public life.

What followed was a struggle for power, dominated by the young and ambitious general Gnaeus Pompeius (Pompey). Given expansive authority by the Senate, he led his mighty army in subduing much of the Mediterranean and Roman Asia. However, while Pompey fought for over six years, the young Julius Caesar was building his own allies among the *populares* in Rome at Pompey's expense. In an effort to head off further civil conflict, the two joined secretly with the wealthy Crassus to form the First Triumvirate in 60 B.C. The three made a formidable but unstable alliance. While Caesar was leading his legions in the conquest of Gaul, Crassus died on a military campaign in Asia in 53 B.C. Meanwhile, the Senate granted Pompey extraordinary powers to control the raging civil strife between *optimates* and *populares*, and the Triumvirate collapsed after a ten-year duration.

In 50 B.C., Caesar learned that Pompey and the Senate had voided his powers. The next year, Caesar took up the challenge by marching his forces across the Rubicon River from Gaul to Rome. When Pompey beat a strategic retreat, Caesar pursued him and defeated Pompey's forces at Pharsalus, Greece. Continuing his campaign into Egypt and further south, Caesar annexed new territory and then returned to Rome to celebrate victory and consolidate power. He assumed a number of the traditional republican positions before a reluctant Senate in 46 B.C. made him dictator for ten years and then, two years later, dictator for life.

By reputation a true military hero and a leader of keen insight, Caesar gathered bountiful honors for his campaigns. In his dress and public manner he openly encouraged adulation. The government struck a coin in his image, built monuments to his victories, erected his statue in the capital alongside those of the kings of Rome, and made him a god. When rumors spread that Caesar himself aspired to reinstitute kingship, he did nothing to allay them and only seemed by his arrogance to encourage them. It was Caesar's unbounded ambition, his great power, and his determination to reshape Rome that frightened the senatorial aristocracy into conspiring against him.

On the Ides of March (March 15), 44 B.C., as the Senate was meeting, a band of conspirators led by Cassius and Brutus descended on Caesar with knives and stabbed him to death. As he slumped down in death, the assassins shouted victoriously that they had restored the Republic; in fact, their desperate act would bring on thirteen more years of civil war.

Caesar left a paradoxical legacy. Both as general and political leader he had built the framework for the Roman Empire, and his keen intelligence had led him to abandon archaic traditions of the early Republic in pursuit of a more cosmopolitan vision. At the same time, by flaunting his power and mocking the republican constitution, he perpetuated the interference in politics by generals. And in exploiting political factions he built a dictatorship, based on a cult of personality, at the expense of a more orderly and balanced political process.

THE ROMAN REVOLUTION

Caesar's assassination touched off a thirteen-year power struggle among his would-be successors as well as profound social and political changes. As the assassins fled Rome, Caesar's friend and colleague Mark Antony took the reins of government. Consul at the time, Antony controlled Caesar's papers, delivered his eulogy, and claimed to be his legitimate successor. However, Caesar's eighteen-year-old great nephew, Octavian, mounted a strong challenge. Caesar's personal heir and adopted son, Octavian reassembled three thousand of his great uncle's troops to demonstrate the seriousness of his ambitions. Quickly Cicero, former consul and Rome's most famous orator, entered the fray against Antony, who, after losing a battle in the new civil war, fled Italy.

In the fall of 43 B.C., Octavian, Antony, and Caesar's cavalry commander, Lepidus, created the Second Triumvirate by formalizing a five-year agreement to stabilize Roman politics. The three began ominously by imposing a proscription list that led to the murder of three hundred potential opponents, including Cicero. They then divided Roman territories among them and pursued Caesar's assassins to the east, where both Cassius and Brutus committed suicide. For five years, the three men struggled to win control of their respective strongholds. Antony, who had built an imposing military force and stabilized his power in Rome, traveled to Egypt on a military campaign. While he was there, stories began to circulate in Rome of Antony's infatuation with Cleopatra, queen of Egypt, and his fascination with Eastern culture and with the idea of moving the capital to Alexandria.

After a serious disagreement, Octavian announced the termination of the Second Triumvirate in January 32 B.C. The next month Octavian took his grievances to the Senate, which eventually removed Antony from power and declared war on Cleopatra. In the fall of 31 B.C., Octavian prevailed in the famous Battle of Actium in the Adriatic Sea, when Antony and Cleopatra retreated to Egypt. Octavian invaded Egypt the next year, took control of the treasury, and reduced Egypt to provincial status. In the process, both Antony and Cleopatra committed suicide. The civil war now ended. Octavian, or Augustus—as he would soon be known from the title the Senate would award him—already in control of much of the Mediterranean, set about consolidating his power in Italy.

AUGUSTUS AND THE DEVELOPMENT OF THE PRINCIPATE

In the forty-four years of Augustus's reign, he cautiously restructured the Roman Empire while maintaining a facade of republican institutions. By the time he claimed victory in the Battle of Actium, dramatic changes had already begun to transform Roman society. The old senatorial aristocracy, badly damaged by the extended political conflict and the resulting social upheaval, now found its ranks dominated by provincial Italians, the middle class, and former *plebs*, many of them quite wealthy. Most of the new ruling class owed allegiance to Augustus, who relied on their support to sustain his quest for supremacy. The decline of the independent farmer continued, as estates worked by slave labor grew and specialized in sheep herding, cattle ranching, and olive and grape cultivation at the expense of grain production. Augustus now fashioned a campaign in the name of restoring the virtues and values of the old Republic. If saving the Republic was impossible, his own ascendancy was assured.

The year before Augustus returned from the east to a hero's welcome, the Senate made him special tribune for life. By 29 B.C., Augustus had begun to establish a firmer grip on power and to reform Roman administration. He achieved greater peace and security by expanding Rome's alliances and making diplomatic initiatives with bordering territories. Inside Italy, he strengthened the Roman patriotism of cities without sacrificing regional or local identity.

The city of Rome was now sprawling beyond its earlier defensive walls, prompting Augustus to expand Caesar's urban development projects in an effort to solve basic problems while providing the capital a fitting presence. He built and repaired temples, theaters, roads, aqueducts, and a drainage system, and he generally modernized the city and gave it a monumental appearance while at the same time intentionally restoring old monuments to make a public gesture toward the old Republic. Augustus claimed that he had found Rome a city of bricks and left it a city of marble. Furthermore, he attended to the needs of the populace by managing the distribution of food and instituting a program of public entertainment in the newly constructed amphitheater.

Augustus called the product of his reforms the Principate (to signal he was Rome's *princeps*, "first among citizens"). Although impressed with the traditions of Eastern monarchy, he moved more cautiously than Caesar to integrate Eastern elements into Roman government. The most serious challenge Rome faced was to develop a formula for providing peace and stability in a very large empire held together by only the most delicate bonds. Republican institutions were both inadequate to this task and badly eroded. Appealing to the nostalgia for the old city-state and to the vanity of the senatorial aristocracy, Augustus invoked Roman traditions in his campaign to build public support for his disguised despotism. He appealed to the conventional morality of the old Republic, sponsoring literature that glorified the past and enforcing new laws of rigid morality. Some of his reforms enjoyed only marginal success. For example, in spite of legislation that emphasized marriage and family and provided incentives for bearing children, Augustus's policies failed to reverse the declining birth rate. Families remained small, in part, because of the widespread use of contraceptives, including condoms. Nonetheless, Augustus pursued his reforms while skillfully avoiding Caesar's mistakes.

A man of immense personal fortune, Augustus had strengthened his grip on power by assembling a fighting force of sixty legions—a professional army, many of whom served twenty-year enlistments and fought battles in his name. At the same time, he accumulated a series of republican offices, including those of consul, *imperator* (military commander), and *pontifex maximus* (chief priest), and the power of tribune (although not the office). The state constructed an arch in the Forum to honor him, extended him religious honors, and proclaimed him "savior of the state." Based on the census of 28 B.C., Augustus replaced one-third of the Senate, which in turn granted him the power to speak first in that body and thus influence debate. The next year he dramatically proclaimed that he was restoring the powers of government to the Senate and the Roman people. The Senate, refusing this gesture to lay down his powers, instead granted him titles: Augustus, "the exalted one," which became his preferred title, and *pater patriae*, "father of the fatherland." In reality, although the Senate retained a certain reputation for its role in the early Republic, much of its power over domestic and foreign affairs had been lost to Augustus.

Augustus's dominance was both calculated and expansive. Not only did he control Rome, but he both extended its territory and sang its praises. In addition to peacemaking operations in Africa, Asia, Spain, along the Rhine and Danube frontiers, the Adriatic coast, and Alpine regions of Italy, Augustus added the province of Galatia. Indeed, Augustus's enormous territories encompassed perhaps fifty million people. To his credit, his administration gave the Mediterranean world an extended period of peace, the *pax Romana*.

The extended period of Augustan peace encouraged further economic development. Local industries flourished, particularly in glassware and pottery, as did the larger scale iron and construction industries. Such production contributed to a thriving international trade, as Romans, for example, imported silk from China, spices from India, and linen from Egypt. Free from battle, the Roman navy escorted its merchant ships safely through the Mediterranean Sea. Moreover, the spreading dominance of Roman currency and Roman banking and credit systems further contributed to the expansion of the economy. Eventually, however, the continuing spread of commerce and wealth to the provinces undercut the domestic economy, making it more difficult for local manufacturers to sell their products in provincial markets.

One of the strengths of the Augustan system was its acceptance of existing cultures and social structures, while recruiting local elites to assist the small Roman provincial bureaucracy. Augustus subdivided the territories, improved the road system to promote communication, and created a new imperial council and a few specialized advisers to assist him. He extended to the more than five million residents of Italy a privileged exemption from property tax, substantial local autonomy, and regional elections. In contrast, the provinces outside Italy paid taxes in various forms to proconsuls (former consuls who served to govern them) with the exception of Egypt, which the emperor governed directly. Remarkably, Augustus created an administrative system that was flexible, efficient, and durable.

To build and sustain support for his authoritarian regime, Augustus subsidized leading Roman writers who celebrated the virtues of early republican culture and praised Rome's great gift to the world. "Thou, O Roman," wrote Vergil in the *Aeneid*, " . . . thy role is to lead the nations by thy authority; for this is thy skill, and also to keep peace under thy control." Augustus commissioned Livy to write the extensive and heroic *History of Rome*. At the same time, Augustus took a personal interest in restoring traditional Olympian deities such as Apollo and Mars.

Naming a successor to inherit his great empire proved difficult. Augustus particularly wanted to continue to avoid the appearance of monarchy and had no sons of his own blood. When a series of arranged marriages to his only daughter and adoptions of her sons failed to produce an heir, the emperor turned finally to his stepson Tiberius in A.D. 4. Ten years later, at age seventy-six, Augustus died. In the aftermath Romans struggled to preserve the extended peace, the *pax Romana*, that was Augustus's great legacy. Each of his successors would be measured against his legendary greatness.

THE JULIO-CLAUDIAN DYNASTY, A.D. 14–68

When Tiberius succeeded his stepfather in A.D. 14 at age fifty-five, he sustained the Augustan line, so that each of his three successors would be dynastic descendants of Julius Caesar. No longer would emperors carry on Augustus's pretense that the old Republic lived. Although initially each made gestures of collaboration toward the Senate, in the end they all commanded power in the name of the Roman Empire, sometimes approaching absolute power. In general, the Julio-Claudian emperors followed Augustus's lead. They refined and expanded the Empire's central administration and adhered to Augustus's foreign policy of maintaining the existing boundaries of the Empire through careful diplomacy, judicious use of the military, and cultivation of satellite territories. Each of them faced opposition from the senatorial aristocracy as well as provincial revolts against taxation and other aspects of Roman rule. Significantly, the military played an ever more active role in the politics of the Julio-Claudian era, routinely interfering in the selection of new emperors.

In the realm of religion, each of the Julio-Claudians maintained the emperor cult and presided over a number of religious groups, including Judaism, various mystery cults, and Christianity. Jews managed to reach an agreement with the Roman authorities by which they were exempted from military service and state religious ceremonies and given jurisdiction over certain legal cases. Although discriminated against in public life and subjected to a special tax, Jews were allowed to co-exist.

In contrast, Roman authorities considered the followers of Jesus a political threat. Jesus, born in Palestine during the reign of Augustus (c. 6 B.C.), taught the virtues of charity, humility, and love, and his followers regarded him as the Messiah or Christ. In about A.D. 30, Pontius Pilate, prefect of the Palestinian province of Judea (taken from the Jews thirty-three years earlier by Roman legions), tried and executed Jesus. His small band of followers maintained their commitment, and one of them, a convert named Paul of Tarsus, traveled throughout the eastern Mediterranean region establishing Christian congregations. Ultimately, Paul reached Rome. According to Christian tradition, Paul was martyred in Rome, as was the Apostle Peter, but only after founding the cornerstone of the Christian Church. Although the earliest Christians in Rome were regarded as just one of many new, exotic religious sects, the emperor Nero would single them out for abuse. Only later would systematic persecution begin.

Tiberius seemed the ideal candidate to follow Augustus. Experienced in governmental and military affairs, educated, fiscally conservative, and committed to the Republic, Tiberius nonetheless failed to rally Romans to his cause and ended by abusing his power. After a decade of quelling provincial revolts and managing political intrigues, Tiberius retired to the island of Capri, where he continued to govern. From a distance, he managed both domestic and international affairs but became increasingly antagonistic in punishing would-be conspirators. In A.D. 37, Tiberius died an embittered man without having named a successor.

Based on his Julio-Claudian ancestry, the young Caligula laid claim to imperial power amid an outpouring of enthusiastic, but short-lived, public support. In his short, four-year reign, Caligula wholly mismanaged Rome, depleting its treasury, bungling an invasion of Britain, and alienating Jews by his attempt to place his own monument in the Temple at Jerusalem. In January 41, conspirators assassinated Caligula. Among them were the praetorian guard, who moved to preempt the Senate by selecting the inexperienced and cerebral Claudius.

Although widely ridiculed by his contemporaries, Claudius proved to be an exceptionally competent emperor. Having spent his life writing more than sixty volumes of history, Claudius now turned to public affairs with considerable skill. Rejecting the title *imperator*, he reorganized the administration, renewed Augustus's religious reforms, and launched an ambitious public works program of roads, aqueducts, and swamp reclamation that included the construction of the port of Ostia. In foreign affairs, he completed the conquest of Britain and succeeded in adding new colonies such as Judaea and Anatolia.

In 49, Claudius married his niece Agrippina and adopted her son Nero, who, as a result, became the heir apparent. When Claudius died in 54, probably poisoned by Agrippina, the praetorians named the sixteen-year-old Nero emperor. With the assistance of his mother and others, Nero gained the confidence of the Senate. Ancient as well as modern historians have portrayed this emperor as, on the one hand, the cruelest of tyrants who murdered his own mother, while, on the other, a cultivated patron of the arts and poet. Wherever the truth lies, he clearly became more authoritarian after Agrippina's death and more confrontational toward the Senate in his quest to reshape Roman culture. When Rome burned in 64, he enacted plans for a new capital. Three years later, when he was declared public enemy by the Senate at age thirty, Nero committed suicide.

THE FLAVIAN DYNASTY, A.D. 68–96

Nero's death exposed Rome once again to a civil war, somewhat reminiscent of the wars that had brought Caesar to power. After eighteen months of armed struggles among various factions throughout the Empire, the army of the Danube and the Egyptian legions, along with Nero's sons Titus and Domitian, forced their claim to make Vespasian emperor. The sixty-year-old Vespasian, whose military and administrative career had taken him from Britain to Africa, managed to restore order within two years and to establish his legitimacy. The first emperor of the Flavian family proved a capable manager who set a tone of order and progress throughout the Empire. By 70, he both calmed the tumultuous Rhine frontier and subdued the Jewish revolt, taking Jerusalem, destroying the temple, and thus forcing a new diaspora (dispersion) of Jews throughout much of Europe. He fortified the borders, sponsored building in Rome (most notably its great new amphitheater known as the Colosseum), and informed the Senate that his sons would succeed him.

Vespasian's educated and ambitious son Titus had acquired enough power—serving as consul, censor, Senator, commander of the praetorian guard—that he virtually became co-ruler during the last decade of his father's life. Titus ruled for only two years and, perhaps partly because of his premature death, was subsequently revered by the Roman people. Titus's younger brother Domitian had been largely excluded from power during his father's regime until the Senate granted him the powers of emperor in September 81 at age twenty-nine. While consolidating his own power, Domitian continued his father's policies, restoring monuments and constructing new ones such as the Arch of Titus in Rome's forum. However, as time passed, he expended greater efforts in suppressing uprisings in the provinces, eventually gaining the reputation of an abusive tyrant. Fifteen years after becoming emperor, Domitian was stabbed to death by a band of conspirators, including his wife.

Rome changed significantly under Flavian rule, not only in government but in social structure as well. As the great senatorial families faded, the middle class expanded and provincials from Gaul, the Iberian peninsula, and especially provincial Italy rose to greater prominence. Italian families remained small, particularly in the upper class, and women gradually found new opportunities. Although still deprived of political power, women began during the Empire to practice a number of occupations. They were particularly active in business and the professions, including, for example, midwifery and the manufacturing of piping for Rome's water system.

THE ANTONINE DYNASTY, A.D. 96–192: THE FIVE GOOD EMPERORS AND THE *PAX ROMANA*

The seventy-year-old Nerva succeeded Domitian. Nerva served seriously and prudently and, although little more than a figurehead, by adopting Trajan as successor he managed to provide a smooth transition and to found a line of succession that took Rome to the height of empire. The Antonines exhibited several qualities that together earned them a reputation for providing good government. They viewed themselves as guardians of the Roman state, devoting themselves to respecting and preserving its traditional religion, law, and administration as well as its army and infrastructure, including roads, ports, aqueducts, and monumental structures. In all, the Antonine era extended the prosperity and peace of the *pax Romana*.

Trajan came to power while a military commander on the Rhine, just three months after being named successor. Popular, respected as a general, moderate in his politics, and connected to the Senate, Trajan brought important qualities to the office as Rome's first provincial emperor. Not only did he articulate a vision of good government, but in his administration, his public building campaign, and his military successes he projected and lived up to all the ideals of the good emperor, earning the reputation of "Best Ruler" (*optimus princeps*).

When Trajan died in August 117, the army proclaimed Hadrian emperor, an act that the Senate confirmed. Great nephew and confidant of Trajan, Hadrian quickly developed his own style of governing. He tightened central administration around an imperial council, introduced a number of legal and economic reforms, and traveled widely, directly addressing problems he encountered in the provinces. In an effort to tighten security, he ordered strategic withdrawal from peripheral territories conquered by Trajan. After two decades in power, Hadrian transferred power to Antoninus, fell ill, and died.

Antoninus Pius, a wealthy and well-connected senator from a prominent family, ruled from 138 to 161. In the process, he managed to establish a superb reputation for fairness and restraint in governing a generally peaceful empire. Among his reforms, he abolished most anti-Semitic policies. The few criticisms made of this emperor tend to be insignificant. He lacked imagination, confined himself largely to the capital city, and failed to anticipate growing problems on the frontiers. Nonetheless, he both contributed continuity and preserved the good record of the Antonine dynasty that now bears his name.

During this extended period of peace, Roman architects achieved great distinction by creating a uniform building style throughout the Empire. In cities from Britain to Armenia, residents and travelers alike recognized temples, baths, theaters, stadiums, and courts that were built to Roman standards in a uniquely Roman style. Imperial-age builders made significant advances in the earlier Roman invention of poured concrete, using it in combination with the arch, dome, and vault, thus enabling them to erect much larger structures with vast interiors. Roman housing, increasingly built in the configuration of apartment buildings in the urban centers, often included running water and central heating systems. The emperor

Hadrian, an architect himself, designed and built in Rome the Pantheon, widely admired for its elegance as perhaps the finest example of Roman architecture.

With the death of Antoninus Pius in A.D. 161 came the accession of Marcus Aurelius, who had been trained for the emperorship since childhood. A philosopher and man of principle, he dedicated himself to delivering good government. Unfortunately, he suffered from physical frailty and lack of military experience. The latter would not have been a serious shortcoming in the previous half-century; however, ironically, this philosopher of peace found himself embroiled in military affairs throughout his two decades of power as problems flared on all sides. He dispatched troops to Asia, led others to the Danube frontier, and ordered campaigns in northern Italy, North Africa, and elsewhere. The results were foreboding. Troops brought a devastating plague back to Rome from Asia in 167. On the Rhine-Danube frontier, Germanic ("barbarian") tribes threatening Roman defenses could not be checked. The constant battling brought divisiveness, which in turn led to a policy of less tolerance for Christians as their religion spread both geographically and throughout the social classes.

In this time of disquiet, Marcus Aurelius's death in 180 brought to power his son Commodus, whose brief reign quickly was consumed by his own madness and depravity. He retaliated violently against plots on his life, real and imagined, and then withdrew from governing, content to amuse himself by watching gladiatorial combats and chariot races. His murder on the final day of A.D. 192 left Rome without an heir, dynastic or appointed, and in the throes of deepening crisis.

THE CRISIS OF THE THIRD CENTURY AND THE DECLINE OF THE ROMAN EMPIRE IN ITALY

The end of the Antonine dynasty presaged what historians traditionally called "the fall of the Roman Empire" in the west. Although economic prosperity continued for perhaps another forty years under subsequent emperors, particularly the Severi, indications of change began to appear simultaneously. By the mid-third century, Italy entered an extended period during which Roman governmental, legal, and economic structures gave way to less formal, more decentralized political cultures, heavily influenced by the traditions of immigrating Germanic tribes. Particularly obvious was economic change, which, in the wake of declining commerce, reduced many regions of Italy to subsistence economies. In contrast, the eastern portion of the Roman Empire would retain its basic strength and structure until overrun by Ottoman Turks in the fifteenth century.

Throughout the third century A.D., Roman emperors actually consolidated power while leaving some local autonomy to municipalities. The city of Rome continued to grow and retained its role as financial and commercial center of the Western Empire, while the Italian peninsula experienced uneven development. Much of the South and Center lost some of their earlier prosperity, although certain pockets thrived, such as the port of Ostia, the Carrara marble mines, and the Etrurian wine region. In contrast to the general decline, northern cities, such as Milan, Bologna, Modena, Padua, and Verona, continued to flourish as centers for wheat, wine, and wool trading.

Throughout the third century, growing turbulence on the frontiers sounded a loud warning bell. Roman legions were forced to fight on two fronts to stop simultaneous invasions of Germanic tribes and resurgent Persian armies. The resulting Roman military defeats intensified internal conflict and thrust the military directly into the political process as the troops assassinated emperors to empower new ones. A dizzying succession of emperors, the bulk of them generals, broke down the political process and made impossible any continuity of policy. At the same time, Germanic invaders looted northern towns, disrupting trade routes. The fighting aggravated economic decay, which in turn deepened social problems, especially the suffering of the poor, and touched off a growing malaise among the general population. Emperors fought back, sometimes successfully, as was the case with the victories of Claudius II over invading Germanic tribes in 270. Strapped by increased military demands and economic contraction, emperors resorted to extreme measures, increasing taxes on an already suffering population, debasing the coins, and resuming sporadic persecution of Christians for their alleged disloyalty. Nonetheless, Christianity expanded in third-century Italy.

After this extended period of disruption, two exceptional Roman emperors managed to reorganize the Empire and restore its administrative order. In doing so, Diocletian and Constantine changed the Empire irreversibly; the latter moved the capital to Constantinople, where the Eastern Roman (later, Byzantine) Empire would thrive for over a thousand years. Italy gained almost no direct benefit from this political and economic resurgence and, with a few notable exceptions, was largely abandoned by subsequent emperors to be controlled by a succession of Germanic tribal leaders.

THE REFORMS OF DIOCLETIAN AND CONSTANTINE

In 284, Diocletian took power. This career soldier from Dalmatia seemed an unlikely candidate to carry out sweeping reforms that, together with those of his successor, transformed the Roman Empire. He began by reorganizing and expanding the army, then followed by subdividing the provinces. In 294 Diocletian initiated fiscal and monetary reforms, including restructure of the tax system, revaluation of the currency, and imposition of wage and price controls.

After a year of confusion following Diocletian's retirement in 305, another general, Constantine, claimed power. He extended Diocletian's military and administrative reforms, but it was his dramatic change in religious policy that brought him notoriety. Diocletian had instituted systematic persecutions of Christians. Constantine, converted by a vision on the eve of his victory over his rival Maxentius at the Milvian Bridge in 312, introduced a policy of official religious tolerance and then involved himself directly in resolving conflicts within the Christian Church. In 313, the emperor legalized the practice of the Christian religion. At the same time, Constantine intensified official discrimination against Jews, labeling Judaism a sinister cult, revoking Jewish exemptions from official religious and military obligations, and making intermarriage between Jews and Christians a capital offense.

Ranking alongside his sweeping religious changes in importance was the emperor's founding of a second Imperial capital on which he bestowed his name—Constantinople. Clearly the focal point of empire had now shifted eastward, not only in administration but in economics and culture as well. By the mid-fourth century, the Byzantine Empire (as it is now called) had become a highly centralized, bureaucratic state under which the status of Italy was diminished to the level of other provinces such as Gaul and Spain. In Rome, the former Senate, although still prestigious, was reduced to a municipal council, exercising no authority outside the city; the city itself was now governed by a corps of bureaucrats headed by a prefect. Other Italian cities likewise fell under the jurisdiction of imperial officials but continued to exercise local autonomy and retained varying degrees of prosperity and vitality. Although no longer the political center of empire, Rome, as capital of the Western Empire, actually grew in physical presence. It enjoyed renewed prestige as a result of the ambitious building projects of Diocletian and Constantine and the latter's sponsorship of the first Christian basilicas (specially honored churches) such as St. Peter's and San Giovanni Laterana, Rome's cathedral.

In the countryside, several trends brought fundamental changes in Italian life. Rural folk were increasingly governed by chieftains, usually of Germanic tribes. Such immigrants acquired land through a variety of legal arrangements, often in return for military service. And even though this process strengthened the Roman army and expanded the labor force at a time when both were needed, it presented Roman authorities with a fundamental problem: The Germanic immigrant population was not being assimilated. Italy, particularly in its northern regions, was evolving toward a dualistic culture wherein the Roman population lived under established Roman law while the Germanic population lived under a parallel set of Germanic customs.

Fourth-century Italy experienced a range of social and economic adjustments that accompanied cultural and political change. In rural Italy, expanding estates threatened the well-being of small, independent farmers. This trend toward large estates, or villas, reinforced the class system, as did the state in awarding titles and cultivating a political elite. The trend toward concentration of land also generated migration to the cities by the displaced farmers and a simultaneous emergence of villas as rural economic centers. Furthermore, although statistics are sparse, it appears that the middle class declined in this period, to some extent a victim of increased taxation. Slave labor persisted, not only in rural areas but in the towns and cities as well.

The peace that returned to Italy after the death of Constantine provided renewed economic expansion, so that the peninsula enjoyed a degree of economic revival in the fourth century. Activity at the natural ports revived, with goods being imported and exported at Genoa, Ostia, Naples, and Brindisi while the domestic trade routes connected the ports with the thriving city of Milan and the Alpine passes. Many towns and cities reinforced their defensive perimeters by building walls, but Italian cities remained relatively stable. At the same time, the Roman state intervened more aggressively in the economy, imposing greater economic regulation and competing with private workshops in such industries as pottery production.

In some cases, Italian cities even experienced a degree of cultural revival. Artists, writers, and architects enjoyed renewed patronage, although little of the work was innovative, as it was so strongly rooted in earlier classical forms. As the Christian Church expanded, the local cathedrals often added schools, thereby preserving the classical languages and literatures. Revitalized literary activity resulted, too, from this growth of Christianity, including works of theology such as those of St. Ambrose, bishop of Milan.

The mild economic resurgence in the fourth century A.D. was both sporadic and brief. Some cities seemed untouched. By the final third of the century, a new crisis began to spread that left the Italian peninsula in disarray. The emperor Valentinian I officially divided the Empire in 364 and moved the capital of the west from Rome to Milan. Although he addressed a range of economic and social problems, military threats on the borders demanded much of his attention. Similarly, Theodosius (ruled 379–395) fought invaders on several fronts. He followed military successes with treaties, including an arrangement whereby Goths were allowed to settle inside the Empire. In domestic affairs, Theodosius banned the practice of pagan religions, further entrenching Christianity in Italy.

Theodosius's official incorporation of Germanic peoples into the Empire was a sure sign of change. Theodosius's son Honorius entrusted Rome's security to the Vandal general Stilicho, who won acclaim for his defense against invasions by both Visigoths and Ostrogoths in the early fifth century. Stilicho's prominence was typical of the growing integration of barbarian chiefs and tribal units into the Roman army. A few years later, after Vandals had crossed the Rhine River, Stilicho was captured and executed. Then, in 410, Visigoth invaders under Alaric took Rome itself, marking the end of Roman control of Italy. Rule by a succession of ineffective Roman emperors was followed by that of barbarian chiefs, including the chief of the Hunnic Confederation, Attila, and the Ostrogoth Theodoric. Centralized Roman administration of Italy was reduced to mere memory. Nonetheless, Roman traditions of language, law, and literature would survive, as would the abundant physical evidence of Roman architecture, throughout the peninsula.

3

Italy in the Middle Ages, 400–1300

In the centuries after the political power of the Roman Empire diminished in Italy, life in the peninsula developed along lines that many now recognize as uniquely Italian. Cities and villages emerged from the shadow of Rome to become more important political and economic focal points. In fact, the peninsula would never again, until the nineteenth century, constitute a single, interdependent economic unit with an effective system of communications, and only in the third quarter of that century would it achieve political unification. Because of the diffusion of power in the fifth century, much about Italian culture is to be learned by examining the period that followed, known as the Middle Ages or Medieval era.

Students of Italian history, in contrast with those who study English or French history, for example, do not measure progress primarily in terms of the centralization of political power in the hands of a dynasty whose growth signals the emergence of a modern nation-state. The Italian peninsula developed along different lines. In spite of the collapse of the Roman Empire in the West, Italy retained a significant degree of identity, particularly because its cities sustained their character as civic and economic centers, even when they became more self-sufficient, built defensive walls, and lost their international commercial connections.

In Italy, what was more indicative of development than the rise of a single state was the emergence of an urban nobility that, through intermarriage with the leading commercial families, established the power of a number of separate cities. In each case, this urban ruling class, often featuring rival factions of merchants and bankers, eventually established control over the surrounding countryside, creating a number of economic and political units, each of which served as a population center and a marketplace for crops produced in its environs. Many functioned also as centers of administration for the various ruling powers or for the Church.

Throughout the Medieval era, although some disappeared, a vast majority of Italian cities endured. In fact, it is the importance of its cities that distinguishes Medieval Italy, especially after the rise of the autonomous communes (self-governing cities) in the Center and North. This urban identity contrasts markedly with much of the rest of Europe, where largely self-sufficient rural manors became the dominant feature.

The cities of early Medieval Italy, although they maintained their Roman walls and rectangular street plans, were often less impressive in their architecture than their Roman predecessors. Churches now were relatively small, private housing was constructed of timber or stone, and gardens and fields encroached on the urban landscape. The major streets normally converged at a forum that functioned primarily as a commercial market but had lost its political identity with the decline of civic government. In its stead, the palace and the cathedral now symbolized power.

The commercial character of Italian cities persisted during the Medieval era, even when the volume of inter-urban and international trade declined. Artisans such as goldsmiths, ironworkers, clothmakers, and house builders continued to practice and organize their crafts. Political authorities—even kings and princes, depending on their ability to command power at a given time—imposed tolls, tariffs, and various regulations, including licensing and price controls on products and services. The modern concept of free markets (in which governments avoid interfering with competition) existed in only the most limited sense.

Not only did Medieval Italy retain its urban identity, but, even when divided, it remained better connected to the outside world than any other place in Europe. In no other location did Catholic, Byzantine, and Muslim cultures intermingle so readily as in this hub of East-West interaction. Venice, in particular, maintained its international trade throughout this period, although such ports as Pisa and Genoa were slower to recover and began to thrive only amid the general economic expansion of the eleventh century.

In spite of this trend toward decentralization in the early Middle Ages, the bulk of the Italian peninsula fell under the dominance of a series of kings: Ostrogothic, Lombard, and Frankish. In fact, these kings made serious attempts to reestablish centralized power and, in some instances, enjoyed relative success. All the while, the Roman ideal of unity remained alive, at least in a cultural sense if not as political reality.

It is also the case that the Church, by organizing a hierarchical structure that recognized the bishop of Rome as pope (*papa*, or father of the Church), developed its own powerful network that transcended the peninsula and became, although inconsistently in this period, an international force. As the Roman Empire had done, the medieval Church developed the ideal of unity. Even more important for Italy in many ways was the influence of the Church in formal culture, especially in theology, painting, sculpture, and architecture, and in its social impact through the local parish clergy in Italian villages and cities.

In fact, most people living in Medieval Italy did not use the term *Italy* and did not think of themselves as *Italians*. Their identity remained local, although they may have acknowledged the authority of a particular duke or Germanic king who controlled the territory to which their town was subjugated—and to whose magistrate they paid taxes or appealed for justice. Only in the fourteenth century did the Florentine poet Dante Alighieri provide Italians with a common vernacular language, so that a new *Italian* literature promoted the idea of *Italy*. However, references to Italy or Italians remained restricted largely to the literate population and to merchants and those living abroad who made certain generalizations about the people and culture of the peninsula.

THE OSTROGOTH INVASIONS OF THE FIFTH CENTURY

For a little more than a half-century after Alaric's Visigoths took Rome in 410, a succession of Roman emperors managed to hold power, although ineffectively, from their residence in the Adriatic city of Ravenna. The emperors of the fifth century no longer commanded the army; in fact, several Roman generals held the frontiers against Germanic tribal invasions by allying with bands of Huns and Goths. In the late Empire, Roman generals and Germanic military leaders not only provided security but interchangeably interfered in politics, so that the break between Roman Italy and Germanic Italy was not as great as might be imagined.

The Germanic ruler Odoacer took power in a military coup d'état in 476, a date that traditionally marks the end of the Roman Empire and its succession of western emperors in Italy. Odoacer, ruling the peninsula as king, provided fourteen years of relative peace while maintaining good relations with the Senate and the support of his army. Then, in 489, the Ostrogoth

Theodoric invaded the peninsula with an army of 25,000 and a population perhaps in excess of 100,000. The next year, Theodoric claimed power in the name of the Byzantine emperor and established himself as the most powerful ruler Italy had known in over one hundred years.

Meanwhile, life among the people of the Italian peninsula continued largely uninterrupted, with the exception that Theodoric was more efficient than his predecessors in collecting taxes and rooting out corruption. He also managed to rebuild Roman palaces in Pavia, Ravenna, and Verona. By maintaining peace and prolonging Roman traditions of government, Theodoric won favor with both Roman and Gothic populations.

JUSTINIAN'S WARS, THE LOMBARD INVASIONS, AND THE END OF ITALIAN UNITY

If the change in administration did not automatically disrupt life in Italy, the subsequent warfare did. War devastated much of the peninsula once the Byzantine emperor Justinian withdrew his support of Theodoric and launched a campaign in 535 to reclaim Italy from the Goths. Troops under the command of the brilliant Byzantine general Belisarius occupied Sicily, then drove through the mainland north to the Po Valley, engaging Gothic armies in a series of battles that continued for eighteen years. In the end, Justinian's armies reattached Italy to the Byzantine Empire, but at the cost of famine and greater political and economic confusion than even the Germanic tribes had caused. In the wake of the wars, the Gothic culture was lost along with virtually all archaeological traces of its existence.

Justinian died in 565, leaving his entire empire with serious problems and opening the door to yet another invasion of Italy, now badly battered by two decades of warfare. As a result, when the Lombards swept down from the north in 568, these semi-nomadic, mounted warriors found the peninsula largely undefended. They forced the Byzantines to take refuge in the northeast around the city of Ravenna, in the southern mainland, and on the island of Sicily, while the popes clung to Rome and its environs. The Lombards brought with them a heroic, warrior ideology that elevated the social status and political and economic power of those who understood Lombard culture and could fight. Lombard social norms emphasized kinship, inherited through the male, who in turn exercised control over the women in his family.

However, although the Lombards succeeded in establishing a kingdom that controlled at its peak of power more than two-thirds of the peninsula, they failed to create a unified state. The political unity imposed by the Romans and continued with at least minimal success by the Goths now had ended. The Lombards neglected both the Roman infrastructure and the system of administration, producing, at first, no written records. Consequently, when the Lombards abandoned the system of drainage and irrigation, land formerly drained by Romans reverted to swamps. And because the Lombards had little need to maintain local centers of governmental administration, the cities, particularly those in the North and Center, lost much of their Roman political identity.

However, in spite of another major shift in political control, life for much of the Italian population went on without significant change. The Lombard migration into the peninsula meant that they comprised something less than 10 percent of the population. Instead of imposing their own customs on the Roman population, the Lombards largely adapted to the culture they found. Although most came into Italy as Arian Christians (Arianism had been ruled a heresy by the Church in A.D. 325), many converted to Roman Christianity, thus easing their integration into broader society. They absorbed much of the Latin culture, giving up their own language in favor of Latin and accepting Roman legal traditions and popular styles. In the countryside, Lombard chieftains did little to dismantle the great estates. Instead, they displaced the Roman landholders in a number of instances and converted much of the land from farming to grazing. A higher percentage of Lombards than Romans owned large estates; conversely, a higher percentage of Romans worked as agricultural tenants. In either event, Italian farmers continued to use virtually the same tools and techniques throughout the Medieval era to produce the same crops—grains, wine, and olive oil—that Roman farmers had produced.

The fact that every region of eighth-century Italy reflected social, legal, and commercial differences provides further evidence of the strength of local traditions and the inability of the Lombards to impose their own uniform culture. Under Lombard domination, Italy reverted to its fragmented, pre-Roman conditions. Thus, both rural and urban life varied significantly from village to village and region to region. However, throughout Medieval Italy, a free peasantry persisted together with a class of large estate owners that tended to live in urban areas. Tenants and slaves constituted the bulk of the population, with tenant holdings scattered geographically, meaning that peasants had to move from field to field. But by the tenth century, most farmers in Italy had acquired their freedom. Free tenants now signed fixed-term leases and usually paid rent in money, a sign of a general revival of the economy. All the while, land ownership remained the most important element in determining power.

Eventually the Lombards developed a functional scheme of administration in the North. By the middle of the seventh century, they had placed agents of the king in a number of northern towns. Their capital, Pavia, with its palace, baths, and numerous monumental buildings and churches, provided a vital center for Lombard rule. Lombard kings maintained a system that incorporated their own customs into Roman administrative tradition, minting coins, setting price controls, maintaining city structures, collecting important duties, tolls, port fees, and sales taxes. However, the one Roman tax that the Lombards proved unable to collect was a critical one: the land tax. Without it, Lombard kings were no longer able to fund the army, meaning that the responsibility for providing a defensive force increasingly rested with local Lombard dukes.

Notable among the Lombard kings were Authari (ruled 584–590), Agilulf (ruled 590–616), Rothari (ruled 636–652), Grimoald (ruled 662–671) and Liudprand (ruled 712–744). After surviving three invasions by the Franks and just before dying, Authari issued an anti-Catholic decree in 590, the same year that Gregory the Great was elected Pope. This was to prove an omen, as the papacy would steadily grow more wary of Lombard antagonism and would eventually call for outside help. King Agilulf seemed to fulfill the papacy's worst fears, not only by expanding Lombard control of the Po Valley and Tuscany but by moving on Rome itself. Finally, Agilulf negotiated a series of treaties that stabilized the peninsula for a generation. By the mid-seventh century, Rothari revived Lombard aggression, acquiring Emilia and the Ligurian coast. While in power, Rothari made great strides in formalizing the Lombard presence by issuing a Latin edict of 643 in which he provided an extensive account of Lombard customs. In response, Italians, whether Lombard or Latin, widely accepted Rothari's extensive code, giving Italy a Germanic legal system to parallel the Roman law of Justinian.

When Grimoald seized power in 662, one of more than ten coups d'état in the Lombard era, he embraced Rothari's code, further legitimizing Lombard culture. When he succeeded in staving off the final Byzantine attempt to conquer Lombard Italy, he paved the way for sixty years of peace. Taking power after another series of coups, Liudprand modified Rothari's code, expanding the rights of women to inherit property and legalizing donations to the Church. By carefully incorporating elements of Roman law into Lombard practice, Liudprand contributed to the synthesis of the two cultures. The Germanic methods of resolving disputes by feud and battle persisted, but by the ninth century they had diminished greatly in importance. And in spite of the success of a number of Lombard kings in expanding their power, ultimate judicial power rested with the individual cities. Eventually, Liudprand expanded Lombard influence through much of the remaining Byzantine territory in and around Ravenna (which he eventually abandoned) and infringed on Church territory around Benevento and Spoleto in the South, once again alarming the papacy.

In international affairs, the Lombard kings maintained alliances with the more powerful Franks until Stephen II (pope 752–757), protesting further Lombard encroachment, summoned Pippin III to lead his Franks against the Lombards around Pavia. In the aftermath of a Frankish victory, the Lombards ceded Ravenna and its hinterland to the Pope, constituting the basis of the territories known as the Papal States. The Lombards broke the status quo, however, when they challenged the expansion of the Papal States through the center of the peninsula. In response, Charlemagne led his Franks into Lombard Italy in 773, took Pavia, and crowned himself king of the Lombards.

THE SOUTH UNDER BYZANTINE DOMINATION

If life in Italy continued largely uninterrupted as Lombard rulers replaced Romans throughout much of the peninsula, even greater continuity existed under Byzantine rule in the South. Sicilian and southern Italian ports such as Naples and Bari remained connected commercially through the Mediterranean to the eastern world, while Salerno, Amalfi, and other coastal cities competed and sometimes fought as semi-independent states. A number of southern port cities developed as commercial centers, trading with Arabs, Byzantines, and western Europeans. In general, the Byzantine-controlled southern port cities developed more as hubs of international trade than as markets for the products of their hinterlands, although a linen industry thrived in Naples as did wheat production in Apulia and silk manufacturing in Calabria. In the rural South of the early Medieval era, small-scale agriculture prevailed. Farm production was largely in the hands of tenant farmers who paid their rents in crops, but a minority of independent farmers and a smaller number of slaves continued to farm throughout this period.

The Byzantine emperors controlled political power through much of the South in the Medieval era. However, their success varied over time and place, rising and falling with the fortunes of various imperial armies in confronting localized resistance and in countering Arab incursions. Naples and other cities such as Benevento continued to resist outside authority, while Arabs controlled Sicily through most of the ninth century. Byzantine cultural influence also varied, relative to such factors as political control, density of the Greek-speaking population, and volume of trade. Thus, for example, the Byzantines influenced Calabrian culture more than Apulian. Throughout this period, the Byzantines managed to collect taxes. However, many cities operated autonomously, each led by a local prince or a powerful family, until, in the middle of the eleventh century, Normans acquired control of much of the South.

THE INTERVENTION OF THE FRANKS IN THE NORTH AND THE CREATION OF CAROLINGIAN ITALY

Charlemagne's successful invasion of Italy in 773–774 destroyed the Lombard kingdom after a little more than two centuries and set a precedent for northern European rulers of Italy: They would govern in absentia. Once he returned home after his Italian victory to rule the Carolingian Empire, Charlemagne crossed the Alps into Italian territory only four times. The most noteworthy occasion was his trip to St. Peter's Basilica on Christmas Day A.D. 800, when Leo III (pope 795–816) crowned him "Emperor." He and his Carolingian successors would control most of the North and Center as the Kingdom of Italy for seventy years.

Another pattern is clear. Once again, in spite of conquest by an outside power, Italians experienced little change in their everyday lives. In many ways Italy continued to be a decentralized territory, with Carolingian dukes and counts now replacing Lombards and governing in the name of the Carolingian emperor. Social class structure, economic patterns, and means of making political and judicial decisions remained largely unaffected by the Carolingians, who migrated across the Alps in relatively small numbers. Control of land by urban noblemen, the Church, and the monarch remained a key to power, as it had been.

The Carolingian kings of Italy were generally a forgettable group, primarily because only one, Louis II, actually lived in Italy throughout his reign and because none of them clearly defined the place Italy occupied within the Empire. When Charlemagne returned to Francia (the former kingdom of the Franks), he placed his young son Pippin in control of Italy under the supervision of several agents. In 814, the Carolingian emperor Louis the Pious, who never visited Italy, granted Italy to his young son Lothar. Eight years later Lothar traveled to Italy, where he spent much of the remainder of his life, essentially in exile from Francia. However, Lothar seemed more interested in northern Europe than in Italy, and accordingly he contributed little to expanding Carolingian influence over Italian life.

In 844, Lothar sent his son Louis II to Italy. Shortly thereafter, Louis launched a campaign to consolidate Carolingian power, first in the North, and then further south. He brought many of the bishops of Italy under his control while issuing decrees to remedy the most pressing problems that had developed under more than a half-century of neglect by Carolingian emperors: thievery, abuse of power by authorities, and deterioration of roads and bridges.

With varying degrees of success, the Carolingian kings maintained control of Lombard Italy, but not even Louis II acquired much more territory. However, because Pippin and Charlemagne had been invited by popes, they and their successors claimed authority over most of the Papal States outside the vicinity of Rome. Carolingian troops in several instances moved on southern cities, but they never did establish permanent control. In particular, Louis II, now Carolingian emperor, took a large army south in 866 to drive the Arabs out of Bari and expand his influence. After five years of indecisive campaigning, Louis was captured and held prisoner for a month, which forever undermined his prestige and thus his effectiveness in the South. When Louis II died in 875, he left no male heir. The dispute to succeed him touched off thirty years of conflict that essentially ended Carolingian control of the Italian peninsula.

In spite of the continuity of Medieval Italian life and the durability of Latin culture, the Carolingians did leave a mark. In part because the kings themselves were generally weak, Carolingian political influence was most effective at the lower administrative levels. Carolingian dukes and counts continued to collect tolls and tariffs and to derive their power from control of the land, as the Lombards had done. Charlemagne and other emperors began to rely also on bishops to carry out their decrees, a departure from Lombard practice. And because bishops and counts derived their power from land, they often competed for influence throughout much of Carolingian Italy. The later Carolingian rulers, especially Berengar I (ruled 902–924), gave away substantial land and privileges in order to solidify support against Hungarian raids, thus further weakening Frankish central authority and turning over the defense of Frankish Italy to the private armies of counts and bishops. Consequently, although the later Frankish kings found it more and more difficult to exercise power, they did play a role in allocating power in many localities. The Carolingians favored bishops over counts, giving bishops virtual control of a number of northern cities. By about 900, a pattern developed in the North and Center whereby political power in Piedmont and Tuscany was held by counts, whereas bishops controlled the Veneto, Emilia, and much of Lombardy. At the same time, throughout much of the peninsula, particularly the South, the building of fortified castles continued and power remained dispersed.

By the 920s, the Carolingian rulers of Italy were so weak that they contracted with Hungarian mercenary troops to protect their power; in turn, northern noblemen turned to Burgundy and Provence for help, dividing northern Italy accordingly. Hugh of Provence (ruled 926–947) made a bold effort to force control of much of the North and Center and to strengthen his defenses against the prospect of German raids, using military forces and leaving family members and bishops to consolidate his power. The crowning of Otto I as king of Germany reaffirmed Hugh's earlier fears, especially when Otto crossed the Alps in 951 and crowned himself king of Italy. Berengar II (ruled 950–962), the last of the Carolingian kings of Italy, was then reduced to ruling in Otto's name, and seeing his power diminishing even further, he resorted to force, as Hugh had done. Over their final decade, the Carolingians saw their judicial and administrative authority over Italy virtually disappear.

ARAB CONQUESTS IN THE SOUTH

The attacks by the Carolingian Louis II against Arab forces in Bari constituted only one response to the growing Arab presence in Sicily, southern Italy, and much of the Mediterranean world in the ninth century. After taking North Africa in the seventh century, Arabs had expanded across the Mediterranean in a series of raids on Sicily and the southern mainland. They invaded Sicily in 827, proceeded to take Palermo and Messina from the Byzantines, solidified their power, and then used the island as a staging area for attacks on the southern peninsula, raiding the territories of Apulia, Calabria, and Campania. By most accounts, Sicily thrived under Arab rule, particularly its capital Palermo, which became known for its many brilliant mosques. The Arabs mined and marketed silver, lead, and sulphur while introducing new crops and such new technology as reservoirs and water towers.

In about 840, Arabs launched attacks against a number of cities on the southern mainland. In 843, they took Bari, where they maintained their emirate (Islamic domain) for three decades. However, throughout much of the eighth, ninth, and tenth centuries, in spite of Arab raids, a number of southern cities continued to act semi-independently, their autonomy limited only by the success of the outside powers that controlled portions of the peninsula at any given time. The princes of Benevento and Salerno, for example, governed during portions of the ninth and tenth centuries on the authority of the Byzantine emperor.

Eventually Byzantine forces under Emperor Basil I retaliated against Arab control, taking Bari in 876 and the rest of the region of Apulia by 888, and essentially driving the Arabs from southern Italy. By 925, most of the cities of the South had regained substantial autonomy. A familiar pattern now repeated itself. The Arabs, like the Franks, Lombards, and Goths before them, had fallen short of creating a unified Italy. But in the wake of their failure, neither was anyone else able to fill the void by imposing centralized political organization on the peninsula. Once again, political and economic power was most effectively exercised at the local level.

THE POWER OF THE PAPACY

One power that aspired to wider control over Medieval Italy was the papacy, whose officials, predominantly Italian, had begun to dominate Rome. Throughout the early Medieval era, the city of Rome and its contiguous territories reflected characteristics that generally fit into the southern Italian tradition. Largely because of the international influence of the popes and the expansion of papal bureaucracy, the Church wielded growing control over Rome and the Papal States. In the process, bishops in many cases began to exercise powers that might normally have been claimed by the state. At the same time bishops built fortified castles alongside those of the local nobility, so that much of Italy south of Tuscany was by the end of the eleventh century dotted with walled and towered bastions, many of them owned by the Church. Shortly thereafter, throughout much of the South, local free peasants migrated inside the walls, creating fortified villages where they made rental agreements for land to farm.

THE GERMAN EMPERORS AND NORMAN DOMINANCE OF SOUTHERN ITALY

When Otto I named himself king of Italy in 951, he required Berengar II, the last of the Carolingian kings of Italy, to travel north to accept authority to rule Italy in the name of the Germans. In 962, Otto I annexed Italy and replaced Berengar II as king. Primarily on the strength of his army, Otto I imposed some centralized control, actually removing two hostile popes (John XII and John XIII), holding court, and initiating legislation. However, when he died in 973, German power waned in the peninsula as political disorder spread. Like the Lombards and the Carolingians before them, the German kings had attempted unsuccessfully to impose Roman-style centralized control without the Roman tax system or ideology and without ever understanding Italian society or culture.

A succession of German emperors would subsequently claim Italy for about sixty-six years. They attempted, with limited success, to extend their control over southern Italy while governing from north of the Alps. Both Otto II and III led armies to the South, and their princes managed periodically to control a number of southern cities. However, sensing weakness in central power, a number of local counts, aristocrats, and powerful urban merchants and landholders challenged the German emperors, who even lost financial control over Italy by 990. Inability to collect taxes and enforce their imperial orders proved their greatest frustrations. In turn, the emperors called on the bishops—including their own German appointees—to counter the ambitious local leadership. Largely as a result of the ineffectiveness of the German emperors, and even in the midst of political confusion, many Italians towns and cities began to recover a sense of civic pride that had not flourished on a wide scale since the Roman era. Almost always the urban leadership consisted of landed aristocrats who no longer served in the emperor's government but discharged their civic responsibility at the local level instead. Most of the surviving Roman cities still showed evidence of their origins, particularly the street grids, walls, and forums. And although many Roman buildings had fallen into disrepair, churches now sprang up as the new symbols of the Medieval urban landscape.

In the tenth-century cities of the North and Center, historians have found that the growth of civic identity was accompanied by signs of economic expansion. Several cities illustrate these trends. In the 890s, the bishop of Modena began to exercise civil authority. However, Modena's defenses were so weak and the government so disorganized that the residents abandoned the city in 899 in the face of a Hungarian invasion, only to return when the Hungarian raiders moved on. When Otto I established German control in the 960s, the population of Modena and other northern cities stabilized and prosperity returned. In 1099, Modena's majestic Romanesque cathedral began to rise on its foundation.

In the former Lombard capital of Pavia, which in the ninth and tenth centuries served as a political center for the Franks, Frankish palace officials exercised extensive regulation of the city's economy. As part of their administration, they granted monopolies and tariff exemptions to guilds (trade associations) of craftsmen and merchants, and they licensed and taxed foreign traders. Such widespread regulation testifies to an expanding economy even prior to the major economic revival of the eleventh century. However, with the weakening of German imperial power in Italy, citizens of Pavia in 1024 laid waste to the palace as a symbol of exploitation and corruption. After the German emperors abandoned Pavia as a capital, the city organized itself as a commune shortly after 1100.

Particularly important among Medieval Italian cities was Venice, which continued to develop along unique lines influenced by the Byzantine Empire. By the eighth century, the people of the Venetian lagoon had begun to cluster on the islands near what later was named the Grand Canal, and the elected *doge* (head of state) established his quarters at the current site of the Doge's Palace. There his chapel claimed to house the bones of St. Mark, from which the name of the cathedral was later derived. Venice emerged in the eighth and ninth centuries to dominate the sea trade between northern Europe and Constantinople. In the process, the Venetians expanded their influence through the coast of the Istrian peninsula and the Adriatic Sea and became powerful enough to wrest commercial privileges from the Byzantines in the form of lower tariffs and tolls. In Venice, as in other Medieval Italian cities, a commercial oligarchy (ruling group) dominated a growing urban population, augmented by the movement of free peasants to the cities.

However, historians find even stronger evidence of tenth-century expansion in rural Italy than in the cities. Early in the century, many of the great rural estates controlled by landlords and monasteries remained uncultivated, even in the fertile Po Valley. But sometime before 1100, tenants began to contract to clear portions of the estates, with the result that the average rural unit of land was smaller, more intensely cultivated, and more valuable than it had been a century earlier. This change was accompanied by a general opening up of landlord-tenant-laborer relationships. Peasants, formerly bound to landlords, now managed in many cases to acquire land, and slaves secured their freedom. With the increased freedom of laborers and the return of the free peasantry, the power of the land-owning noble classes, which had peaked between the fifth and eighth centuries, now subsided. At the same time, scientific improvements in agriculture occurred, especially in the Po Valley, with the introduction of a more efficient scythe and plow and the draining and clearing of land for cultivation. In general, the improvements in both town and country, although relatively minor, set the stage for the economic transformation of northern and central Italy with the emergence of the communes in the eleventh century.

In the South, the impact of Norman expansion also contributed, if only indirectly, to the economic development of the eleventh century. Various southern Italian cities had used Norman soldiers-of-fortune against their enemies, only to see the Normans begin to seize land in the South after about 1025. By 1091, the Normans had wrested control of southern Italy from the Germans and had driven the Arabs completely out of Sicily. Only Naples retained its autonomy.

When North African Muslims retaliated against Normans and Italians alike, a number of Italian port cities, including Pisa, Genoa, and Amalfi, joined forces and launched a naval raid of North Africa in 1087. After a successful campaign, the Italians not only enriched themselves with substantial booty but, more important, took control of the western Mediterranean Sea.

At the same time, the Normans challenged the Byzantines in the Balkans, forcing the Byzantines to employ the Venetian fleet at the cost of granting Venice free trade rights in both the Mediterranean and Aegean seas. Then, in 1096, the First Crusade created new opportunities for fleets from Venice, Genoa, and Pisa. When they delivered knights to the Holy Land, the Italian fleets obtained commercial rights and port facilities that opened up the lucrative import trade in spices, silks, and dyes. Ironically, at the same time much of the South lost its independence to the Normans in Sicily, several Italian coastal cities took control of the Mediterranean trade from the Byzantines and Arabs who had dominated it in the ninth and tenth centuries.

ITALIAN COMMUNES AND THE REVIVAL OF TRADE

In northern and central Italy, but only to a lesser degree in the South, a vast majority of Roman towns and cities survived the early Middle Ages. These urban areas led a surge in commercial and financial activity that produced remarkable economic expansion in Italy from the eleventh to the fourteenth centuries. In turn, economic growth further freed the cities from imperial control, so that by the 1020s, Italians generally disregarded the German emperors altogether. In the North and Center, communes emerged to fill the political vacuum. Communes developed in many places in western Europe, but nowhere as dramatically as in northern and central Italy. It is, in fact, the development of communes that distinguishes Italy in the late Middle Ages, not only from the rest of Europe but from its own past.

The agricultural progress of the tenth century provided much of the impetus for the impressive growth in eleventh-century Italy. The large estates of the early Middle Ages continued to be subdivided by peasant landowners and an emerging rural middle class. This middle class of landlords was now free to practice trades, take positions in communal administration, or even relocate to a nearby city, while supporting itself by renting the newly acquired land. The new farms, developed from previously untilled land, produced surpluses and profits, which in turn increased the accrual of capital. Greater prosperity boosted the population and freed peasants to migrate to the cities, where opportunities were improving.

The population of Italian cities grew also in response to the expansion of import-export business with the Middle East and Asia. As a result, in many Italian cities a commercial and land-owning elite emerged to assert its political power, often soliciting support from ordinary town dwellers (known as the *popolo*) in opposition to the authority of the local bishop or count. Struggles persisted among lay and religious leaders for control over defense of the town walls, public works, the legal system, and the surrounding countryside. The movement by the new merchant oligarchy to take power enabled a number of cities finally to break away from control of the German emperor and his bishops and to establish the autonomy of the local communes. By 1150, all the major cities of the North and Center, including Milan, Genoa, Pisa, Florence—and even Venice and Rome—had organized as communes. However, the communes developed gradually and informally, usually undermining authority instead of challenging it directly. In fact, often the bishops and counts, from whom the communes were taking power, found a way to reconcile themselves to the new communes.

Systems of urban government varied widely, some showing little or no evidence of organization. Only gradually did communes develop formal systems with legal standing separate from the individuals who held the power. Except for a vague tone of democracy, no particular ideology drove the movement, only the pragmatic choice of a way to govern locally in the void left by the German emperors. However, some important general features stand out. In those cities that developed communal systems, the officers of the commune, usually called *consuls*, attempted to build allegiance to the city and to rally its residents against common external enemies. Each took an oath to protect the commune's well-being. Often the consuls invoked a local saint or the local cathedral as a rallying point for the city's population, or summoned the secular glories of the Roman past. In turn, the authority of the consuls to govern came not from above, as had been the case with emperors and popes in previous centuries, but from the urban community that participated widely in local politics. Usually political participation was limited to long-time residents who owned property. Gradually, most communal consuls provided defense and justice, administered public areas such as markets and docks, redefined and amended existing law, and supported their services by taxing and borrowing.

However, the communal system proved unstable and particularly vulnerable to disputes among local factions of affiliated noble families, each claiming a *piazza* (square) or a neighborhood, and each manning its own defensive tower. In the thirteenth century, Florentines could count more than one hundred such towers, some reaching well over two hundred feet in height. As a result, a number of Medieval Italian cities were wracked by partisan fighting in the streets, retaliatory raids against property, and attacks from the towers by bow and catapult. In the decade of the 1170s, for example, government in Florence broke down almost entirely.

In spite of such recurring internal political instability, the communes of the twelfth and thirteenth centuries enjoyed an extended period of economic activity in response to the crusader trade to the east and the trans-Alpine trade to France. Nothing better illustrates this economic growth than the evolution of the guilds. Often the merchant guild, the original local economic association, began to spin off more specialized guilds, so that by the thirteenth century a wide variety of guilds represented trades, crafts, and professions. The communes attempted to use the guilds to regulate quality and prices of goods in the interest of the residents, while the guilds, although excluding common laborers and the poor, acquired political power in the name of the *popolo*.

Urban populations continued to increase, and prosperity spread not only among the merchant oligarchy, urban nobility, bankers, and guilds but, although unevenly, among shopkeepers and ordinary workers as well. Many of these groups maintained connections with the surrounding rural areas, either by owning farms or by acquiring raw materials for local industry. Economic progress was most dramatic in the northern port cities of Venice and Genoa and more deliberate among the inland cities, where prosperity often depended more on local industry than on international trade. In many thirteenth-century Italian cities, universities contributed to the development of a secular culture, particularly in the fields of rhetoric and law, which, in their study of Roman texts, laid some groundwork for the later advent of Renaissance culture. Largely on the strength of its law school, Bologna became the intellectual center of Italy during the thirteenth century.

The general growth of the communes in the twelfth and thirteenth centuries led to intensified internal struggles for power and the emergence of the *popolo* as a real political force. As a typical northern or central city increased in population, expanse, and economic activity, the *popolo*, now a broad-based faction or party, primarily organized under the banners of crafts guilds, began to challenge the consuls for power. Often the *popolo* resorted to armed force in their drive for power, demanding fairer taxes, lower food prices, limits to the power of the local church, and an end to the ravages of internal feuding among the noble families. Eventually, in most communes, the *popolo* selected a captain whose duty was to protect the people from abuse and injustice. In the process, the *popolo* managed to acquire significant influence and, in so doing, involved thousands of Italians in communal government by the middle of the thirteenth century. This marked a dramatic expansion of the political base of the communes, where perhaps a few hundred at most had participated at the time of their founding 150 years earlier.

The rise of the *popolo* can best be understood as the reintroduction of representative government to the Italian peninsula. However, because the *popolo* restricted political participation to the property-owning middle class, they never gained full acceptance among the working class and cannot be credited with a democratic revolution. Partly because of their unwillingness to include the working poor, they were unable to sustain these republics for very long.

As the republics took shape, they vastly increased the number of communal officials, with a typical city employing numerous judges, lawyers, accountants, and security officers. However, official communal authority generally remained in the hands of a few consuls until the emergence of the *podestà* (the chief executive, or "the power"). By the mid-thirteenth century, a *podestà* had assumed power in most communes, often a foreign appointee of the resurgent German emperors and an object of contempt in the eyes of the local population. The *podestà* led the communal republic into a somewhat adversarial relationship with the captain of the *popolo*, each supported by his own council. In time, the communal leadership began to recruit its own *podestà* for a fixed, one-year term, with defined judicial, administrative, and military powers and an obligation to mediate among local factions. Ironically, the institution of *podestà* remained a permanent fixture in Italian communes well after the German emperors abandoned Italy.

THE HOLY ROMAN EMPIRE CHALLENGES

The revival of the Medieval German or Holy Roman Empire, as it was now called, created a threat that both strengthened the communes and induced them to cooperate, further reinforcing the communal tradition in Italy. When Frederick I ("Barbarossa") was elected emperor in 1152, he launched a series of military campaigns to regain control of northern Italy, ultimately destroying Milan in 1162. In response, the northern communes formed the Lombard League, a defensive coalition that counterattacked the imperial armies. In the celebrated Battle of Legnano in 1176, the Lombard League's infantry defeated Frederick Barbarossa's troops and forced the emperor to the bargaining table. At the Peace of Constance (1183), the emperor conceded the autonomy of the communes, a benchmark in Italian history.

In the second quarter of the thirteenth century, Emperor Frederick II attempted to succeed where his grandfather had failed. Launching a campaign to unify Italy from his home in Sicily (which the German dynasty had inherited from the Normans), Frederick II instead ran afoul of the stalwart popes Gregory IX (pope 1227–1241) and Innocent IV (pope 1243–1254), who were determined to build on the work of Innocent III in establishing the independence of the Papal States. The result was a war between German emperor and pope that lasted almost three decades and, in the process, drew the communes into the conflict.

In each northern city, similar partisan factions assembled. Guelphs supported the pope; Ghibellines backed the emperor. Outside the Romagna (a region of the Papal States), the Ghibellines and the emperor's forces enjoyed little success. At Frederick II's death in 1250, he had made scant progress toward his goal and had won few supporters among the northern communes. Instead, he had intensified partisan turmoil and spread extended warfare—local feuding often in the guise of Guelph versus Ghibelline—that once again brought devastation to the Italian peninsula.

Manfred, illegitimate son of Frederick II, renewed his father's campaign only to be countered by Urban IV (pope 1261–1264), who solicited the forces of Charles of Anjou, brother of the king of France. On the pope's promise of Sicily, and hoping to build a Mediterranean empire of his own, Charles invaded southern Italy. At the Battle of Benevento in 1266, Charles's Angevin armies defeated the Germans and killed Manfred in the process. The failures of Frederick and Manfred marked the final attempt to impose unity on the Italian peninsula until the northern Italian House of Savoy succeeded in doing so six hundred years later.

What survived as the Medieval era drew to a close, in spite of regional variations, were certain cultural characteristics that can be identified as Italian. In contrast with much of Europe, where the manorial pattern prevailed, fourteenth-century Italy reflected a primarily urban culture that featured many forms of landholding. The aristocracy typically lived in cities, derived power from controlling the hinterland, and engaged in commerce and banking in an economy that retained its ties to the outside world even at its low ebb. Much more than in northern Europe, Italian culture remained connected as well to its ever-present classical roots, not only in its artistic traditions but in such practical respects as the use of Roman roads, ports, and laws. And in Italy literacy and education were spreading, much less the private monopoly of the clergy than elsewhere. These very qualities provided the context for the Italian Renaissance that lends its name to the period beginning in the fourteenth century.

4

Renaissance Italy, 1300–1500

What are the origins of the artistic and literary awakening known as the Italian Renaissance? Historians continue to debate this question. During the fourteenth and fifteenth centuries, styles and subjects of painting and sculpture changed as artists, architects, and writers turned to classical themes for inspiration. Italians also began to write in a single literary language modeled on the work of the Florentine poet Dante Alighieri. These innovations led to an explosion of secular and sacred art and architecture, much of it commissioned by the urban nobility that changed the face of Italian cities and churches. Fifteenth-century Italian writers labeled this rediscovery of classical values the Renaissance, or "rebirth," in order to distinguish themselves from Medieval intellectuals. Modern scholars have found in the Renaissance the themes of individualism, nationalism, and capitalism.

Much of the art, literature, and science of the Italian Renaissance focused on the human condition, leading historians to emphasize the re-emergence of classical humanism. Other historians, however, noting artistic themes tied to the immediate past, see as much continuity as change in the early Renaissance. Exactly when the Medieval era ended and the Renaissance began in Italy will continue to stimulate debate, especially because that discussion involves issues much broader than painting, sculpture, architecture, literature, and science. For the sake of convenience we will mark a new era here, but we will focus first on the continuity in Italian political, economic, and social life.

The great burst of creativity in fourteenth-century Italy was intimately connected to the traditional public life of its cities. The intramural power struggles of the thirteenth century eroded republican government and removed the *popolo* from power in most communes. In many northern and central cities, aristocratic despots (*signori*), usually supported by merchant oligarchies (governments controlled by a few prominent local businessmen), usurped power to dominate public life for the duration of the Renaissance era. In fact, the Renaissance, for all its celebrated artistic achievement, brought widespread abuse of power, infighting, and increased violence to the Italian peninsula. The advent of this new epoch in artistic creativity raises the additional question, particularly important to contemporary students of history, as to how the Renaissance affected the entire community—not just the male artists, writers, and their patrons, but women and the countless poor.

ITALIAN CITIES IN THE AGE OF DANTE

The impact of the poet Dante Alighieri (1265–1321) was so significant that his name is often identified with the period around the beginning of the fourteenth century. He is in many ways a transitional figure. Born in the Medieval era, he wrote one of the masterpieces of that time, the epic *Divine Comedy* (c. 1320). The horrific nightmares of the section of the *Divine Comedy* called *The Inferno* reflect the brutishness and suffering of the fourteenth century. At the same time, the realism of Dante's writing, his criticism of the excessive politics and corruption of the Church, and his standardization of the Italian vernacular language made significant contributions to the advent of the Renaissance. His writing also reflects the turbulence of his native Florence, which he represented as a diplomat and from which he was forced into permanent exile in 1301 as the result of a factional power struggle.

Two other Tuscan writers, Boccaccio and Petrarch, contributed significantly to the emergence of the Italian Renaissance. Giovanni Boccaccio (1313–1375), a Florentine, published in his *Decameron* a series of one hundred short stories, designed simply to entertain and be free of the religious or moral purpose that had characterized Medieval writing. The *Decameron*, full of earthy humor, colorful characters, and beautiful lyric poetry, is generally regarded as the first and best work of prose in the Italian Renaissance. Boccaccio lived in both Naples and Venice, but he returned to Florence where, at the end of his life, he lectured on Dante.

Petrarch (Francesco Petrarca, 1304–1374), from the Tuscan town of Arezzo, spent much of his life copying ancient manuscripts and writing in a variety of genres, sponsored by the papacy in Avignon, the Carrara family in Padua, and the Visconti in Milan. Using the classics as a source of inspiration, Petrarch wrote letters of advice, polemical essays, and moral philosophy in which he probed a range of questions about religion and the human condition. Petrarch also became famous for his love poetry, especially a collection called *Canzoniere* in which he employed the new Italian language to write in very human terms about his passionate devotion to a woman he had met in Avignon named Laura. Petrarch's work earned him recognition for the development of an Italian literary language, especially what came to be called the Petrarchan sonnet, and his reputation among contemporaries as a man of letters provided the paradigm for the humanist scholar and writer. Lesser known scholars also contributed to the emergence of this new literary tradition. Francesco Filelfo (1398–1481), supported by the Visconti, translated Plato's *Republic* into Latin in the 1440s; Guarino da Verona (1374–1460), subsidized by Nicholas V (pope 1447–1455) and a Venetian nobleman, translated Strabo's *Geography*. Their translations of classical works supplemented the accomplishments of Dante, Boccaccio, and Petrarch in developing the humanistic world view of the early Renaissance.

By the time Dante was born, the German emperors were losing any hope of unifying Italy and only periodically came south looking for subsidies. With their collapse, the Italian cities of the North and Center exercised their autonomy with great enthusiasm. The cities rid themselves of many of the traditional privileges that landlords and the Church had exercised. They developed comprehensive laws and new systems of taxation and accounting, and they took responsibility for trying and punishing crimes. Coins and measures were regionally standardized, easing trade. However, beneath the surface lay confusing contradictions in authority. Pervasive legal inequality among classes contributed to the increasingly bad reputation of urban judicial systems. Likewise, the wealthy routinely evaded taxes, leaving public finances in a shambles. One result was that the merchant oligarchy, particularly in Genoa, Florence, and Bologna, made loans to the cities, at interest, and then administered the budget themselves, a clear conflict of interest.

Only the papacy held any prospect of exercising widespread influence throughout the peninsula. However, much of its crusading spirit had been spent by overuse and its moral authority had been eroded by political partisanship. Because of turmoil in Rome, the new French pontiff, Clement V (pope 1305–1314), moved the papacy to Avignon in 1305. The popes remained in France until 1377 when Gregory XI (pope 1370–1378) returned to

Rome, thus ending a period known as the Babylonian Captivity (taking its name from the forced migration of ancient Jews). The contested election of Urban VI (pope 1378–1389) prompted the selection of a second pope, Clement VII (first antipope 1378–1394), and the subsequent thirty-nine year split in the Church known as the Great Schism until the Council of Constance re-unified the papacy.

With both the empire and the papacy weakened, the *signori* consolidated their power, amassing enough influence and constitutional authority to maintain control through the Renaissance and, in many cities, beyond. These despots, including the Visconti in Milan, the Medici in Florence, the Carrara in Padua, the Este in Ferrara, the Malatesta in Rimini, and the Della Scala in Verona, wielded greater centralized executive authority than had the communes, while claiming public power as a private privilege. However, many historians doubt that the *signori* were as powerful or efficient as their reputation suggests, or that the republics were as democratic as they claimed. In fact, all these governments, in spite of nominal differences, had a great deal in common: All were dominated by powerful oligarchies.

The growth and prosperity of cities under the *signori* continued to typify the Italian peninsula. At the beginning of the fourteenth century, Milan, Venice, Florence, and Genoa probably numbered more than 75,000 residents each, matched in northern Europe only by Paris. More than twenty Italian cities—but only four in northern Europe—exceeded 20,000 inhabitants. Whereas the prosperity of the largest can be attributed to international commerce and banking, dominated throughout Europe by Italians, many of the cities of the second tier thrived primarily as markets for agricultural products from their own environs. Although agriculture remained the largest sector of the Italian economy, the wealth produced by agriculture flowed directly to the cities. Demand for luxuries, particularly silks, household furnishings, and the works of artists, drove the urban economy. The growing prosperity of Italian cities infused the commercial oligarchies with the newly enriched and led to the building of spectacular palaces. In the *Divine Comedy*, Dante laments the new wealth and the disruption of a quieter, more secure Florence, but in fact the city had long been undergoing profound social and economic change.

FAMINE AND THE "BLACK DEATH"

By the middle of the fourteenth century, most of Europe had become tragically engulfed in famine, plague, and warfare. In Italy, after more than two hundred years of growing prosperity and expansion of the best developed economy in Europe, these catastrophes were particularly damaging.

The Hundred Years' War between France and England (1337–1453) inter-rupted trade on the continent, while marauding mercenary armies, living off the land beyond the control of any political authority, used Italy as a staging area from which to attack France. Even more costly and destructive, Italian cities began to attack each other (Florence vs. Pisa, for instance), em-ploying mercenary forces to supplement their own communal militias. The prevalence of soldiers-for-hire not only drove up communal taxes and prices but contributed to political instability, particularly in cities other than the strongest Italian republics. The city of Lucca, for example, was sub-jected to five different rulers in the 1330s alone. To compound the problems of war, taxes, and inflation, Italians suffered through failed harvests in 1345 and 1346, with little recovery in 1347. In spite of imports, food prices soared and hunger spread, seriously weakening the poor population of much of the continent and making it vulnerable to the devastation that lay ahead.

A pandemic known as the "Black Death" (the plague brought to Italy by merchant ships) ravaged the European continent in recurring waves. Via trade routes through southern ports, the plague first swept through Italy in 1347–1348. When it subsided two million Italians had died, over one-third of the population. Magistrates in a number of Italian cities handled the cri-sis with intelligence, imposing quarantines, regulating public gatherings, protecting the food supply, and providing medical attention. Milan es-caped the catastrophe altogether, but in a number of cities the mortality rate exceeded 50 percent. In Pistoia, an estimated 70 percent of the residents per-ished; in Siena, perhaps 80 percent; in Orvieto, 90 percent. Many survivors endured psychological trauma when faced with the profound destruction and resulting chaos. Worse in the long run than the singular disaster of 1348 was the persistent recycling of plagues that struck throughout the penin-sula, hitting Palermo twelve times and Florence eight times before the end of the fifteenth century.

In addition to the massive human fatalities, the crises of the fourteenth century produced serious economic, political, and social consequences. Italian bankers incurred huge losses in the Hundred Years' War, particu-larly the Florentine houses of Bardi and Peruzzi that had underwritten the English crown. Not until the rise of the Medici did Florentine banking re-cover. The banks' losses in turn brought credit restrictions, which led to fur-ther business failures. In the face of these horrible crises, cities turned increasingly to the *signori* to marshal resources.

Some historians point out the irony that in the long term, the decline in population resulting from the plague brought higher wages and greater prosperity to all classes. Nonetheless, the immediate results proved unset-tling. In a series of uprisings, workers embittered by economic hardship challenged authority in Bologna, Siena, Lucca, Perugia, Ferrara, and Florence. The best known of these was the Ciompi uprising of 1378 in Florence. The plague had drastically reduced demand for wool cloth, leading manufacturers to cut production by two-thirds and impose austerity measures, including layoffs and wage controls. The Ciompi (woolworkers) rebelled, demanding that jobs and wages be restored and that they be represented in the local government. After some temporary success by the Ciompi, the merchant oligarchy regained control of Florence. In general, Italian society suffered through a loss of confidence. However, historians still debate the long-term economic and social impact of the Black Death. Scholars now have begun to focus primarily on cultural and psychological results of the plague, not only interpreting works of art and literature (Boccaccio's *Decameron*, for example) but comparing records from different cities, taking note of change with the passage of time.

RENAISSANCE SOCIETY IN THE ITALIAN CITY-STATES

Among the changes that accompanied the Renaissance in Italy was a tightening of access to political power, particularly with the advent of the *signori*. The wealthy, prominent families of the local political elite engaged readily in conspicuous consumption, particularly in expensive fashions, lavishly decorated homes, and elaborate weddings and funerals. Fearing that the great aristocratic families would exhaust their fortunes on excessive spending, Renaissance cities imposed—but rarely enforced—"sumptuary laws" to limit such extravagance.

Some changes occurred also in the lives of Renaissance women. Although more is known about the upper classes than about the urban work force, the results were mixed in both cases. Partly as a result of larger dowries, upper-class women acquired greater wealth and influence, new liberties, and expanded educational opportunities. However, new restrictions appeared as well. Renaissance society reimposed patriarchal customs from classical culture. For working-class women as well, setbacks accompanied new opportunities. Because men dominated the guilds in the woolen and silk industries in Florence, they relegated women to lesser jobs, moving toward a more modern delineation of gender roles. Ironically, when the Medici suppressed the guilds, new and more desirable jobs opened to women. Meanwhile, in the countryside, the expansion of wine and olive oil production enabled women to enter into the labor force.

In this age when many Italians became more secular and materialistic, important religious changes swept through the peninsula. The number of preaching friars (especially Franciscan and Dominican) increased dramatically, along with their reputation, particularly among members of the working class. Throughout Italy new religious confraternities appeared, committed to charity and civic participation, thus providing a strong sense of fellowship, particularly to many ordinary parishioners disillusioned by the sullied reputation of the organized Church. The confraternities developed public rituals that combined civic pride with religious festivals, particularly saints' days such as the festival of St. John in June, when they celebrated by lighting fires in streets and markets. Often city governments, in an attempt to control such ceremonies, organized and supported them. Such was the case in Venice, where the Piazza San Marco provided a home for both church and government and was the site of many pageants, masquerades, and fireworks displays accompanying the Carnivale (the pre-Lenten festival).

THE EARLY ITALIAN RENAISSANCE

Just as Dante's writing provided a literary transition from Medieval to Renaissance culture, so the altarpieces and frescoes of the Florentine Giotto di Bondone (c. 1266–1337) represented a similar transition in the visual arts. Both Dante and Boccaccio applauded his genius. Giotto is particularly recognized for the three-dimensional realism, drama, and emotion he brought to his paintings, most notably in the renowned frescoes in the Arena Chapel in Padua, the frescoes in the Church of Santa Croce in Florence, and the *Ognissanti Madonna* (found in the Uffizi, Florence). While retaining some Medieval conventions, these works depart in other ways to break new ground in painting.

Among other forerunners of the Renaissance were Nicola Pisano and his son Giovanni, whose works are found in northern Italian cities, and the Sienese brothers Ambrogio and Pietro Lorenzetti. Nicola Pisano (c. 1220–1284) gained distinction as a sculptor by incorporating Roman influences in his famous pulpit for the baptistery in Pisa. The emphasis on three-dimensional individuality in his sculpture parallels the innovations of Giotto's painting. In utilizing both classical and Gothic elements in his pulpits in Pistoia and Pisa, Giovanni Pisano (c. 1250–1314) influenced Renaissance sculptors such as Lorenzo Ghiberti (1378–1455) and Donatello. The Lorenzetti brothers brought the influences of Giotto and Giovanni Pisano to Sienese painting, particularly in their experiments with three-dimensional images. Pietro Lorenzetti (c. 1280–1348), more conventional than his brother, brought emotion to his painting, particularly his altarpiece in Arezzo, his frescoes in the lower church at the Basilica of St. Francis Assisi, and his triptych of the *Birth of the Virgin* in the Cathedral Museum in

Siena. Regarded as the more original and influential brother, Ambrogio Lorenzetti (1290–1348) painted the famous allegorical frescoes *Effects of Good and Bad Government* in the Town Hall in Siena, an early visual statement of the new civic humanism.

POLITICAL AND ECONOMIC POWER IN THE FIVE MAJOR RENAISSANCE CITY-STATES

By the beginning of the fifteenth century, a number of communes had so extended their power that they acted as virtually sovereign states. These Renaissance city-states have sometimes been regarded as new and distinctive political systems—secular, based on new class structures, and absolute in their exercise of power—although some historians see strong continuity with the past. With *signori* having replaced the *popolo* as the ruling force in city government, the old noble families survived to dominate most important positions. Niccolò Machiavelli (1469–1527), the most renowned thinker of the Italian Renaissance, observed that no prince could govern without his noblemen. Like Dante before him, Machiavelli served as a diplomat, a vital function in Renaissance Italy where emissaries were highly valued for their skills in negotiating the peaceful resolution of conflict.

Not only did the Renaissance states compete and negotiate, they often went to war. Florence, for example, had conquered neighboring Fiesole in 1125; Siena, in turn, achieved its height of political power by defeating Florence in 1260. Later, Milan would impose its power over a number of northern cities, sometimes by force, and its army would drive south to the gates of Florence. The Venetians would expand throughout much of northeastern Italy, at times using force to dislodge the Milanese, at times forming alliances. In each case, cities assembled fighting forces combining a communal army, a few mercenaries, and supporters of the bishop, the leading nobles, and the local guilds. By the fourteenth century, however, most of the city-states were financing mercenary armies by taxation. In 1427, Florence imposed its first income tax, in part to fund defense.

By 1400, five city-states dominated the peninsula. Three had been Medieval communes: Milan and Venice prevailed in the North and Florence in the North-Center. The Papal States now ruled the Center; the Kingdom of Naples, the South. Smaller cities and towns were pressured to align with one of the five principal city-states, each of which acquired a unique place in the history of Renaissance Italy.

In Milan, Archbishop Ottone Visconti seized power from the Della Torre family in 1277. By the end of the fourteenth century the Visconti had made themselves hereditary dukes, establishing a reputation for heavy-handed dynastic rule over most of the cities of northern Italy. Galeazzo II (1320–1378), a friend of Petrarch, was known for patronizing the arts and founding the University of Pavia. The tyrannical Duke Gian Galeazzo Visconti (ruled 1395–1402) began building the Cathedral of Milan and consolidated the Visconti territorial holdings, taking Bologna in 1402. Gian Galeazzo's death from the plague stalled further Milanese expansion. The Visconti revived their campaign in the 1420s, driving again to the gates of Florence only to be stopped by forces from Venice, which regarded itself, like Florence, as another of the "free states" of Italy. Soon Genoa and Lucca joined this alliance of "free peoples" against Milanese aggression.

Upon the death of the last of the Visconti, Filippo Maria (ruled 1402–1447), the Milanese also declared a republic. Having no experience with republican institutions, however, the new government proved short-lived and was replaced three years later by that of Francesco Sforza (ruled 1450–1466), who established the Sforza dynasty. By signing a treaty with Florence and Naples, Francesco cooled tensions in north and central Italy. Ludovico (ruled 1479–1500), the most famous Sforza, infused his court with humanists and Renaissance artists, including Leonardo da Vinci and Donato Bramante (1444–1514). He launched a building campaign and employed a number of architects to complete the brilliant Cathedral.

An oligarchy of several hundred successful merchants governed the long-established republic of Venice, which continued to exploit its dominant position in long-distance trade throughout the Renaissance era and beyond. Venetians used a complex pattern of elections for *doge* and Great Council, initially dominated by noblemen of prominent families but eventually expanded to include non-nobles as well. In 1310, Bajamonte Tiepolo attempted, in the name of the people, to set himself up as a despot. When the revolt failed, Tiepolo and his supporters were forced into exile by the emergency Council of Ten, confirming the solidarity among the Venetian aristocracy. The Council of Ten exercised full powers including the use of secret police and a court whose decisions were final. By the fifteenth century, membership on the Great Council itself granted noble status, and almost two hundred families shared power under Doge Pietro Gradenigo.

Venetian power peaked in the fifteenth century when Venice controlled the Adriatic, many trade routes to the East, and the Mediterranean kingdoms of Morea, Cyprus, and Crete. Upon the death of Gian Galeazzo Visconti of Milan, Venetian forces launched a campaign that netted them the cities of Verona, Vicenza, Padua, and Bassano. Then, in the 1420s, after its troops defeated Milanese Duke Filippo Maria Visconti, Venice acquired Udine, Brescia, and Bergamo, giving them a major presence through much of northern Italy and a "breadbasket" from which to feed their expanding population. Later in the century Venice secured control of the Veneto region by winning Rovigo in a war against Ferrara.

These Venetian gains in Italy, however, were offset by the ominous expansion of Ottoman Turkish power in the Balkans. The Venetians countered the threat but suffered defeat at the hands of the Turkish fleet in 1430. When the Ottoman Turks laid siege to Constantinople in 1453, the Venetians, along with the Genoese, supported the futile attempt to protect the city. The expansion of the Turkish Empire threatened Venetian prosperity—at times Venice itself—and led to a prolonged war (1463–1479) in which the Turks prevailed decisively. In the subsequent Treaty of Constantinople, the Venetians lost territory and agreed to pay an annual tribute to trade in the Black Sea.

The fourteenth century brought momentous change to Florence as well. In the wake of a military crisis, the twenty-one guilds engineered a popular revolution in 1343 to overthrow a reigning despot. The guilds then revived the Florentine Republic and restricted the political power of the upper classes. In the final decades of the fourteenth century, Florentines further bolstered pride in their Republic by repelling expansionist campaigns by both the papacy and the Visconti of Milan. It was also in the fourteenth century that Florence won a reputation for its republican institutions and democratic values, the foundation of its civic pride. Despite this, no more than 5 percent of Florentines were eligible to vote, and fewer than 1 percent qualified for office. Yet Florence was as democratic as any of the other cities of its day.

Emerging from the guild movement, the Medici family of bankers seized power in 1434 and controlled the city throughout much of the fifteenth century. In the process, the Medici broadened political participation in the guise of expanding republican institutions, with perhaps 20 percent of the population now eligible to vote. Despite appearances, they limited access to power so that the guilds lost most of their previous influence. Most important positions were chosen by lot from among a small elite.

By patronizing artists and writers, Cosimo, Piero, and Lorenzo de' Medici lifted Florence to its height of power in international banking, commerce, and Renaissance culture. In the process they built a powerful patronage system that provided organized support for their political interests. "Lorenzo the Magnificent" (ruled 1469–1492) not only earned his reputation for devotion to art and learning but distinguished himself as the best of the Medici rulers. Not even Lorenzo, however, was immune from organized political challenge in the tempest that was Florentine politics. In 1478, he survived his greatest political test when he uprooted the infamous Pazzi conspiracy (in which the Pazzi family conspired to replace the Medici as papal bankers) whose tentacles reached the Vatican itself. The Medici were eventually condemned for alleged violation of the ordinances of Florence and were expelled from Florence in 1494. They returned to power in the next century when Spanish Emperor Charles V and Pope Clement VII made Alessandro de' Medici Duke of Florence in 1530. Upon Alessandro's assassination seven years later, Cosimo I de' Medici (1519–1574) succeeded him, then was named Grand Duke of Tuscany by Pius V (pope 1570). With Spanish support, Cosimo I extended Florentine control over much of Tuscany. In the process he established a reputation for centralized administration, support for industry and agriculture, and, in the family tradition, patronage of the arts.

South of Florence, Rome and the Papal States had progressively fallen under localized secular control while the popes were living in Avignon during much of the fourteenth century. During the "Babylonian Captivity," as rival popes competed for power, Rome itself was shaken by revolt, enabling independent local lords to regain control of the Papal States. The papacy began to reunify in 1414 at the Council of Constance but was not fully secure in the Vatican until around 1450. Thereafter, a series of popes began to employ a combination of politics, diplomacy, and warfare to restore the Church's supremacy. Meanwhile, they lived in luxury while providing only minimal spiritual leadership. In fact, the Renaissance popes in general were products of the age, providing valuable support to artists and architects. Pope Nicholas V, a scholar who founded the Vatican Library, recruited humanists to Rome, including the papal secretary Poggio Bracciolini, the famous architect Leone Battista Alberti (1404–1472), who rebuilt St. Peter's Basilica and the Vatican, and Lorenzo Valla, Rome's most notable humanist.

Among the politically aggressive Renaissance popes was Sixtus IV (pope 1471–1484), known for patronizing the arts and building the Sistine Chapel in St. Peter's, but also for extravagant spending and excessive pursuit of power. He joined the Pazzi Conspiracy in war against Florence, then supported Venice against Ferrara. More successful in reestablishing Vatican control over the Papal States was Pope Alexander VI (pope 1492–1503), from the powerful Borgia family, who seized territories in the Romagna from local landlords and tyrants. The "warrior pope" Julius II (pope 1503–1513) unified and expanded the Papal States, organizing the League of Cambrai against Venice, then forming the Holy League against France. Known for his keen intellect and vast energy, Julius convened the Lateran Council in 1512 to reform abuses of the Church. However, his papacy is perhaps best known for his active building campaign and his patronage of the arts, including support of Raphael, Bramante, and Michelangelo. Pope Leo X (pope 1513–1521), son of Lorenzo de' Medici, proved skillful in politics and diplomacy and continued to patronize the arts. In fact, Leo's lavish spending, including support for Raphael and Bramante and the rebuilding of St. Peter's Basilica, led directly to the Protestant Reformation of Martin Luther, whom Leo excommunicated in 1521. Another Medici pope, Clement VII (pope 1523–1534), was drawn into European warfare, leading to the sack of Rome and his own capture. In spite of his support for Michelangelo, Raphael, and Benvenuto Cellini (1500–1571), his political and diplomatic misfortunes brought an end to Rome's prominence as a Renaissance city. In the 1550s, after the papacy had launched the Counter-Reformation, several popes returned Rome to its Renaissance fame, especially Julius III (pope 1550–1555) and Pius IV (pope 1559–1565), who continued to patronize Michelangelo. Sixtus V (pope 1585–1590) continued the tradition of extravagant spending on public buildings, most notably in the construction of the Lateran Palace.

Farther to the south lay the Kingdom of Naples, which included the island of Sicily. The history of Naples and Sicily was especially contentious, with the French (Normans and Angevins) engaging in a protracted struggle with the Spanish (Aragonese) that lasted over two centuries. The Normans had conquered the Duchy of Naples in the twelfth century and had consolidated it with Sicily in the Kingdom of the Two Sicilies. In 1266, Charles of Anjou became king of Naples and Sicily. His oppressive policies provoked the violent uprising known as the Sicilian Vespers of 1282, by which the Sicilians drove the Angevins out of Sicily in favor of Pedro III of Aragon. The Aragonese maintained an extended and stormy presence in the Italian South.

While giving up Sicily, the Angevins maintained control of Naples until the mid-fifteenth century. It was at the Angevin court that the Neopolitan tradition of arts and letters first bloomed. Among the Renaissance artists who worked in Naples were Giotto, employed as a court artist for King Robert of Anjou in 1332, the Sienese artist Andrea Vanni (c. 1332–1414), and the Milanese artist Leonardo da Besozzo. In 1435, Alfonso V of Aragon (ruled Naples 1443–1458), supported by the Visconti and the pope, wrested Naples from the Angevins, unifying Naples and Sicily and making Naples the center of Spanish power in Italy. The Aragonese continued the artistic court tradition, as the Renaissance patron Alfonso recruited the painter Pisanello (c. 1395–1455) while supporting poets at the Academy of Naples.

In a struggle with the papacy, the notorious Ferdinand I of Naples (ruled 1458–1494) won control of the city and its hinterland with the assistance of Francesco Sforza and Cosimo de' Medici. As the Spanish crown unified, their military defeated the French at Garigliano in 1503, securing control of Naples for Spain in the process. Although the Spanish kings of Naples were unpopular, their power remained virtually unchallenged until the insurrection of Masaniello in 1647.

THE HEIGHT OF THE ITALIAN RENAISSANCE

Although there was no clear break with the past, Italian culture still acquired an identity—political, economic, and artistic—that fifteenth-century Italian intellectuals as well as modern scholars believe differentiated Italy from the rest of the world. A major reason that Italian cities of the Renaissance developed a unique place in history was the abundant patronage of art provided by the Church, private organizations, and prominent individuals. Again, like other aspects of the Renaissance, patronage for artists had many precedents. The Church, in particular, had long utilized artistic representations to embellish its rituals and buildings, just as guilds had paid artists to enhance their prestige.

What distinguished Renaissance patronage was its growing popularity and stunning results. In Florence, for example, Brunelleschi designed and constructed the famous *duomo* (cathedral) on a commission from local cloth merchants. The Medici hired Sandro Botticelli to paint the *Adoration of the Magi* (1475) to celebrate the family tradition and bolster its legitimacy, just as *signori* and prominent individuals all over Italy employed artists to do the same for them. They hired architects, sculptors, painters, and scholars to enhance their homes and glorify their accomplishments. In turn, a number of Renaissance artists enjoyed growing prestige.

Patrons supported Italian writers as well, not only to flatter powerful individuals and families but to celebrate the prestige of various cities. In fact, one unique element of the Italian Renaissance was the application of humanist writings to public life. As Petrarch and others related history and philosophy to urban politics, their work became valued as "civic humanism," particularly their ability to synthesize a set of beliefs about the exceptional merit of their respective cities. Thus, humanist writers Coluccio Salutati (1331–1406) and Leonardo Bruni (1370–1444) generated myths to celebrate broad democratic participation in Florence, while Venetian humanists such as Giorgio Merula, Giorgio Valla, and Marcantonio Sabellico (all non-natives) glorified the contributions of the Venetian leadership elite to the life of the city. Likewise, humanists from the Visconti court in Milan and the court of the king of Naples sang the praises of their respective dynasties. In Rome, Lorenzo Valla (1407–1457) devoted much of his life to translating ancient manuscripts while serving in the papal secretariat under Pope Nicholas V. Despite individual loyalties, these humanist writers shared a perspective that celebrated intellect, achievement, and active par-

ticipation in the political life of the city as a great virtue. Their ideals circu-
lated from city to city, dispersing a new intellectual culture throughout the
peninsula. Among their principles was a strong commitment to education,
based on the belief that the aristocratic youth had to prepare themselves to
rule.

Perhaps the most brilliant humanist of his day was the Florentine Pico
della Mirandola (1463–1494), patronized and defended by Lorenzo de'
Medici. Pico learned five ancient languages in order to study history in the
original texts. Eventually he tried to summarize all human learning in his
Oration on the Dignity of Man. Another Florentine, Francesco Guicciardini
(1483–1540), became the most celebrated of the Italian Renaissance historians. Like Dante and Machiavelli, Guicciardini had worked as a diplomat
and his experience led him to believe that Italy had suffered from a shortage
of wise, educated rulers. He relied upon original documents to write his
History of Italy (1564), a careful comparison of the city-states that set the
standard for Renaissance historical scholarship.

In spite of the successes of the humanist writers, it is the visual arts that
gave the Italian Renaissance its glorious reputation. The prosperity of Florence and the patronage of the Medici brought a burst of creativity among
architects, sculptors, and painters that spread Florentine influence
throughout much of Italy and the European continent. Particularly important in the early fifteenth century were Filippo Brunelleschi, Masaccio, and
Donatello. Brunelleschi (1377–1446), an engineer, architect, and sculptor,
traveled to Rome to study classical building techniques, then returned to
Florence to construct his masterpiece, the wondrous dome of the cathedral.
He was among the first to employ linear perspective in his sculpture, notably in the bronze panel submitted in the competition to cast the doors of the
cathedral's baptistery. Of his many influential accomplishments, none is
more admired than the Pazzi Chapel at the Church of Santa Croce in Florence, known for its symmetry and elegance of design.

Another Florentine, the young Masaccio (1401–1428) is regarded as the
first great painter of the Italian Renaissance, particularly because of the influence of his revolutionary style. He applied Brunelleschi's linear perspective and his own mathematical system to give painting its "modern" style,
more committed to three-dimensionality and simplicity than to mere deco-
ration of flat surfaces. Most notable are his frescoes in the Florentine
churches of Santa Maria Novella (*The Holy Trinity*) and Santa Maria del Car-
mine (*The Expulsion from the Garden of Eden* in the Brancacci Chapel). In the
former, he employed scientific perspective for the first time in Italian painting. In the latter, painted at the end of his brief life, Masaccio portrayed nat-

ural light and dark to create a realistic, memorable, and moving image of the familiar biblical story.

A contemporary of Masaccio, the Florentine Donatello (1386?–1466) became one of the most original and influential of all sculptors. An associate of Brunelleschi, Ghiberti, and the architect-sculptor Michelozzo (1396–1472), Donatello drew upon classical models, especially in his early sculptures such as *St. Mark* and *St. George,* carved between 1413 and 1417 for the Church of Orsanmichele in Florence. The realism and individual expression conveyed in each sculpture—the introspective St. Mark and the dauntless, youthful St. George—demonstrate Donatello's modern approach. Around 1425 he made another breakthrough, using linear perspective to create the illusion of depth in his bronze relief panel of *The Feast of Herod*. After a sojourn to Rome where he worked in St. Peter's Basilica, Donatello returned to Florence to create his most celebrated work, the nude bronze of *David*. Donatello's work influenced not only sculptors but painters such as the Paduan Andrea Mantegna (1431–1506).

By the second half of the fifteenth century, several notable painters carried on the early Renaissance tradition while others broke new ground. Domenico Ghirlandaio (1449–1494) used traditional techniques to paint biblical scenes in Florentine settings. His most famous painting is *Scenes from the Life of St. Francis* (1485, Church of Santa Trinità, Florence). Piero della Francesca (c. 1420–1492), in contrast, experimented with light and with mathematical calculation, apparent in his series of striking frescoes entitled *Legend of the True Cross* in the Church of San Francesco in Arezzo. In two renowned paintings commissioned for Medici villas, *Primavera* and *Birth of Venus*, Sandro Botticelli (1445–1510) combined themes from classical mythology and Christianity, typical of the intellectual atmosphere of the Medici court that commissioned a number of his works.

In the 1490s, changing political conditions moved the focus of Italian Renaissance activity from Florence to Rome, which led to the era of brilliance known as the High Renaissance. The French invasion of 1494 dislodged the Medici from power, restored the Florentine Republic, and plunged Florence into extended warfare and turmoil. With the demise of the Medici, the Dominican preacher Fra Girolamo Savanarola (1452–1498) led a campaign condemning what he described as the decadence of the city. While Savanarola's moral crusade created a hostile environment for artists and intellectuals in Florence, the popes increased their patronage, attracting a number of artists to Rome.

The three most celebrated figures of the High Renaissance in Italy were Leonardo da Vinci, Raphael, and Michelangelo. Leonardo (1452–1519) was a man of sweeping intellect who became in his lifetime a painter, sculptor, architect, engineer, and scientist. Educated in Florence and apprenticed to the painter and sculptor Andrea del Verrocchio (1435–1488), Leonardo painted several famous masterpieces, especially the fresco *The Last Supper*, commissioned by the Duke of Milan for the Monastery of Santa Maria delle Grazie in Milan. Equally renowned is the portrait of *Mona Lisa*, also known as *La Giocanda*, which hangs in the Louvre. After French troops drove the Sforzas from Milan in 1499, Leonardo took a position as chief engineer for Cesare Borgia, duke of the Romagna, then returned to Florence to serve in the same capacity for Florence in its war with Pisa. He divided the decade 1506–1516 among Florence, Milan, and Rome, serving the French King Louis XII, who lived in Milan at the time, then Pope Leo X. In 1516, at the invitation of King Francis I, Leonardo moved to France, where he lived the final three years of his life.

Among Leonardo's wide-ranging contributions to the Renaissance were his many drawings, demonstrating his virtuosity in depicting humans, plants, animals, sculptures, and architectural features. His scientific observations and experiments in hydraulics, geology, meteorology, aerodynamics, and human anatomy foreshadowed a number of modern discoveries. Taken together, Leonardo's achievements qualify him as the embodiment of Renaissance genius.

Born in Urbino, Raphael (1483–1520) studied under the Umbrian painter Perugino before moving to Florence in 1504, where he absorbed the influences of Leonardo and Michelangelo. As a painter in Florence, Raphael is remembered for his numerous Madonnas, none more exquisite than the *Madonna of the Goldfinch*. Once summoned by Julius II (pope 1503–1513) in 1508, Raphael spent the remainder of his life working in Rome on papal commissions. His most famous fresco, *The School of Athens*, depicting discussions among famous classical philosophers, decorates a wall in the Vatican palace. When Pope Julius II died, his successor, Leo X, appointed Raphael chief architect for St. Peter's and director of antiquities for Rome.

Michelangelo Buonarroti (1475–1564), sculptor, painter, architect, and poet, shares with Leonardo the distinction of being the most influential force of the Renaissance. Although he turned to Plato for inspiration, Michelangelo defied the constraints of classical form in favor of his own inspired vision in executing his work, most notably in shaping marble to "release" the reality of the human spirit. A Florentine who studied with Ghirlandaio and at the Medici school of sculpture, Michelangelo spent most of his adult life in Rome working on papal commissions. Already well known when the Medici were driven from Florence in 1494, he moved to Bologna and then to Rome, where he produced his first famous work, the *Pietà*, in which the young Mary holds the body of the dead Christ. After completing the *Pietà* by age twenty-five, Michelangelo returned to Florence to work on his monumental *David*. Completed in 1504, it stood more than fourteen feet tall in the Piazza della Signoria in Florence.

A year later, Michelangelo was summoned back to Rome by Pope Julius II to paint the expansive ceiling of the Sistine Chapel and to create the pope's tomb. Michelangelo's Sistine ceiling remains his most influential achievement. For four years, the artist lay on his back atop scaffolding to create colossal and brilliantly colorful images from Old Testament narratives, centering on *The Creation of Adam*.

By the time Michelangelo reached his mid-forties, he had begun to concentrate on architectural designs, in both Florence and Rome. In Florence, he devised two notable projects for the Church of San Lorenzo: the Laurentian Library and the Medici tombs. In Rome, he designed the Campidoglio (1534), the political capital of the city, and his greatest architectural success, the dome of St. Peter's Basilica. The soaring achievements of this genius remain unsurpassed.

Whereas Renaissance artists of Florence and Rome clearly influenced each other, the painters of Venice remained largely independent because of the republic's historical orientation toward the Eastern world. Venetian painters, most significantly Giovanni Bellini, Titian, and Tintoretto, used oil paints to create distinctive color and natural light. Bellini (1430?–1516) is known best for his series of monumental altarpieces, especially his *Madonna with Four Saints* painted for the Church of San Zaccaria. Titian (Tiziano Vecellio, 1477?–1576) was the undisputed master of sixteenth-century Venetian painting. As a young artist he worked with Bellini and Giorgione (1478?–1510), then began to paint independently. Among his most famous works are the serenely beautiful *Venus of Urbino* and the numerous portraits he painted as he traveled in the 1530s and 1540s. When Titian returned to Venice in 1550, he began to produce mythological and religious paintings, notably an *Annunciation* in the Church of San Salvatore. Tintoretto (Jacopo Robusti, 1518–1594), who became estranged from his former master Titian, produced dramatic paintings with techniques that anticipated the baroque style of the next century. Always in demand, his paintings grace the walls of many of Venice's churches and palaces. Among the best known is the series on the miracles of St. Mark created for the Scuola di San Marco in the 1560s.

THE ITALIAN LEAGUE

In the second half of the fifteenth century, the five dominant city-states finally managed forty years of relative political stability by forming the Italian League at the Peace of Lodi (1454) and agreeing to maintain separate spheres of influence. The threat represented by the Ottoman Turks' successful siege of Constantinople and the high cost of warfare among the city-states finally brought cooperation among Alfonso of Aragon, Cosimo de' Medici, Francesco Sforza, Pope Nicholas V, and the Venetian Senate. Although the city-states agreed among themselves, they continued to expand at the expense of smaller cities. Nor did the respite guarantee domestic harmony, as evidenced by uprisings against the Sforza in 1476, the Medici in 1478, and Ferdinand of Aragon, king of Naples, in 1486. Ferdinand's reign proved particularly disruptive, instigating civil wars and conflicts with Popes Callistus III (Alfonso Borgia, pope 1455–1458) and Innocent VIII (pope 1484–1492).

Although the major city-states avoided head-to-head confrontation, they readily negotiated support from such outside sources as the kings of France, Serbia, and Hungary in an effort to expand their influence. When a Turkish fleet landed at Friuli in northern Italy in 1475 and Otranto on the southern coast in 1480, various cities agreed to negotiate with the sultan while at the same time lamenting the spread of Islam.

THE FRENCH INVASION OF 1494, THE ITALIAN WARS, AND THE END OF THE RENAISSANCE

The French invasion of Italy in 1494 proved the first step in their prolonged battle against the Habsburg dynasty, the Austrian royal family whose diplomacy and marriages eventually gave them control of Spain, the Netherlands, and parts of Germany and the Italian peninsula. The Italian Wars, touched off by an appeal to France by Ludovico Sforza of Milan, lasted sixty-five years, thrust Italy squarely into the center of European diplomacy, and ultimately spelled the end of the independent city-states.

King Charles VIII of France (1470–1498) brought his armies south in the spring of 1494 in response to Ludovico's plea to protect Milan from a conspiracy between Florence and Naples. In a poorly planned campaign, Charles attacked Florence, forcing the Florentines to relinquish control of Pisa and other towns, then moved on Rome and Naples. The French king captured Naples from the Aragonese, but his expansive success frightened Milan into joining Venice, Pope Alexander VI, and Ferdinand in an anti-French coalition. In 1499, French forces under King Louis XII (ruled 1498–1515) renewed their campaign, captured Milan, and imprisoned Ludovico Sforza. The French armies then returned to battle the Spanish in a contest over much of the South. After several decisive Spanish victories, the French surrendered in 1504 at Gaeta, ensuring Spanish control of southern

Italy. Only partially successful, the French armies, merely by their presence, had reignited old hostilities among Italian cities.

Meanwhile in the North, the French led a coalition of European powers in a campaign against Venice that touched off a dizzying array of battles and diplomatic maneuvers extending over a half-century. After numerous shifts in allegiance and diplomatic exchanges among popes, Henry VIII of England, and even the Swiss cantons (states), the French were badly beaten at the Battle of Novara in June 1513. In the process, the Medici were restored to power in Florence and the Sforza in Milan. Francis I (ruled 1515–1547) and his successors on the French throne renewed the Italian Wars. A French victory at Marignano in 1515 won back Milan, which was further secured by treaty with Charles I of Naples (soon to be Emperor Charles V of Spain) in which the French dropped all claims to Naples.

In 1522, Emperor Charles V retaliated against France in the first of the Habsburg-Valois (Spanish-French) Wars that would once again subject the Italian peninsula to extended conflict and ultimately afford the Spanish dominance. After losing most of their Italian strongholds, the French sent reinforcements and, in February 1525, lost the Battle of Pavia, the most important single engagement in the half-century of warfare. But Spanish success touched off a combined reaction, as Francis I, the pope, Florence, Venice, and the Sforza formed the League of Cognac in opposition. The Spanish responded by forcing Sforza out of Milan and, in early 1527, moving south, where they sacked Rome with great vengeance and captured the pope in the process. Amid the confusion, both Florence and Genoa reestablished republics, as Florence once again evicted the Medici and the Genoese expelled the French. The settlements, however, proved transitory because the Treaty of Cambrai returned the Sforza and the Medici to power and made Charles V king of Italy, affirming Spanish control of much of the peninsula.

The French would launch several final attempts to take Italian territory. When Francesco Sforza died in 1535, the French challenged Charles V's claim to Milan. Twenty years later, Henry II of France conspired with Paul IV (pope 1555–1559) to take Naples, but they failed. As a result of French failures, the Spanish resumed direct control of Milan while the French abandoned Italy except for the city of Turin, bringing the protracted and damaging Italian Wars to a close.

It was against the background of the French invasion and the Italian Wars that Machiavelli, a Florentine experienced in both politics and diplomacy, wrote the most original political treatise of the Italian Renaissance. In *The Prince* (1532), Machiavelli used the infamous Cesare Borgia as the model ruler. Machiavelli advised that any prince who wished "to conquer by force or by fraud, to make himself loved and feared by the people, . . . to destroy those who . . . are likely to injure you" should follow the example of the ruthless Borgia. Machiavelli's great fame is in part explained by his audacious rejection of humanism and conventional morality. More important, Machiavelli explored the possibilities and limits of power within a modern, realistic framework, devoid of moral or ethical constraints.

Historians sometimes view the changes they detect in late sixteenth-century Italian culture as ushering in a new era. Urban aristocracies further consolidated their power and used it more arbitrarily. Wealthy families built lavish rural villas and began to invest more in land than in financial or commercial pursuits. As a result, they were criticized for abandoning humanistic values by retreating from civic responsibility. However, it now appears that the aristocracy never permanently exited the cities but simply shifted their investments in response to changing market conditions. When the Italian Renaissance came to an end, the cause may have been changing international conditions: the invasion of Italy by foreign armies, the spread of authoritarian religious policy in the Counter-Reformation, and the shift of economic activity from the Mediterranean to the North Atlantic.

5

Early Modern Italy, 1500–1789

The sweeping changes that overwhelmed Renaissance Italy around the beginning of the sixteenth century initiated a long period during which political and economic progress slowed on the peninsula. The French invasions of 1494 opened the door to more than two centuries of foreign occupation and conflict when many of the improvements of the previous century were abandoned, along with Machiavelli's idea of a unified "Italy." At the same time, Italians also experienced important positive developments, particularly by the middle of the eighteenth century when notable progress was made in Tuscany and Piedmont, and when Italian intellectuals, inspired by the European Enlightenment, proposed sweeping modern reforms.

SPANISH DOMINATION

The military campaigns that drove armies of aggressive European monarchies into Italy before 1500 ended in Spanish victory. By the mid-sixteenth century, Spain had taken control of Sicily, Naples, Sardinia, and Lombardy and had restored the Medici to power in Florence as Grand Dukes of Tuscany. The Treaty of Cateau-Cambresis of 1559 confirmed the status quo: Venice, Genoa, and Lucca remained republics; a number of hereditary duchies were created, including Savoy, Parma, and Modena; and the Vatican controlled the Papal States. In short, the Spanish dominated the peninsula, either directly or indirectly. The map of Italy would retain this configuration throughout the entire period of Spanish control. With European powers expanding and little history of cooperation among the weakened Italian states, hopes of Italian national unification had to be deferred indefinitely.

From Naples in the South and Milan in the North, the Spanish Empire maintained control of Italy for more than 150 years. Until the Peace of Utrecht ended the War of Spanish Succession in 1713, the Spanish presided over Italy in a period of general regression punctuated with some advances. Historians disagree as to the precise cause of the decline. The failure of Italians to thrive under Spanish rule is attributable to a combination of factors, including warfare, economic recession, and the stifling influence of the papacy.

Spanish cultural influences unquestionably contributed to the general deterioration. A number of Spanish aristocrats moved to southern Italy in particular, bringing with them conservative customs that emphasized ceremony, chivalry, and piety. Consequently, the Catholic Church grew wealthier and stronger, exerting a smothering influence on economic development and secular modernization. Under the influence of Spanish bias against commerce, Italy's bankers and merchants became less productive landed aristocrats, losing their aggressive role in European finance and trade. In order to raise money in the face of economic slowdown, Spanish officials sold land, titles of nobility, and privileges to wealthy Italians, reinforcing their abandonment of commerce. Consequently, the Italian urban elite became more dependent on these obsolete, medieval legal privileges and immunities and less responsive to market conditions. Not only did urban business activity suffer, but the landlord class strengthened also at the expense of the peasantry, particularly in the South. Many historians argue that by introducing such policies and values, the Spanish "refeudalized" Italy.

Clearly, the Spanish were not entirely to blame for the general decay of the sixteenth and seventeenth centuries. Some historians are quick to point to economic recession as a cause, as well as an effect, of the decline. As early as 1600, a number of sectors of the Italian economy showed signs of weakening. Banking, textile manufacturing, shipbuilding, and agriculture all suffered, forcing Italian merchants to import finished products from northern Europe while depending more on the export of raw materials, olive oil, and wine. As world economic activity shifted from the Mediterranean toward the Atlantic basin, greater problems in the Italian domestic economy surfaced. The guilds, long a force in Italian cities, now became a detriment as they artificially protected prices and wages in the face of stiff competition from lower-priced northern European goods. And the ever-growing concentration of wealth in a landed aristocracy left a poorer underclass of peasants, workers, and jobless who were unable to afford Italian goods. Poverty and suffering spread, the plague returned, and population declined. In the countryside, the trend toward absentee ownership of land left aristocrats neglecting the fields and peasants losing land and falling to the status of tenant farmers and day laborers. Farming methods and technology regressed, productivity suffered, and Italians actually became partly dependent on imported grain.

The complications of war, particularly in northern Italy, intensified economic difficulties through the first half of the seventeenth century. In turn, the armies of Savoy engaged the French; the Venetians fought the Austrians, French, Spanish, and the dukes of Savoy; and France and Savoy allied with several Italian duchies against Spain. Furthermore, an increase in piracy further undermined the economy of the peninsula. As Italians found themselves aligned with the Spanish in international affairs, Italian merchant ships were more readily victimized by Spain's opponents. The continuing conflict not only further weakened trade but compounded the problem of government debt and drove taxes higher, thus aggravating the problem of under-consumption.

Under the influence of Spanish political control and in response to the spread of Protestantism, the Catholic Counter-Reformation ordered severe repression in sixteenth-century Italy. The Vatican imprisoned suspected heretics and imposed censorship on Italians, introducing the first Index of Forbidden Books in 1559, while book burnings abounded. The Roman Inquisition decreed intellectual conformity, sentencing Galileo to life imprisonment in 1633 (commuted to house arrest) for publishing a book on Copernicus's theory that the earth revolves around the sun. In reaction to the Church's heavy-handed practices, a number of Italian scholars, artists, political thinkers, and religious reformers fled into exile, depriving Italy of vital intellectual energy.

NEW DYNAMICS IN THE ARTS AND IDEAS: MANNERISM, THE BAROQUE, AND THE ILLUMINISTI

In spite of what is generally regarded as suffocating Spanish political and economic domination, Italians managed to make progress in a number of areas. In retrospect, one can appreciate the importance of incremental progress, although, at the time, results were not always readily apparent. For example, in combating the Protestant Reformation, the Vatican patronized the most accomplished painters, sculptors, and architects to transform Rome into a showplace for the glories of Catholicism. Thus, Rome provided a striking exhibition of Mannerism and the Baroque, the dominant post-Renaissance styles. Mannerists such as Giulio Romano (1499–1546) typically painted with technical mastery, using elongated figures and exaggerating the dramatic use of light and dark. In the second half of the sixteenth century, early Baroque artists such as Annibale Carracci (1560–1609) and Caravaggio (1573–1610) returned to classical and humanist influences in a more elegant style of painting. Carracci's paintings adorned the ceiling of the Farnese Palace; Caravaggio's paintings of the life of St. Matthew, *Conversion of St. Paul*, and *Crucifixion of St. Peter* embellished Roman churches. Most dramatic were the works of the sculptural master of the high Baroque, Gianlorenzo Bernini (1598–1680). Examples are found in St. Peter's Basilica, numerous palaces and piazzas, and in the architectural designs for churches. Most celebrated are his sculptural masterpiece *Ecstacy of St. Teresa* in Santa Maria della Vittoria and the *Fountain of the Four Rivers*, the focal point of the Piazza Navona in Rome.

Alongside Mannerist and Baroque artists, Italian scholars made progress in spite of general repression and isolation from the mainstream of European thought. Among the first Italians to apply ideas from the northern European Enlightenment, the intellectual movement based on reason and science, was the Benedictine monk Benedetto Bacchini. Under the influence of the French Benedictine Jean Mabillon, Bacchini and his students Ludovico Muratori and Scipione Maffei meticulously collected historical documents in an effort to examine the Italian past. The proponents of the Italian Enlightenment were called Illuministi.

Their systematic inquiry led the Illuministi to criticize the Church for what they viewed as its role in stifling human progress. Among the most outspoken critics was Pietro Giannone, a lawyer from Naples who published in 1723 a history of Naples in which he presented a strong indictment of the Church. In retaliation, Giannone was driven into exile where he died in prison. By the early eighteenth century, when Spanish power began to wane, criticism by the Illuministi spread throughout much of northern Italy and began to focus on the role of the Church in secular affairs. The champions of the Italian Enlightenment began to circulate allegations of the Church's misgovernment of the Papal States, its perpetuation of superstition, and the regressive economic influences of its numerous religious holidays and its control of uncultivated lands. In the 1740s, Girolamo Tartarotti continued the attack on magic, arguing that the belief in witches contradicted the new spirit of scientific inquiry.

By mid-century, the Illuministi had begun to win the attention of other Europeans, particularly in the case of two intellectuals from Milan. Most influential was Cesare Beccaria's *Of Crimes and Punishments* (1764), in which he advocated extensive reforms including equal justice for all classes, speedy trials, the right to face one's accusers, and an end to cruel punishment, including torture and the death penalty. Seven years later Pietro Verri's *Meditations on Political Economy* attacked the assumptions of the Physiocrats, the influential French economists who had advocated free trade and a single tax on land. Verri's claim of internal contradictions and flawed logic within the Physiocrats' positions created widespread controversy. Both Beccaria and Verri contributed to the best-known journal of the Italian Enlightenment, *Il Caffé*. Although published for only three years in the 1760s, *Il Caffé* managed to present powerful arguments for fundamental reform of Italian society. In all, the Italian Enlightenment, less well known than its French counterpart, made a significant contribution to both the development of European thought and the reform of antiquated political and economic traditions in Italy.

A HALF-CENTURY OF PEACE: REFORMS IN GOVERNMENT AND BUSINESS

During the first half of the seventeenth century, European warfare had forced the frequent realignment of the map of Italy, shifting the allegiances of various regions primarily between Spain and Austria, with the House of Savoy expanding its influence through clever diplomacy. In 1748, the European powers signed the Treaty of Aix-la-Chapelle, establishing a formula that provided the Italian peninsula a stable political configuration and an extended period of peace. The Austrians largely displaced the Spanish, taking Lombardy and controlling Tuscany indirectly. The Spanish temporarily governed Naples, Sicily, and Parma through Bourbon surrogates. However, the European balance of power meant that the new rivals for control of Italy—Austria and France—maintained a rough equilibrium until the French armies invaded in 1792.

It is significant that the region of Piedmont, under the reign of the House of Savoy, emerged in the second half of the eighteenth century to assume a position of independence. By appealing to the desire of the British to prevent both Austria and France from controlling the peninsula, the Piedmontese managed to attain the status of a sovereign kingdom (1713) and to acquire the island of Sardinia (1720) and the western part of the Duchy of Milan (1748). It was primarily the Piedmontese drive for expansion that led the dukes (now kings) of Savoy to promote reforms. In an effort to produce more abundant revenues through a more productive economy and greater administrative efficiency, the Savoy dynasty began in the eighteenth century to institute changes.

The dynasty began with a thorough land reform program, designed to recover from the Church and the aristocracy massive uncultivated and untaxed acreage. Once the surveying and accounting were completed, the Piedmontese government took back idle land, lifted tax exemptions, and instituted a more efficient system of tax collection. Much of the confiscated land was distributed among the royal family's supporters, entrenching their political base in a subservient landed aristocracy. At the same time the government revamped the school system, introducing modern, secular reforms that further weakened the Church's hold on the culture of the region. And in a limited effort to boost Piedmontese businesses, the king introduced protective tariffs. As a result of these reforms, the dynasty greatly strengthened the power of its centralized government and its ability to support a large standing army. Thus, by the time that new political theories from the Enlightenment reached Italy—such as the rights of people to select and limit their government—Piedmontese reforms were firmly in place. Along with them came repressive policies that crushed all forms of political opposition for the foreseeable future, including advocacy of more fundamental reform. Deprived of further change, Piedmont remained a military state. Insulated from the influence of the Enlightenment, the region was mired in an inefficient agricultural system and an economy unable to benefit from the extensive modernization introduced to other parts of Europe and Italy in the name of free trade and scientific progress.

Elsewhere in northern Italy authorities worked somewhat more closely with Illuministi, if only in an effort to preserve power. In Lombardy, Austrian authorities introduced reforms for reasons similar to those that motivated the Savoy dynasty to the west. Attempting to increase economic activity and revenues, the Habsburg queen, Maria Teresa, initiated comprehensive changes, including a land reform program and the elimination of internal trade barriers. The results aroused great interest among the Illuministi and businessmen of Milan. At the same time, the fertile Po Valley opened to profitable agricultural development by enterprising farmers, while the middle class in Milan and other smaller cities expanded their commercial activity. Throughout Maria Teresa's reign, Piedmontese intellectuals and entrepreneurs cooperated with Austrian authorities. However, her son and successor, the Emperor Joseph II, with more interest in centralized power than economic reform, reversed the trend, alienating the Piedmontese middle class.

Most notable among other regions that instituted reforms in the eighteenth century was Tuscany, particularly under the regime of Grand Duke Peter Leopold (Habsburg-Lorraine). When he inherited power from his father in 1765, Tuscan agriculture remained underdeveloped, with land owned primarily by the Church and the aristocracy and farmed by a class of poor tenants. Peter Leopold, partly under the influence of Illuministi, promoted the development of agriculture by encouraging the sale of fallow lands, revoking the nobility's medieval privileges, and opening agricultural markets. At the same time, the Grand Duke's administrative reforms decentralized power and redistributed taxes. However, his efforts to drain the Maremma marshes, transfer land to the peasantry, and limit the power of the Church met only limited success. In 1790, Peter Leopold left Tuscany to succeed his brother as Austrian emperor. His successors as Grand Dukes of Tuscany, ever mindful of the insurgency in France, backed off from reform in fear of encouraging the spread of revolution to the peninsula.

In the neighboring duchies of Parma and Modena, Enlightenment ideas spread widely, most notably represented by the highly original historical research of Muratori and his students and the restrictions placed on the Church's influence in Parma. However, reform efforts met even less success in Venice and Genoa. In the northernmost portions of the Papal States, only the Romagna, connected through Bologna and its great university to the currents of European thought, engaged in any significant reforms.

Central and southern Italians, as well, experienced varying degrees of reforms in the eighteenth century. The Papal States, even much of the rural Romagna, remained in a state of agricultural and commercial backwardness, with progress arrested by the smothering influence of the Vatican and the landlords who dominated the region. The Church, threatened by modern, secular reform, reacted defensively to the Enlightenment, adopting only minor adjustments in the system of taxes and tariffs just before the end of the century. Rome itself remained economically retarded, relegated to the role of great symbolic center of Christendom and nucleus of the Church's vast bureaucracy.

In the southern kingdoms of Naples and Sicily (Kingdom of the Two Sicilies), notable Illuministi in the tradition of Pietro Giannone advocated a range of modern reforms in the face of stalwart tradition. Among the advocates of reform were Antonio Genovesi, Gaetano Filangeri, and Bernardo Tanucci. Genovesi, a priest and economics professor at the University of Naples, provided much of the intellectual stimulus for Neapolitan reform, based on modernizing trends from northern Europe. In the second half of the century, Tanucci, chief minister of the Bourbon king Charles, placed limits on the Church's control of land, abolished the Inquisition, reorganized the prisons, and expelled the Jesuit order. However, Charles's gestures toward land and tax reform met resistance from the tradition-laden landlord class and the Church, rendering all such attempts futile. Naples, the principal southern city, remained a busy port but primarily exported raw materials in exchange for finished goods, as agriculture remained unchanged and industry failed to develop. In Sicily, large grain exports provided a sounder economic base, particularly evident among the privileged aristocracy.

Modest changes came to the Kingdom of the Two Sicilies toward the end of the eighteenth century, only to be curtailed. Charles's successor, Ferdinand IV, deferred first to Tanucci, then to his wife, Austrian princess Maria Carolina, and her trusted aide, the English adventurer Lord John Acton. Maria Carolina and Acton implemented a number of reforms, as had Tanucci. In Sicily, the viceroy, Domenico Caracciolo, attacked what he viewed as the island's fundamental problem, the special privileges of the nobility to exploit the peasantry. In reaction, Sicilian landlords mobilized the peasantry against the reforms, blaming them on a power-hungry king in Naples. After very limited success, reform efforts ran aground as the French Revolution frightened the king and his aides into backtracking. Consequently, the kingdoms of Naples and Sicily remained less developed than any region on the peninsula.

ITALY ON THE EVE OF THE FRENCH REVOLUTION

In spite of the failure of the Illuministi and their allies to introduce fundamental reform, peaceful conditions alone represented an improvement in the lives of many Italians. Nonetheless, life remained largely bound by tradition and deprivation, driving many Italians to protest. Conditions varied by region and from town to countryside, with Northerners and city-dwellers generally faring somewhat better than others. In the South, peasants often lived in simple huts, landless and trapped in debt. Serious food shortages in the 1760s reduced many tenant farmers to day laborers and drove others to the cities, creating a homeless class of urban beggars. Vast discrepancies of wealth left most peasants in poverty, while privileged landowner and merchant classes provided the cities with visible signs of prosperity.

Education, which would become increasingly important in the nineteenth century, remained largely the private privilege of a few. No Italian states had yet introduced public education, leaving the vast majority of the population illiterate. Formal education was provided by private tutors, Jesuit schools, or, after the expulsion of the Jesuits in 1773, by other Catholic orders such as the Congregation of Pious Schools. The latter adopted a more pragmatic curriculum with a greater emphasis on the Italian language than their predecessors had.

Italian women led lives confined in many ways by custom. Educational opportunities remained severely limited, marriages were arranged, and divorce was difficult. Nonetheless, there are a number cases in which highly accomplished women, as in France, hosted salons that became the favored gathering places of Italian intellectuals. And in Italy, in contrast to much of Europe, some women managed to attend universities as well as the new scientific academies.

As the eighteenth century entered its final decade, the intellectual ferment that contributed to the overthrow of the old regime in France was notably weaker in the Italian peninsula. In Piedmont, after flirting with pragmatic reforms, the Savoy dynasty dug in its heels and resisted change, entrenched in absolute power. And at the other end of the peninsula, in Naples, failed experiments in reform left an economy mired in archaic privilege. Neither political, social, nor economic transformation seemed likely. In response, frustrated by the futility of their efforts, a number of reformers organized groups of Illuministi and Freemasons (members of fraternal lodges pledged to humanist, secular values) dedicated to fundamental challenges to authority, and intellectuals of various preferences grasped for new and sometimes radical ideologies. Among the new ideas, interest developed in republican, democratic, and communistic alternatives. At the same time, other intellectual and political leaders proposed as a bold solution to existing problems nothing less than the political unification of the Italian peninsula.

6

The French Revolution, Napoleon, and the Restoration of Austrian Power in Italy, 1789–1848

The seeds of change planted by the ill-fated Italian reform movements of the eighteenth century were given life by the unrest that swept throughout much of Europe at the close of the century. It is with the French Revolution and its Napoleonic aftermath that both domestic reform and the prospect of Italian national unity found their most ardent expression to date. Yet the subsequent defeat of Napoleon and the establishment of a reactionary European settlement under the Austrian foreign minister, Prince Klemens von Metternich, conspired to bury most reforms—although he found some necessary—dashing hopes and effectively postponing change in Italy for a generation. Nonetheless, the nationalistic and progressive aspirations that awakened in Italy during the 1790s would not die. The result was a period of constant probing, intellectual disquiet, organized resistance to the status quo, and ever more numerous attempts to find a formula that would ensure Italian independence.

INFLUENCES FROM THE REVOLUTIONARY TRADITION

Among the Italians whose ideas influenced this period of intellectual and political ferment was the renowned Neapolitan philosopher Giambattista Vico (1668–1744). As Enlightenment theories of natural rights and popular sovereignty spread, Italians turned to the writings of Vico. Earlier in the eighteenth century Vico's study of various cultures had led him to propose highly original theories of "cycles of history" and "nation-hood," most notably in his *Principles of a New Science Concerning the Common Nature of Nations* (1725). A number of Italians, most notably his student An-tonio Genovesi, turned to Vico's work for inspiration in shaping their ideas of the common cultural characteristics that contributed to the development of "Italy." Along with Genovesi, the work of Benedetto Bacchini, Ludovico Muratori, and Scipione Maffei (see Chapter 5) provided an intellectual framework for the emerging argument that Italians shared adequate "na-tional" traditions to pursue unification.

Because the Enlightenment was international by nature, Italian scholars and political reformers were attuned to the French intellectual currents that dominated the movement. Thus, the outbreak in 1789 of the closely moni-tored French Revolution provided an immediate jolt to politics in Italy, just as it affected much of the continent. Furthermore, as economic issues fueled conflict in France, so the surge in European prices severely eroded living standards in Italy, spreading popular unrest. However, by late 1792 initial Italian enthusiasm dampened and continued to falter in 1793 and 1794 as the French Revolution turned more radical, escalating beyond moderate re-form to the Reign of Terror when the Committee of Public Safety guillo-tined opponents, assailed religion, and threatened capitalism.

Italian enthusiasm for the French Revolution was strongest in the Masonic lodges, universities, and salons. Among the Italian champions of the early Revolution was the Milanese dramatist Vittorio Alfieri. Then, ap-palled by the growing fanaticism in Paris, Alfieri left in 1792 for Florence, where he wrote his satirical *Il Misogallo*. Like Alfieri, many Italians shrank from sympathy for the Revolution as it unfolded; others declared them-selves "Jacobins," supporting the Revolution. One result was that Italian intellectuals and newspapers that had advocated reforms were discredited by the inference that the new militancy and violence in France were direct by-products of Enlightenment philosophy. Consequently, the kings, princes, and dukes who ruled the various Italian states recanted all previ-ous flirtation with progressive reforms, ordering police to enforce censor-ship rules and to suppress Freemasons and Jacobins. Equally troubling in the eyes of the authorities were spreading incidents of peasant militancy in Italy, which, although local in origin and focus, suspiciously resembled the rural violence that accompanied the revolution in France.

Italian authorities' fears intensified in 1792 in light of the outbreak of war in Europe. War threatened to compound internal discord, especially if Italy became a battleground. In fact, France's war against Austria and its allies quickly disrupted the generation of peace that had been enjoyed in the Italian peninsula. First, the French revolutionary government laid claim to Savoy and Nice as part of an attempt to expand French boundaries to protect the First Republic from counterattack by the monarchies. The Italian states responded by allying with the anti-French coalition of Austria, England, and Prussia.

NAPOLEON BONAPARTE IN ITALY

In the spring of 1796, after a three-year lull, the French government dispatched the young Corsican general Napoleon Bonaparte across the Alps into northern Italy where he won a series of victories and quickly imposed his presence. After his armies defeated the Piedmontese and the Austrians in northern Italy, Napoleon signed the Treaty of Campo Formio with Austria in October 1797, validating his control of Italian territory in exchange for Austria's acquisition of Venetia, and creating resentment among many Italians. If there had been doubts about Napoleon's intentions, few remained: He had undertaken the course of expansion. Before leaving Italy, he began to reorganize much of the Italian peninsula. By 1798, he had divided Italy north of Naples into Cisalpine, Ligurian, and Roman republics, driving the pope into exile. In the spirit of revolution, Neapolitan patriots, with outside assistance, drove the Bourbon king out of Naples to Sicily and proclaimed their own republic.

In the midst of the fervor stirred by the overthrow of the old regimes of monarchs who had previously controlled the various Italian states, Italian Jacobins organized revolutionary and patriotic movements throughout the peninsula. In some cities the Jacobins gained power, but internal disagreements prevented them from moving to unify the peninsula politically. In spite of the fact that the Jacobins had now been overthrown in Paris in a series of counterrevolutions, Italian Jacobinism thrived, most prominently in the person of Filippo Buonarroti, a former member of the Jacobin government in Paris. Buonarroti organized an insurrection in Piedmont that, although a failure, alerted both the Italian people and the French government to the prospect of political unification.

Napoleon decided to use Italy to support his expanding military campaign. Unwilling to tolerate resistance, he subdued Italian Jacobins and nationalists, driving many out of northern Italy and postponing further insurgency. In place of dangerous radicals, Napoleon installed a highly centralized government, modeled on the French system, that would enable him to raise revenues and soldiers from Italy.

Napoleon's reforms, particularly in northern Italy, proved ultimately very influential. In order to support his war effort as efficiently as possible, he swept aside many laws and customs of medieval origin that stood as barriers to modernization and efficiency. In their place he imposed reforms derived from the French Revolution. Feudal obligations were abolished in favor of legal equality. Much of the Church's land was confiscated and redistributed, and the Church's courts were replaced by civil courts.

Although many of Napoleon's reforms promoted progress, the means by which they were imposed—by an authoritarian foreign power—left many Italian democratic and patriotic groups angry and disillusioned. In turn, protests invited further repression by French authorities. The most dramatic anti-French, counterrevolutionary movement came in Naples, where French forces had driven the Bourbon king Ferdinand IV into exile and created a republic in early 1799. The republic's Jacobin leaders introduced reforms, including land reform, constraints on Church activities, and tax increases, measures that offended the sensibilities of the region's conservative peasants. In reaction, Cardinal Fabrizio Ruffo led his Christian Army (Sanfedista) of peasants to capture Naples from the French and restore Ferdinand. When French troops were transferred north to the Austrian front as the European war flared, the Jacobins of Naples were left defenseless in the face of Ruffo's assault. Taking the city, Ruffo guaranteed the protection of the surrendering Jacobin patriots; however, the restored King Ferdinand carried out their execution, which deprived Naples of much of its middle class and intellectual leadership, including the remarkable republican writer and editor Eleonora Pimentel.

The fate of Italians hung in the balance as Napoleon first seized control of the French government in November 1799, then consolidated his power, making himself First Consul for life in 1802 and Emperor in 1804. Shortly after the coup, Napoleon renewed his military campaign against the First Coalition by attacking Austrian forces in Italy. Napoleon won the Battle of Marengo in June 1800, then followed up with a string of victories that forced Austria to give up its Italian territory to France in the Treaty of Lunéville in February 1801. Until he abdicated in April 1814, after his disastrous invasion of Russia, Napoleon controlled the entire Italian peninsula with the exception of the islands of Sardinia and Sicily.

Regarding Italy as essential to his vast military and economic ambitions, Napoleon resumed his program of innovation. He once again reorganized Italy in several stages, ultimately creating the Kingdom of Italy in the North, the Kingdom of Naples in the South, and several large territories governed directly from Paris.

In and of itself, Napoleon's reorganization facilitated long-term change by breaking down the structures of existing governments, most of them foreign. Throughout Napoleonic Italy, he and his agents—including the innovative Milanese liberal Francesco Melzi d'Eril and the emperor's stepson, Eugene Beauharnais—modernized Italy's infrastructure and its administration, clearing the way for progress. Improved roads and docks opened European markets, and the standardization of currency, weights, and measures and the creation of a large free-trade zone stimulated new industrial and commercial activity. A new French-style civil law code protected private property rights, including investments. To facilitate modernization, Napoleon imposed French-style centralization of government, leaving little room for the regional and local differences that had traditionally characterized Italian public life. Not surprisingly, his agents encountered rigid resistance to change, particularly in the South.

A number of Napoleon's policies did prove successful, providing opportunities for many Italians while opening the peninsula to economic and social development. A new generation of young Italians responded, expanding the middle class and replacing the older aristocratic office-holders with a more aggressive, better educated, and better trained class of young bureaucrats. Once having tasted the power of the state, especially the ability to introduce reforms, these young men would be reluctant to relinquish the power and, once replaced, anxious to re-acquire it. In the rural areas, Napoleon's ban on feudal privileges deprived the nobility of traditional sources of income. However, when Napoleon's regime sold land it had confiscated from the Church, the nobility frequently purchased it, impeding any significant land reform and in many cases improving their own economic position. In the North this enabled ambitious families to acquire fallow land, which they converted to profitable agricultural production. In the South, in contrast, it was often the small-town middle class of bankers, lawyers, and merchants who benefitted most, aggressively purchasing available land but rarely cultivating it.

At the same time, a number of Napoleon's policies continued to produce widespread opposition in Italy, particularly the institution of military conscription and the reintroduction of the death penalty. While implementing his Continental System (economic embargo of England's European markets), Napoleon prevented Italians from exporting to France or England, damaging much of the economic progress he had energized. It was the emperor's governments, rather than the old regimes they replaced, that perfected the use of extensive police surveillance.

To the south, Napoleon ordered a French army into Naples in 1806, driving Ferdinand IV into exile. The emperor replaced the Bourbon king, first with his brother Joseph Bonaparte, then in 1808 with his brother-in-law Joachim Murat. The French kings of Naples implemented Napoleonic reforms in law, public finance, commerce, education, the military, and the affairs of the Church. Murat, in particular, managed to move Naples toward greater autonomy, promoting Neapolitans in his government and lending some support to the proponents of Italian independence. Still, most of the progress occurred among the middle class in Naples and Palermo; the reforms failed to address the pervasive conditions of rural poverty throughout the rest of the South.

THE SPREAD OF ITALIAN NATIONALISM

During the Napoleonic era, evidence of Italian nationalism began to appear in several guises, in some cases inspired by the ideals of French nationalism, in others reacting against Napoleon's heavy-handed government. Particularly active under Murat's regime in the South were secret societies, driven underground by the police. The most important was the Carboneria, whose members were called *carbonari*, a name probably derived from their habit of meeting secretly in caves around charcoal fires.

At the same time, Italian writers expressed renewed enthusiasm for Italian nationalism, at least in a romanticized, abstract form. Among these editors and essayists the best known was the poet Ugo Foscolo, who generated interest in Italy's past in his most famous works, *Dei Sepolcri* (Of Sepulchres) and *Le ultime lettere di Jacopo Ortis* (The Final Letters of Jacopo Ortis). Clandestine political organization and literary and artistic expression kept alive, at least among a small elite, the ideals on which more realistic forms of nationalism would later build. But the nationalistic cause would struggle even more mightily in the next generation.

THE IMPACT OF AUSTRIAN REACTIONARY POLICIES

When Metternich convened the Congress of Vienna in 1815, the powers that had overcome Napoleon designed a "Concert of Europe" that restored "legitimate" monarchs to power in an attempt to roll back the changes introduced over the previous quarter-century, especially constitutional restrictions on the absolute power of monarchs. The Restoration produced a mixed record. On the one hand, there is convincing evidence of immediate and lasting regression in Italy. However, historians have recently reassessed this era. It is clear, and not surprising, that nowhere in Italy did Metternich fully achieve his aspirations, nor did he encourage the adoption of the most extreme reactionary policies. Whether regarded as intelligent conservative or as reactionary, he developed the strategy of encouraging "legitimate" rulers to pursue more efficient management of governments in the hope that constitutions and elections would lose their appeal. In fact, in a number of places, influences from the Enlightenment, the French Revolution, and the Napoleonic era contributed to the continuation of progressive reforms. It may also be that Bourbon administrative reforms in the South actually contributed to economic and political development in spite of the general view of Bourbon government as repressive. Regardless of the debate over the impact of Restoration governments, Italian nationalism and liberalism continued to develop, if gradually and unevenly.

As a major tenet of his European system, Metternich maintained control of most of the peninsula. The Austrian Empire annexed Lombardy and the Venetian Republic, placed Austrian dukes in power in Parma, Modena, and Tuscany, restored the pope's power in the Papal States, and reinstated the reactionary Bourbon Ferdinand IV to the throne in Naples and Sicily (Kingdom of the Two Sicilies) on the condition that he keep a defensive alliance with Austria. However, in line with his principle of supporting "legitimate" rulers, Metternich allowed the one native dynasty, the House of Savoy, to add the Republic of Genoa to its Piedmontese territory. In fact, throughout the entire peninsula, only Piedmont (known as the Kingdom of Sardinia) remained independent of Austria.

Problems imposed by Austrian rule were unmistakable. Economic progress promoted by Napoleon's consolidation of territory into large free-trade zones was lost when regional fragmentation led to the revival of customs barriers. In the Papal States, Pius VII (pope 1800–1823) and Cardinal Consalvi resisted reactionary pressures, refusing to restore the nobility's privileges or to retake land that the French had confiscated from the Church. However, when elected pope on the death of Pius VII, Leo XII reversed his predecessor's policies and thrust the Papal States into severe decline. He and his successors, Pius VIII and Gregory XVI, imposed strict censorship and religious persecution while tightening the Church's grip on education.

Even more repressive was the Piedmont, where the restored King Vittorio Emanuele obstinately turned back the clock by wiping out Napoleonic reforms in a single decree. The king imposed internal tariffs, brought back the Jesuit order to control education and censorship, forced Jews into ghettoes, reversed legal reforms, purged the civil service and the military, and granted to the aristocracy privileges that had been revoked. Similarly, Duke Francesco IV of Modena brought back the Jesuits and replaced all of Napoleon's officials with appointees from the old nobility, indicating a major step backward. Privilege of birth now replaced Napoleon's emphasis on talent as the test for recruiting and promoting state employees. It was precisely in those regions where reactionary policies were most extreme that insurrections tended to occur with greatest regularity during the Restoration era.

At the same time, indications of change persisted. Just as Consalvi had brought progress to the Papal States, so Ferdinand III of Florence and Ferdinand IV of Naples embraced a number of Napoleonic reforms. Consequently, the titles to newly acquired land were widely accepted, many of Napoleon's appointees retained their positions, and Napoleonic legal and commercial reforms remained in place. Even the Austrians, determined to avoid provoking Italian nationalist resistance in Lombardy and Venetia, developed a reputation for competent administration. Nonetheless, in spite of some progress, Italian nationalists and liberals were far from satisfied. Throughout the Metternich era, champions of Italian unity could concentrate their opposition, focusing on Austria as the single force obstructing their path.

RESTORATION CULTURE AND ROMANTIC NATIONALISM

In the face of the restoration of power to Austria and its collaborators, Italian writers, composers, and political activists pursued visions of a future Italy. In the tradition of Foscolo (who had fled into exile upon Austria's return to power), Italians of various political views published their works under the scrutiny of Austrian censors. Two notable journals, *Il Conciliatore* (Milan) and *Antologia* (Florence), expressed an idealistic trust in gradual change. Combined with the works of several prominent writers, Italian intellectuals generally supported a moderate approach to change—incorporating in many cases both the Roman Catholic Church and the Piedmontese monarchy—that would emerge as the dominant model of Italian unification. Among the best known of these Restoration Italian writers were Alessandro Manzoni, Giacomo Leopardi, and Cesare Balbo. Manzoni published his famous romantic, historical novel *I promessi sposi* (The Betrothed) in 1827. In describing the lives of Milanese lovers living under Spanish rule in the seventeenth century, Manzoni provided a metaphor for ordinary Italians who relied on their Catholic faith to protect them against alien forces of oppression. Leopardi, often considered the finest lyric poet of his day, published ardently patriotic poems among his less celebrated works. Included among them is *"All'Italia"* ("To Italy," 1818), and other minor poems in which he sympathized with the fate of Italians while condemning Austria and France. Balbo, a moderate aristocrat who would later become a major figure in Piedmontese politics, published his best-known work in 1844. In

Le speranze d'Italia (The Hopes of Italy), Balbo advocated a diplomatic approach to Austria, by which the Hapsburgs would withdraw from Italy in exchange for territory in the weakening Turkish Empire.

Among the composers who expressed overtones of romanticized nationalism in their works were Gioacchino Rossini and Vincenzo Bellini. Although primarily known for the genre of *opera buffa* ("comic opera") and *bel canto* ("beautiful song"), Rossini composed a strongly patriotic tale in his last opera, *William Tell* (1829). The Sicilian Bellini also became famous for *bel canto* and, like Rossini, produced in his final opera, *I Puritani* (The Puritans, 1835) an opera more readily open to political interpretation. Although premature, these two operas provided a model that Giuseppe Verdi would later use to communicate Italian patriotism more forcefully.

RESTORATION SOCIETY AND THE ORIGINS OF NATIONALIST INSURRECTION

The economic problems brought on by the policies of Austria and its collaborators contributed to a prolonged period of stagnation and hardship that was particularly prevalent in the countryside. Combined with alarming growth in population and peasant indebtedness, rural migration to the cities lowered standards of living and compounded problems of poverty, famine, disease (cholera and malaria in particular), and crime. Government imposition of taxes and military conscription complicated the problems of the poor. Consequently, authorities feared mass uprisings and sharpened political repression, in turn driving protest underground. Influenced by Freemasons, *carbonari*, and other groups surviving from the Napoleonic era, secret societies spread a network of nationalism and reform throughout much of the peninsula. But plagued by ideological disagreement and organizational disarray, the clandestine movements remained largely ineffectual throughout the period of Austrian control.

Although very different in origin, insurrections erupted in several places in the 1820s and 1830s. As might be expected, there were no signs of coordinated effort and little agreement in either ideology or method. All were localized, and none produced permanent change. The first uprising occurred in Naples in the summer of 1820 when a group of dissident army officers toppled the government and forced the Bourbon king to introduce the Spanish Constitution of 1812. However, splits in the ranks of the insurgents undercut the gains and weakened the movement so that Metternich was able to crush the revolt with Austrian troops. Meanwhile, Sicilian workers in Palermo seized the opportunity to revolt against the king of Naples, building on pent-up hostility toward Bourbon rule. The workers' inability to cooperate with either the Sicilian nobility or the Neapolitan rebels doomed their revolution as well. Neither 1820 uprising contributed to Italian unification except to demonstrate pockets of southern political resistance.

Meanwhile in northern Italy, liberals, straining under the heavy hand of Austrian rule and hoping to appeal to the Savoy dynasty's expansionist aspirations, conspired in an attempt to drive the Austrians out of Lombardy. Plans involved moderates in both Lombardy and Piedmont. Austrian authorities, aware of spreading discontent, intensified repression, arresting hundreds on suspicion of conspiracy. Among the many arrested in 1820 was Silvio Pellico, the young publisher of the liberal literary journal *Il Conciliatore*. Pellico was sentenced to fifteen years of hard labor at the Austrian fortress of Spielberg in Moravia. In 1832, Pellico published his memoir, *Le Mie Prigioni* (My Prisons), which sold widely throughout Europe as a stunning literary testimony to his own religiosity, the brutality of life in an Austrian prison, and an affirmation of early Italian nationalism.

As opposition to Austria spread, a young Piedmontese cavalry officer, Santorre di Santarosa, engineered a coup d'état in the spring of 1821 that unseated King Vittorio Emanuele. Santarosa and his compatriots believed that Carlo Alberto, the young heir to the throne, would support an agenda of liberal reform and Piedmontese expansion. Again, confusion and lack of support doomed the effort. After agreeing to adopt the Spanish Constitution of 1812, Carlo Alberto reneged in the face of reactionary pressure from Charles Felix, Vittorio Emanuele's brother. On the request of Charles Felix, Austrian troops smothered the revolt and imprisoned its leaders. Santarosa fled into exile.

The failures of the revolutions of 1820–1821 dramatized certain realities about the prospect of change in Italy. The movements for change were disparate and ill-prepared, and their challenges to authority would be met with force greater than they could muster. However, there were at the same time hopeful signs. Throughout Europe, where assistance was possible, Italian political exiles made the patriotic case. In northern Italy, middle-class groups stepped forward to sponsor change based on precepts of moderate programs of constitutional monarchy and economic reform. Their resources were substantial, assuming that they could marshal the forces of the Savoy dynasty behind a campaign to expand Piedmont. Throughout the 1830s, this group of northern moderates established itself as a force for change and began to articulate a case for an expanded northern Italian state. At the same time, more radical forces throughout Italy championed a grass-roots revolution committed to democracy and social reform. By 1840, these two groups—one moderate, one more radical—represented in the most general sense two divergent paths to the future of the Italian peninsula.

The French Revolution of July 1830 touched off another round of European insurgency. As the French overthrew the Bourbon dynasty and Belgians, Greeks, and Serbs won their independence, Italian nationalists gained inspiration and encouragement. Through the center of the peninsula, Italian revolutions erupted in 1831, organized in part by Ciro Menotti, a liberal from Modena who called for a constitutional monarchy. In Parma, Modena, and the Papal States, patriots waved the green, white, and red flag and, in parts of the Papal States, briefly succeeded in overthrowing the government. Vainly hoping for intervention from Louis Philippe, the new "King of the French," Italian patriots were gravely disillusioned and, once again, overwhelmed by Austrian troops.

GIUSEPPE MAZZINI AND THE DRIVE FOR A DEMOCRATIC REPUBLIC

As the various Italian patriotic movements foundered in the 1830s, one man emerged to provide focus, intellectual energy, and legendary spiritual presence that would sustain the drive for national unification for decades to come. Even in exile, Giuseppe Mazzini (1805–1872) inspired a zealous following while striking fear in the hearts of authorities. Born in Genoa, the only son of a medical doctor and an educated, devoutly religious mother, Mazzini proved a precocious child, enrolling at the University of Genoa at age fourteen. While a student, he was deeply moved at the sight of participants in the failed 1821 revolution fleeing for their lives. Born under French control and now resentful of Piedmont's acquisition of Genoa, the young Mazzini developed revolutionary sympathies that would make him famous. After completing a law degree, he joined the *carbonari* in 1827. Four years later, after serving a prison term in Savona, he fled into exile in France and left the *carbonari* in favor of a group he founded in Marseille, Giovane Italia, or Young Italy. His stated purpose was to fight for "independence, unity, [and] liberty for Italy."

It was in this period that Mazzini developed his fundamental ideas as a man of "thought and action," expressed in the creed of Young Italy. Italians, no less than all peoples, shared a divine right to freedom. Against the forces of repression, a new generation had to win its freedom through popular insurrection, bringing to their knees the princes and emperors that tyrannized them. Mazzini advocated a mass revolt, using guerrilla warfare tactics to force the Austrians, their surrogate rulers, and the papacy out of power. Although some complicity with the French might be useful, Italians would have to rely upon themselves (*"L'Italia farà da sè"*). The campaign would enlist the masses in producing an Italian democratic republic.

Mazzini's supporters organized Young Italy groups throughout northern Italy, Tuscany, the Papal States, Naples, and Sicily. Their first insurrection, organized in 1832 within the Piedmontese army, failed miserably. Sentenced to death in absentia and banished from France, Mazzini fled to Switzerland (1833), then England (1837), where, except for several clandestine trips to Italy, he spent the rest of his life. His "patriotic" supporters remained a small, embattled minority that failed to rally mass popular support.

In opposition to Mazzini's radical vision, northern moderates articulated several alternatives. Most forcefully expressed was the proposal of a former Mazzinian priest from Turin, Vincenzo Gioberti. Gioberti's *On the Moral and Civil Primacy of the Italians (Il Primato)* called for Italians to rally behind a rejuvenated papacy in the drive for unification, thereby providing moderate Catholics an appealing choice by reconciling church and state. Other Northerners, reluctant to solicit the Church's leadership, reached out to Carlo Alberto, king of Piedmont, to lead a campaign of Piedmontese expansion that would produce an Italian federation of states. The most convincing case for a moderate, secular approach was Balbo's *Delle speranze d'Italia*. Balbo proposed a diplomatic solution to Italy's future, rewarding Austria with Turkish territory in exchange for Austria's exit from Italy, allowing Piedmont to create a northern Italian kingdom. Most emphatic was Balbo's focus on Austria as the foremost obstacle to Italy's progress.

By the mid-1840s, a major shift had occurred within Italian political culture. The drive to establish some form of national unification and constitutional government had built momentum, not only among intellectuals but among the middle class and a substantial part of the aristocracy in the North. No better example exists than the influence of Massimo D'Azeglio, a multi-talented, politically moderate Piedmontese nobleman. D'Azeglio had painted romantic landscapes and written two historical novels with nationalist overtones, *Ettore Fieramosca* (1833) and *Nicolò de' Lapi* (1841). A cousin of Balbo, D'Azeglio had traveled extensively through Italy and was thus better informed about Italian politics than other Piedmontese. While traveling in the Papal States in 1845, D'Azeglio met revolutionaries, including Luigi Carlo Farini, who shortly thereafter led an abortive revolution in Rimini. Returning to Turin, D'Azeglio sought out King Carlo Alberto to recount his new revelations. Surprisingly, the king expressed great sympathy and commitment: "When the occasion presents itself, my life, the lives of my children, my arms, my treasures, my army, everything will be spent for the Italian cause." The next spring, D'Azeglio published *Degli ultimi casi di*

Romagna (On the Latest Events in the Romagna), in which he argued that Farini's insurrection had been a mistake. In one of the important works of Italian unification, D'Azeglio rejected violent revolution in favor of a persistent campaign of public opinion supporting the cause of nationalism.

In spite of the northern moderates' growing support for the patriotic cause, many questions remained. Gioberti and his followers found Gregory XVI (pope 1831–1846) both unwilling and unable to lead a movement. Evidence of Mazzinian insurrection continued to alarm moderates, while Mazzini himself was reduced to huddling with fellow exiled conspirators in Marseille, Geneva, and, after 1837, London. And in Piedmont, reformers found more questions than answers.

Ironically, it was changing conditions in Italy's most repressive regions that provided Italian liberals signs of promise. The election of Pius IX (Pio Nono, pope 1846–1878), encouraged Gioberti's followers. Pio Nono moved quickly to introduce a number of reforms to the Papal States—so quickly as to alarm Metternich. Among his changes, the pope loosened restrictions on the press and on Italian Jews and granted amnesties to political prisoners. Meanwhile, in Piedmont, King Carlo Alberto, reluctant to lead a drive against Austria, introduced reforms in the army, public finance, civil and criminal law, commerce, and education, a tortuous attempt to combine economic liberalism with political absolutism. Thus, the record of repression and reform in the Metternich era is, like much of Italian history, dependent on local conditions. Ironically, these pragmatic concessions, made primarily by autocrats to preserve their hold on power, created new tensions that contributed to the demise of their dynasties. These tensions—among classes, regions, political ideologies, government and civil society, church and state—would persist throughout the Risorgimento ("Resurgence"), as the Italian independence movement would be called, and into the newly created Italian kingdom.

THE REVOLUTIONS OF 1848 IN ITALY

As was true throughout much of the European continent, 1848 marked another round of revolutionary disturbances in Italy as well, more widespread and forceful than those of 1830. Like other Europeans, Italians had suffered from economic depression in the 1840s. However, when the upheavals occurred in 1848, the various Italian insurgents focused primarily not on economic change but on overturning the existing political order. There had been a number of scattered foreshadowings of the 1848 revolutions, all of them failures. The boldest was an assault on the Kingdom of the

Two Sicilies by the Bandiera brothers and a few confederates that ended tragically in their capture and execution.

The Italian revolutions of 1848 first erupted in Palermo, Sicily, in January, then quickly jumped to Naples, stunning the King of the Two Sicilies, and thus convincing him to grant immediate concessions. In the face of pressure from nationalists and reformers, Ferdinand II issued a constitution providing for a parliament that placed limitations on his powers, hoping to satisfy the reformers while driving a wedge between Sicilians and Neapolitans. As occurred over much of the European continent where centers of power teetered, the Italian revolution quickly spread, from region to region and from city to countryside. Demonstrations in Turin and Genoa forced King Carlo Alberto in February to issue a similar constitution, *Il Statuto*, derived in part from the French constitution of 1830. The Grand Duke of Tuscany and Pope Pius IX quickly followed suit, and soon every Italian state was granted a constitution, with the exception of Lombardy and Venetia, where Austrian authorities held the line.

Then, to the shock of much of the world, Prince Metternich fled into exile in the face of the revolution in Vienna, throwing into disarray not only Austrian government but also the entire European system that he had crafted and that had dominated the continent for a generation. In a number of the Hapsburg Empire's great cities, confusion spread throughout Austrian military ranks, creating an opportunity for the forces of change to strike. In Italy, where about 40 percent of Austrian infantrymen were Italians and another large contingent were sympathetic Hungarians, the command grew uncertain of the troops' loyalties. Furthermore, the collapse of the conservative, Catholic Hapsburg government in Vienna weakened the protection of the pope's enormous holdings in the center of the Italian peninsula and made the Spanish Bourbons' hold on the Kingdom of the Two Sicilies appear vulnerable as well.

7

Unification of Italy: The Risorgimento and the "Making of Italians," 1848–1900

The "year of revolutions" that jolted the foundations of nineteenth-century Europe at mid-course brought to Italy a series of traumatic disturbances that promised to throw off the yoke of outside repression and move the peninsula toward progressive reforms. As European insurgents forced change in Paris, Vienna, Berlin, Budapest, and Prague, so Italians seized opportunity. Most emphatic were the "Five Days of Milan." Under a Council of War headed by the republican and federalist Carlo Cattaneo, citizens of the Lombard capital erupted in fierce fighting to force Austrian general Josef Radetzky to order his 75,000 troops to abandon the city on March 22, 1848. That same day, Venetians led by an Italian Jewish lawyer and nationalist, Daniele Manin, took control of the city and, as the Austrians capitulated, declared the Republic of St. Mark. The next day, responding to popular demands from Lombardy and hoping to seize control of an unstable and threatening situation, the irresolute King Carlo Alberto of Piedmont declared his support for the Milanese and moved his troops into Lombardy. In retrospect, although it was not always apparent at the time, these were important steps in the evolution of the Risorgimento. And the same northern initiative that drove the first phase of unification would position northern political leaders to place their stamp on the emerging nation.

THE REVOLUTIONS OF 1848 AND THE ITALIAN WAR OF LIBERATION

Carlo Alberto's motivation for intervening against Austria derived in part from a realistic fear that Mazzinian and other republican forces hoped to use the "people's revolts" against Austria as leverage to establish republican governments. Thus, Piedmontese liberals such as Count Camillo Benso di Cavour (1810–1861) emphatically urged the king to take control of the rebellions. Carlo Alberto calculated that military leadership against a hated foe would boost his prestige.

Thousands of Italian workers and peasants rallied to the cause, giving Mazzinians hope that a spontaneous popular war would liberate Italians. In April, urged by D'Azeglio, the commander of the papal armies marched his troops north in support of the Piedmontese, infuriating the pope and provoking a rebuke that, in turn, placed Pius IX in opposition to the nationalist revolt and disillusioned his nationalist supporters.

In Lombardy, after initial successes, Carlo Alberto's armies fell decisively to the Austrians at the Battle of Custoza on July 24, 1848; subsequently, Piedmont signed the armistice of Salasco, returning Lombardy to Austrian control. Facing intense criticism and ignoring Cavour's advice, Carlo Alberto renewed warfare the next spring, only to be defeated again at the Battle of Novara. Humiliated, he abdicated in favor of his son, Vittorio Emanuele II (1820–1868).

Undeterred—even encouraged—by Piedmont's loss of the "war of the princes," Mazzini saw an opportunity to turn Carlo Alberto's failures to the advantage of the republican cause. Roman nationalists capitalized on the pope's opposition to the war of liberation by establishing their own government, forcing Pius IX to flee south to Gaeta in November 1848. Electrified by the news of the pope's flight, Italian independence fighters converged on Rome. Among them were Mazzini and Giuseppe Garibaldi (1807–1882). Garibaldi, the son of a poor fisherman from Nice, was bound for true heroism in the patriotic tradition. A sailor and international freedom fighter, he returned hastily from campaigning in support of Latin American independence to lend his considerable skills as a guerrilla leader to the Italian unification movement. He had first offered his services to King Carlo Alberto; when refused by the monarch as a risk, the guerrilla fighter joined the revolt in Milan, where he was made a general in the Milanese army. When that revolution collapsed, Garibaldi turned south to rally in support of the Roman Republic, where he had just been elected to its constituent assembly.

Mazzini organized the government of the Roman Republic along democratic lines, governing with skill and restraint in the face of upheaval. He abolished much of the Church's antiquated and repressive structure and began the process of transferring Church land to peasants. Revolution continued to spread. By the end of January 1849, Tuscans had driven the Grand Duke Leopold II into refuge in Gaeta. Similarly, Modena and Parma installed revolutionary governments and voted to join Piedmont, while revolution flared in Sicily. Consistent with traditional Italian patterns, each of the revolts of 1848 featured local leadership and revolved around local political and economic grievances, making coordination difficult at best. The growing prospect of independence intensified rivalry among various schools of patriotism. Pro-Piedmontese moderates, who favored a constitutional monarchy, clashed with republicans. Even among republican forces, Cattaneo, Manin, and Mazzini disagreed over the fundamental outlines of an ideal Italian republic.

Unfortunately for Italian patriots, by the spring of 1849 Austrian and Bourbon forces began to recover, reversing in order each of the revolutions of 1848 and reinstalling themselves. In May, Austrian forces occupied Tuscany, restored the Grand Duke with brutal force, and moved to rescind the constitution of 1848. Parma and Modena were, in turn, restored to Austrian control. After heroically resisting the Austrian navy's siege and bombardment, Manin and the Venetians surrendered in August 1849.

With resistance collapsing all around them, the Roman Republicans dug in to protect their gains. An expert in military science, the patriot Carlo Pisacane took command of the armed forces, while Garibaldi organized the field defense among his untrained volunteers and doggedly held off counter-revolutionary armies from Naples and Spain. Meanwhile in France, newly elected President Louis Napoleon Bonaparte, nephew of Napoleon the Great, dealt a devastating blow to Italian patriots who had hoped for his aid. In a politically calculated attempt to win support of French Catholics, Louis Napoleon ordered his armies to restore the pope to power. In April 1849, General Nicolas Oudinot led a French invasion force of twenty-thousand in an assault on Rome. For a month Garibaldi's outnumbered volunteers waged an epic defense, only to fall under the weight of French reinforcements. After crushing the Roman Republic, the French in April 1850 ushered Pius IX to his seat of power in the Vatican.

While Venetians and Romans desperately defended their republics, Ferdinand II moved to reverse revolutionary gains in the Kingdom of the Two Sicilies. With the help of Swiss mercenaries, the king disbanded the Neapolitan parliament in the spring of 1849, cautiously waiting until the revolutions failed in other regions before rescinding the constitution and further re-consolidating his power. In September, a Neapolitan army of twenty thousand invaded and bombarded Sicily. Aided by separatist and socialist contingents, Sicilians resisted fiercely until their ultimate defeat in May 1849. Ironically, the severity of Bourbon repression produced a backlash that undercut their ability to maintain the support of the population.

CAMILLO DI CAVOUR AND THE TRIUMPH OF THE PIEDMONTESE MODERATES

The failure of the revolutions of 1848 to establish either an Italian state or any newly independent republics dashed the hopes of a number of patriotic factions and their leaders. Recently voted dictatorial powers by the Roman Republican Senate, Garibaldi narrowly escaped with four thousand survivors, trekking north, intent on reaching the Venetian Republic. The retreat turned disastrous, as his Republican army dissolved, a number of them captured and executed. After his wife and comrade-in-arms, Anita, died during the retreat, Garibaldi managed to escape once again so as to resume the fight another day. Mazzini returned to England, where in 1853 he founded another patriotic group, the Party of Action.

Discredited by the stigma of failure were both Mazzini's plan to create a democratic republic through a popular uprising and Gioberti's design for an enlarged papal state. Their failure allowed the conservative, Catholic forces—the Austrians, the papacy, and the Spanish Bourbons—to impose a "second restoration" of dukes, princes, and other counter-revolutionary rulers and surrogates. However, the ultimate beneficiaries of these failures were not the conservative powers but the moderate constitutional monarchists of Piedmont, who would now emerge to take the initiative in expanding Piedmontese influence in the drive to create an Italian state.

The ability of the Piedmontese moderates to seize control of the Risorgimento was a product of a number of factors found in the European diplomatic system and throughout the peninsula, but primarily in Piedmont itself. The Piedmontese held the enviable position of being a counterweight to both Austria and France in European balance-of-power diplomacy, a factor the British traditionally valued. The brilliant and cunning Cavour understood this very well and, as he emerged in Piedmontese politics, quickly learned to parlay Piedmont's modest resources into a substantial asset. Furthermore, among Italian states, Piedmont's House of Savoy stood alone as the sole independent dynasty, manning the only regular army.

Just as important, however, was the modernization of Piedmont, managed largely by Cavour. Born in Turin, the second son of a Piedmontese aristocratic family (his father served as chief of police in Turin), Cavour was destined to become, along with Mazzini and Garibaldi, an indispensable leader of the Risorgimento. After resigning his military commission, the young Cavour traveled widely throughout Europe, then returned to manage the family's estate, which soon became recognized as a model of scientific agriculture. From a family that spoke French in a state that bordered France, Cavour favored the expansion of Piedmont but was never convinced of the wisdom of unification of the peninsula. In politics Cavour was a committed moderate, rejecting revolution, republicanism, and Mazzinian insurrection in favor of gradual, orderly progress under an English-style limited monarchy; liberal in economic policy, but conservative on social issues. To articulate his reform agenda for Piedmont, Cavour established (along with Cesare Balbo) a newspaper, *Il Risorgimento*. In its pages he advocated such sweeping changes as a secular parliamentary system, free trade, and public subsidies for construction of railroads, docks, roads, and canals. In addition to calling for a constitution, Cavour urged King Carlo Alberto to launch a patriotic war against Austria on behalf of neighboring Lombardy. In the midst of the revolutions of 1848, the king issued a constitution (*Il Statuto*) and, shortly thereafter, ordered the Piedmontese forces into battle. By then, already widely recognized for his achievements as a businessman, Cavour had entered the new Piedmontese parliament.

In much of Italy a backlash of brutal tyranny followed in the wake of the failures of the 1848 revolutions as each of the regimes re-imposed its power and suspended constitutional government. Piedmont proved the lone exception. Originally an underdeveloped and repressive state, Piedmont pursued a path of gradual reform, the first signs of which had appeared even under the old regime of Carlo Alberto. In fact, it was the economic modernization of Piedmont under an evolving liberal constitutional system that thrust the kingdom to center stage in the drive for unification of the peninsula. Under considerable domestic pressure, the ill-prepared new king, Vittorio Emanuele II (reigned Piedmont, 1849–1861; Italy, 1861–1878), maintained *Il Statuto*–despite his preference for absolute monarchy. During the 1850s, the Piedmontese middle class embraced the parliamentary system and by their enthusiastic participation managed to modify the operation of the authoritarian *Statuto*. By developing an energetic Chamber of Deputies that held the king and his government responsible, Piedmontese liberals effectively placed some constraints on Vittorio Emanuele's ability to exercise arbitrary power.

Cavour joined D'Azeglio's government as minister of trade and agriculture in 1850, a benchmark in a career of political leadership that would take him into the broader arena of Italian politics and end only in his death. Already he had made an impact by sponsoring the Siccardi laws that limited the influence of the Church, which Cavour viewed as an impediment to de-

velopment. Once in D'Azeglio's cabinet, Cavour pursued free-trade policies, aligning Piedmont with Britain, France, and other European states
while sponsoring railway construction and reforms in banking, taxation,
and government administration. Cavour's moderate reforms met stiff opposition from conservatives, who managed to defeat several of his proposals. In response, the adroit Cavour hammered out an arrangement (known
as the *connubio*, or "marriage") with Urbano Rattazzi, head of the
Piedmontese moderate left, whereby moderates of both sides could continue to make gradual progress in modernizing Piedmont while maintaining a political coalition that would provide Cavour a power base that
would sustain him into the next decade.

In the process, Cavour orchestrated a move that made him prime minister in 1852, and thus he began to put his stamp more decisively on the politics of Piedmont and the drive for Piedmontese expansion and the
independence of Italy. Among Cavour's progressive initiatives, he sponsored laws designed to expand business and agriculture. Throughout the
decade the Piedmontese railroads developed, farming thrived, and the textile, silk, iron, and machine industries prospered impressively, as did the
export of rice, oil, and wine. He introduced a central bank, the Banca
Nazionale, while encouraging the development of stock exchanges in Turin and Genoa and the expansion of credit through a series of savings
banks. At the same time, the prime minister launched a policy of secularization he called "a free Church in a free state." When Vittorio Emanuele
opposed Cavour on a bill to dissolve religious institutions not committed to
education or charity, Cavour resigned; unable to find a suitable replacement, the king relented, returning Cavour to power. Cavour thereby had
taken a major step in insulating the cabinet from the king's control. At the
same time, the prime minister had further alienated the Catholic Church
from the forces that would unify the peninsula.

As a result of its economic progress and constitutional development,
Piedmont emerged in the 1850s as a thriving model of progress. The state
began to be compared favorably with France and Britain while dramatically overshadowing the rest of the peninsula, which was mired in economic stagnation and political subjugation. This same state that, only
twenty years earlier, had been among the most backward in the peninsula,
now could lay claim to the role of leadership in the second half of the century. It was Cavour's brilliantly innovative, opportunistic diplomacy that
thrust the small state solidly into the midst of European affairs.

In the spring of 1854, the Crimean War provided Cavour an opportunity to expand Piedmont's influence. Suspicious of Russian ambition, England
and France declared war on Russia to check what they viewed as an aggres-

sive Russian move to take the Turkish straits. Cavour, now foreign minister, led Piedmont into the conflict against Russia, thereby ensuring the Piedmontese a seat at any postwar conference that would surely redraw the map of Europe and reorder military alliances. Although historians traditionally attributed this move to Cavour's careful calculation, recent research suggests that the prime minister took Piedmont into the coalition in response to a range of pressing considerations: support among Italian nationalists in Piedmont, pressure from England and France, and fear that Austria might join, thereby isolating Piedmont. As a result of his commitment to the coalition, reluctant as he appears to have been, Cavour attended the Paris peace conference in February 1856. Although rebuffed on specific demands, he did succeed in a broader sense. He enhanced the status of Piedmont as well as his own prestige, particularly in Italy, alerted the Great Powers to the question of Italy's future, and developed a personal connection with French emperor Napoleon III. Significantly, Austria emerged from the conference isolated, the sole defender of the remnants of the system Metternich had created well over a generation earlier. Amid shifting European diplomatic allegiances, Cavour declared Piedmont to be on a collision course with Austria, and now he began to pursue every opportunity to drive the Austrians out of Italy.

As he anticipated, Cavour's involvement of Piedmont in the Crimean War proved popular. Piedmont was at the time the refuge of perhaps fifty thousand political exiles, many veterans of the campaigns of Mazzini, Garibaldi, and Manin; thus, democratic and patriotic sympathies abounded. In sharp contrast to the failures of Mazzini's insurrections, Cavour's diplomatic success provided a strong case for Piedmontese leadership in a campaign to solicit international assistance in driving out the Austrians. Crucial in converting the veterans of the 1848 revolutions to the Piedmontese camp was the Lombard democratic leader Giorgio Pallavicino-Trivulzio. Pallavicino stressed the futility of Mazzini's campaign, convincing many democrats and republicans that the Piedmontese monarchy offered the best hope for Italian independence. From exile in Paris, Manin called for Italian patriots to rally in support of Piedmont, putting aside demands for a democratic republic, on the condition that the House of Savoy pursue not expansion of its dynastic territories, but unification of Italy. In 1857, Manin and Pallavicino organized the National Society. Led by Giuseppe La Farina and other former Mazzinian democrats, the Society recruited to the Piedmontese campaign a myriad of Mazzini's former partisans throughout the peninsula. Although outbreaks of Mazzinian insurgency continued, Mazzini had now lost any realistic hope of providing organizational leadership to the Risorgimento.

Cavour remained unconvinced of the wisdom and success of a unification movement. But nudged forward by the National Society and by sporadic uprisings instigated by Mazzini's followers, the prime minister launched a cautious diplomatic campaign to destabilize the peninsula at the expense of the Austrians. Cavour's diplomatic campaign was also risky in that he had to play the double game of surreptitiously encouraging insurrection while at the same time assuring the French that Piedmont offered the greatest guarantee of future stability on the peninsula. The English government's support of Austria as a counterweight to Russian ambitions in the Balkans presented a potential obstacle.

In 1857, the Piedmontese broke diplomatic relations with Austria. Then in January 1858, Felice Orsini, a left-wing Mazzinian, attempted to assassinate Napoleon III, providing Cavour with another opening that he exploited brilliantly. Having already opened quiet discussions with Napoleon about assisting Piedmont against Austria, Cavour now found Napoleon more intensely sympathetic to the Piedmontese cause, particularly in Piedmont's ability to undercut extremism on the peninsula. Seizing the opportunity, Cavour met with Napoleon at the resort at Plombières and extracted a secret commitment to support Piedmont in a campaign to drive Austria out of Italy. The conditions were that Austria must declare war and that the war not become an Italian revolutionary campaign. In return for their support, France would be given Nice and Savoy and would presumably exercise influence over a new northern Italian kingdom.

In January 1859, King Vittorio Emanuele signaled his willingness to move against Austria. In delivering his now-famous "cry of anguish" speech to his parliament, he acknowledged the pain experienced by fellow Italians. Reading the proclamation as a call to arms, patriots streamed to Piedmont. Two weeks later, Piedmont and France signed a formal military alliance with specific provisions delineating the conditions of war. As European diplomats braced for war, the English intervened with a call for a diplomatic conference. In a stroke of good fortune, Cavour was saved from a diplomatic solution when Austria, unwilling to talk, delivered an ultimatum to Piedmont.

THE SECOND WAR FOR INDEPENDENCE, 1859–1860

Having discussed such an eventuality with Napoleon, Cavour simply refused the Austrian ultimatum and the war began. Italian volunteers rallied to the cause, while Mazzini dropped his demand for a republic in favor of war against Austria. Desperate to win a heroic reputation, Napoleon took field command of the French troops, which, as promised, came to the aid of the Piedmontese in Lombardy. The allied forces defeated the Austrians in the war's two battles, at Magenta and Solferino, ensuring Piedmontese occupation of Piedmont. However, victory came at a great cost in human life. Witnessing the carnage, and without consulting Cavour, Napoleon suddenly negotiated the Peace of Villafranca with the Austrian emperor on July 11. When Vittorio Emanuele II consented to the terms, Cavour resigned in anger and frustration at Napoleon's betrayal and in opposition to his king.

In addition to Napoleon's shock at the bloodshed at Solferino, the emperor acted in response to several other considerations. The Prussian army mobilized, raising the prospect, albeit remote, that if France pushed on to the east, it might confront Europe's best army. Second, the war quickly energized Italian patriots, while Cavour's agents had seized power in much of north and central Italy, suggesting that Napoleon would not be able to contain the conflict to a limited military campaign to create an expanded northern Italian kingdom that he could control. Third, if the war continued to spread to the Papal States, Italian patriots might well drive the pope into exile once again, leaving Napoleon to answer to French Catholic opinion.

Disappointing as the Peace of Villafranca was to Italian patriots, the fluidity of Italian politics suggested that the terms of the treaty would prove difficult to enforce. While France turned over Lombardy to Piedmont, the National Society and such leaders as Farini and the Tuscan Bettino Ricasoli campaigned actively to bring central Italy into union with Piedmont. Sensing difficulty in turning back the tide of patriotism, Napoleon then demanded Nice and Savoy in return for his approval of Piedmont's annexation of central Italy. With the international diplomatic climate now improving, Cavour returned to office in January 1860 to take the reins of the nationalist campaign, now embracing the task of unifying Italy. He successfully sponsored plebiscites (direct ballots) in Tuscany and Emilia that brought them into a new Kingdom of Italy in March.

Although Cavour may have wished to consolidate the recent gains, once again events forced his hand. This time the news came from the South, where, in October 1859, insurgents led by Mazzini lieutenant Francesco Crispi revolted against the Spanish Bourbons, weakened by the death of King Ferdinand II. Although that attempt misfired, the Sicilian rebels persisted. Insurrection flared once again in Palermo the following April and, when quelled, spread to more pervasive anti-government guerrilla action. Crispi then sent out a call for Giuseppe Garibaldi.

In early May 1860, Garibaldi responded. Departing near Genoa, Garibaldi led his "Thousand" volunteers (also known as Red Shirts) on two small ships steaming for Sicily, determined to fight for "Vittorio Emanuele and Italy." The war for Italian unification now shifted south. Most of the Thousand were young men from northern Italy, poorly armed, poorly trained, and inexperienced. The Thousand landed at Marsala in western Sicily and advanced unopposed, picking up a few hundred Sicilian insurgents, until they encountered a larger Bourbon army at Calatafimi. On May 15, using bayonet charges, Garibaldi's intrepid force stunned the Bourbons. Proclaiming himself "dictator of Sicily," the Red Shirt leader mobilized the peasantry not only by winning but also by promising land grants to those who fought for him. News of the heroic victories brought thousands of volunteers into Garibaldi's ranks and lifted morale among patriots throughout the peninsula. Twelve days later, after ferocious fighting, Garibaldi's volunteer force took Palermo, the Bourbon capital of Sicily. Garibaldi's success touched off a pervasive revolt in Sicily, driving the Bourbons in retreat to the northern port of Messina. After a bitter and costly battle at Milazzo, Garibaldi's forces took Messina, completing the destruction of Bourbon control of the island.

Garibaldi's impressive conquest cautioned the European powers as well as Cavour that the guerrilla leader might move on Naples, Rome, and Venice—which is precisely what Mazzini and the Action Party were urging Garibaldi to do. In fact, Cavour feared that Garibaldi had now seized the initiative and might well convert the Risorgimento to a democratic movement, leaving King Vittorio Emanuele a mere figurehead in a new Italian government—or, worse, might convert the South to a democratic republic.

Although both Cavour and the French might have liked to prevent Garibaldi from crossing the Straits of Messina to the Italian mainland, the British fleet refused to block his crossing. On September 7, amid great celebration, Garibaldi entered Naples. The new, young Bourbon king, Francis II, had fled to Gaeta, while his armies retreated to a position north of Naples, on the north bank of the Volturno River. Sensing once again that developing events were threatening his control of the unification movement, and with the support of Napoleon III, Cavour acted decisively. Fearing that Garibaldi's bold campaign might encourage democratic insurgency and provoke international intervention, Cavour interceded through agents in Sicily and Naples to dissuade Garibaldi. When those efforts failed, Cavour ordered Piedmontese armies to head south. Using as a pretext revolts that Cavour had secretly sponsored, Piedmontese forces moved into the Papal States, where they defeated the pope's army at Castelfidardo, northeast of Rome. When King Vittorio Emanuele II joined his armies at Ancona in October, the Piedmontese held over half of the Papal States. As the king's armies moved south, they sponsored plebiscites in which official tallies in central Italy, Naples, and Sicily showed overwhelming support for joining the Kingdom of Italy.

Meanwhile, Garibaldi ordered his expanded Red Shirt forces to attack the somewhat larger and better-equipped Bourbon army of fifty thousand. After heavy losses, Garibaldi's Red Shirts prevailed, creating the possibility that two Italian armies might face off for control of the South. However, Garibaldi's Red Shirts were so weakened by battle that they lacked the strength to hold Naples or to take Rome themselves. On October 26, the king and the guerrilla commander met just north of the Volturno. After a friendly exchange in which Garibaldi acknowledged the king's authority, Vittorio Emanuele demanded that Garibaldi's forces now fight under the Piedmontese command. In a gesture widely admired for its selfless patriotism, Garibaldi agreed, and he accompanied the king on a triumphal march through the streets of Naples on November 7. Shortly thereafter Garibaldi modestly retired to his farm on the island of Caprera, leaving only an implicit threat that he might return to liberate Rome and Venice.

In January 1861, Italians voted by limited suffrage in Italy's first parliamentary elections. In March the new Parliament, meeting in Turin, declared the Kingdom of Italy and acknowledged Vittorio Emanuele II as king. Garibaldi's concession to the king was also a defeat for the concept that unification could be achieved on a basis other than simple annexation by Piedmont. The annexation method, although simpler and more orderly, proved ultimately very costly. In April, Garibaldi spoke to Parliament, criticizing Cavour and making a passionate plea on behalf of the soldiers, particularly his officers who had been denied commissions in the new Italian army. Cavour, meanwhile, focused on what had emerged as "the Roman Question," the status of the Eternal City in the new kingdom. In June, to the shock of Italians and much of Europe, Cavour died at age fifty without having seen the Risorgimento completed.

VENICE, ROME, AND THE COMPLETION OF THE RISORGIMENTO

Before his death, Cavour had committed to acquire the areas around the great cities of Venice (Venetia) and Rome (Lazio). The completion of Italian unification now rested with his successors (known as "the Right" for its relative conservatism) and depended largely on rapidly changing conditions in Europe. In 1866, as Prussian chancellor Otto von Bismark moved to complete the unification of Germany, Italy signed with Prussia a treaty of military alliance against Austria. During the Seven Weeks' War (June–July

1866), Italy engaged Austrian forces on land and sea; Prussian victory forced Austria to cede Venetia to Italy at the Peace of Prague (August 1866).

Italian acquisition of Rome, fraught with complications, depended similarly on Bismark's drive to unify Germany. Garibaldi had pledged to take Rome, a prospect that Cavour and his successors feared would prompt the wrath of France and a number of other predominantly Catholic states. In 1864, the Italian government managed to negotiate a withdrawal of the French troops that had protected the pope since 1849; in return, Italy pledged to respect Rome's borders. However, "the Left" (as the political opponents of the governing Right were now labeled) demanded Rome, and Garibaldi twice assaulted Rome, prompting the return of French troops to the Eternal City.

The turning point came in September 1870 when Prussia decisively defeated France. With the outbreak of war Napoleon had withdrawn French troops from Rome, opening the city to occupation by Italian troops on September 20. The Risorgimento was now complete. Sadly lacking, however, was a sense of monumental triumph. The Italians had completed unification only by virtue of the military successes of the French and the Prussians. The heroic mythology and popular idealism generated by Mazzini and Garibaldi were now replaced by the more prosaic King Vittorio Emanuele, who, upon his first visit to Rome, reportedly commented: "We have finally arrived." Such an anticlimax reflected the transition from the era of unification to a more banal period of nation building.

BUILDING AN ITALIAN STATE

When the government relocated the capital (temporarily Florence) to Rome, Pope Pius IX reacted decisively. In 1868, the Vatican decreed the *Non Expedit*, prohibiting Catholics from participating in Italian national politics. By 1870, priests were condemning the Italian government from their pulpits. The Roman Question had now placed a considerable strain on the new government.

Under considerable pressure, the Right issued in 1871 the Law of Papal Guarantees, separating church and state, ensuring protection of the Church and extending to the pope privileges equivalent to a head of state along with an annual stipend. Arguing that the legislation could be revoked at any time, Pius IX spurned the offer and declared himself a "prisoner in the Vatican." Nonetheless, the Law of Papal Guarantees remained in place. The Vatican generally accepted the privileges and protection granted to it, while the government did not move to amend it. Thus, although Italian Catholics did participate in national politics, the Roman Question remained an issue for the next sixty years, only partly laid to rest by Parliament.

The Roman Question was only one of many issues that troubled the new Italian state. As the Right struggled with the imposing task of building a nation, Massimo d'Azeglio's famous statement—"We have made Italy; now we must make Italians"—now hung ominously over the new generation's leadership. Among the problems confronting the government were widespread poverty and economic underdevelopment, not easily resolved by the Right's philosophical commitment to the tenets of nineteenth century laissez-faire liberalism by which Cavour had relied on free-market capitalism to correct economic problems. Allegations of widespread corruption at all levels of government persisted, undermining much of the trust that might have been generated by the Risorgimento's heroic mythology. A perception lingered that the Piedmontese had "conquered" the peninsula, leaving power in the hands of a northern elite. Realistic or not, this view perpetuated political apathy, particularly in the South, at the very time when patriotism was needed. Among the most fundamental problems facing the new government was what became known as "the Southern Question."

THE SOUTHERN QUESTION

When Garibaldi liberated the South from Bourbon control, he unleashed a series of expectations. Southern peasants expected land reform, while many landowners looked to the Piedmontese moderates to restore order and protect them from rural insurgency. Sicilian separatists pushed for autonomy. Mazzinians demanded a democratic republic at the same time that socialists pressed for economic transformation. Garibaldi's soldiers expected to be integrated into the army of the Kingdom of Italy; Cavour, in contrast, regarded the Garibaldini (Garibaldi's followers) as a greater security threat than the Bourbon reactionaries. These conflicting expectations and the resulting internal discord prevented the new government from making a smooth transition and accentuated the real difficulties of building an Italian nation. In turn, the confusion in the South created a wave of crime known as the "Brigands' War" during which armed bands seized control of entire towns, only to be stopped by the intervention of the Italian army.

Historians view this disorder as a continuation of the southern social, economic, and political crisis: The same dynamics that had contributed to the downfall of Bourbon government now challenged Cavour and his successors. Furthermore, the continuing chaos in the South led the new Italian government to impose a military solution, dispatching over half its troops to the South, suspending civil liberties, seizing local governments, and dispensing justice through courts-martial and summary executions. It was in this effort to impose order that, in the 1860s, the Italian military reported encountering in Sicily a band of organized criminals known as "the *mafia*." In the long term, the Brigands' War undermined confidence in the new government, both at home and abroad, and created a lasting image of the South as a separate and dangerous place. Thus, the concept of the Southern Question (or Southern Problem)—endemic poverty, anarchy, and crime—has troubled Italian governments for more than a century and remains today an important political issue.

THE "PARLIAMENTARY REVOLUTION" OF 1876 AND THE ERA OF *TRASFORMISMO*

In March 1876, Prime Minister Marco Minghetti's government of the Right lost a vote on the *macinato* (grain tax), forcing new elections which the Left won. Like the Right, more a coalition of interest groups than a disciplined political party, the Left differed in its anti-clerical views, its opposition to free trade, and its support for expanding the right to vote. Two leaders dominated the Left in the remaining decades of the century: former Mazzinians Agostino Depretis and Francesco Crispi.

Depretis came to power in the so-called parliamentary revolution of 1876; in fact, the "revolution" proved to be less significant in ushering in fundamentally new policies than in changing the personnel and image of the governing group. Committed to a program of popular initiatives that included radical reforms of taxes, public education, and voting laws, the Left confronted a number of obstacles that limited its ability to deliver. They failed to provide promised subsidies for economic development of the South or to repeal the Law of Papal Guarantees. On the other hand, the Depretis governments did more than triple the number of eligible voters and introduced a series of legal reforms.

Several of their successful efforts can be attributed to support from the Right, a fact that Depretis acknowledged publicly in 1882 by announcing that he would welcome members of the Right into future governments, because they had been "transformed." The cabinets of the late nineteenth century began to include members of both Left and Right, an acknowledgment of the consensus that had developed between two middle-class groups, differentiated largely by labels. This phenomenon, known as *trasformismo*, implied that decisions were made not along the lines of distinct policy disagreements, but through a series of corrupt deals among a group of middle-class politicos who were out of touch with the masses of the population.

FRANCESCO CRISPI AND THE CRISES OF THE 1890S

Depretis's successor as leader of the Left was a former Garibaldi agent, the Sicilian Francesco Crispi (governed 1887–1891 and 1893–1896), who would dominate Italian politics in the last decade of the century. After rising in the ranks to Minister of Interior during the Depretis era, Crispi suffered a scandalous setback in his career, only to be brought back by Depretis as his heir apparent. Upon Depretis's death, King Umberto I (reigned 1878–1900) asked Crispi to form a government. In his early years as prime minister, Crispi made significant progress in social and economic reforms. Overcoming resistance, Crispi managed to pass significant reforms in the criminal code, developed by Interior Minister Giuseppe Zanardelli, including abolition of the death penalty and easing penalties for crimes against property. Committed to opening up the political system, Crispi expanded the right to vote in local elections. Other hallmarks of domestic achievement included Crispi's laws that reformed public health and charitable organizations.

Had Crispi's reputation rested on his domestic reform program, he would perhaps be better remembered today. In fact, in the face of growing civil unrest, Crispi exercised extraordinary powers, opening himself to charges of abuse of authority—a dangerous precedent in a constitutional system still in its first generation of development.

Crispi's reaction came in response to the emergence of an outburst of radicalism throughout much of the peninsula. In the North, it took the shape of Marxism and anarchism. The Russian anarchist Mikhail Bakunin had incited a failed uprising in Bologna in 1874. Eight years later, Andrea Costa had founded the Workers' Party and won a seat in Parliament, the first socialist to do so. Ten years later in Genoa, worker organizations founded the Italian Socialist Party (PSI). The group split into factions, some ideologically committed to revolutionary Marxism, and others, like Filippo Turati, pursuing a strategy of social reform through the political process. Also represented in the Parliament were a group of leftists known as the Estrema ("Extreme") that pursued social change, a group of Republicans, Radicals, and Socialists who remained outside the confines of *trasformismo* until the turn of the century. Meanwhile, socialist ideas spread rapidly throughout the universities, widely embraced by Italian intellectuals.

Especially troubling to many Italian political leaders was the widespread outbreak of insurgency among peasants in Sicily, where a depression in sulfur mining and agriculture provoked strikes and spreading violence in the 1890s. In response to the Fasci Sicliani, as the Sicilian workers' organizations were known, Crispi at first used restraint, as did his successors. However, Giovanni Giolitti's decision to suppress the Fasci led to the deaths of ninety-two Sicilian peasants, compounding the criticism of Giolitti based primarily on a damaging bank scandal. In November 1893, Giolitti's government fell, bringing Crispi back to power.

Promising to rescue Italy from both fraud and civil disorder, Crispi won an overwhelming vote of confidence from the Chamber of Deputies (the lower house of the Italian Parliament). He acted decisively, suspending civil government and dispatching forty-thousand troops to his native Sicily, saying that if necessary he would govern without Parliament. In the process of a crackdown that lasted for more than a half-year, Crispi's government dissolved the Socialist Party, arrested its leaders, handed out harsh sentences that sent a thousand Sicilians to the penal islands, and purged from the rolls more than one in four Italian voters, most of them poor.

Even more damaging to Crispi's reputation were his foreign policy initiatives. Already at odds with France, Italy held designs on Tunisia that set it on a collision course with the French in Algeria. When France colonized Tunisia, Italy turned to Germany as an ally, only to find that Germany insisted on alliance also with Austria, Italy's recent adversary. Contradicting its Risorgimento legacy, Italy agreed and signed the Triple Alliance in 1882. Crispi's friendship with German chancellor Bismark strengthened Italy's commitment to the Triple Alliance. In support of this expanded foreign policy, Crispi launched a military buildup that alarmed France, leading to a war of words and a ten-year tariff war.

Meanwhile, Crispi pursued his plan to acquire Ethiopia. Partly at Crispi's urging, Depretis ordered Italian troops into the interior highlands of Ethiopia, only to suffer the loss of five hundred troops at Dogali in 1887. Returning to office later that year, Crispi signed the Treaty of Ucciali (1889) that awarded Italy a protectorate, then proceeded to announce the Italian colony of Eritrea on the Red Sea. Temporarily replaced by the conservative Antonio Di Rudinì and then Giolitti, Crispi returned to power in 1893 and moved aggressively to colonize all of Ethiopia.

Although supported by Parliament, Crispi was already confronting resistance at home to his imperialistic policy when Italians read in March 1896 the shocking news of defeat at the hands of the Ethiopians in the Battle of Adua. Undersupported, outnumbered, and lacking even accurate maps, more than five-thousand Italian troops lost their lives, a greater loss than had been suffered in all the wars of the Risorgimento combined. While retaining its colony of Eritrea, Italy otherwise withdrew from the Horn of Africa.

The humiliating defeat produced finger-pointing among politicians and journalists and subjected Crispi to heightened opposition from such disparate groups as industrialists and socialists. More important, the disastrous Ethiopian campaign pointed out the limitations on Italy's ability to support an expansive imperial policy, and further marginalized Italian diplomatic influence in Europe. The public humiliation of defeat also created, particularly among Italian nationalists, a desire for revenge. Facing attacks from former supporters in Parliament, Crispi resigned from office, ending an era of reform, centralized power, social unrest, and nationalistic adventurism.

Acknowledging the national crisis, King Umberto turned again to Di Rudinì. Political turbulence continued in the face of economic suffering, while Marxism gained support in rapidly expanding northern cities and the Estrema in the Parliament demanded social change. As bread prices rose, violence and disorder continued into 1898. Mobs terrorized Parma, Florence, and even Rome, where martial law was proclaimed. The worst violence, known as the *fatti di Maggio* ("events of May"), occurred in Milan, where General Bava-Beccaris ordered his troops to fire into an unarmed mob, killing more than eighty. In the aftermath, attributing the problems to organized socialism, Di Rudinì's government arrested Socialist leaders, including Turati, closed major universities, disbanded numerous organizations, and suspended the publication of newspapers and journals in general disregard for the constitution and the rights of the Italian people.

When the king refused to dissolve Parliament, Di Rudinì resigned. Hoping to send a message of authority, Umberto turned once again to a general, Luigi Pelloux, a Piedmontese conservative with a record of restraint in the civil use of military power. For the first half-year of his term, the general refused to exercise martial law; however, as pressures rose, he attempted to restrict the press and limit public meetings. Then in June 1899, Pelloux made the audacious announcement that he planned to govern by royal decree. When Socialists in Parliament protested, they were arrested and Parliament was suspended.

What stopped General Pelloux's authoritarian initiative was a wide-ranging combination of opposition. First, the high court ruled Pelloux's decree order (*decreto legge*) unenforceable without Parliamentary approval. Then the Socialists and Estrema joined liberals and conservatives in opposition. Newspapers, including the leading moderate daily, *Il Corriere della Sera* (Milan), joined the protest. Although he held a small majority after the general elections of June 1900, Pelloux chose to resign. Departing from precedent, the king selected a senator, Giuseppe Saracco, to succeed Pelloux. Days later, an Italian anarchist from New York, Gaetano Bresci, assassinated King Umberto, abruptly ending what had been for Italians a tumultuous century.

Some historians would later see in the authoritarian methods of Crispi, Di Rudinì, and Pelloux precedents to Fascism. Others would view the last decade of the nineteenth century as a time when the still developing Italian constitutional system was put to a severe test. The system survived, but not unscathed, because at no time did the Parliament or the courts fully establish independent authority, thus leaving the monarchy with broad, if ill-defined, prerogatives. More important, fundamental economic, social, and political problems that had contributed to the disturbances of the 1890s remained unresolved.

8

The Era of Giolitti and World War I, 1900–1918

When Vittorio Emanuele III inherited the throne on the violent death of his father in 1900, he assumed the position as head of state that he would hold through two world wars and the Fascist era. Loyal to his country, he failed at several critical points to provide leadership; in fact, he was not widely admired by Italians, and his failures would eventually doom the House of Savoy to oblivion. Political leadership in the first half of the twentieth century in fact was exercised most decisively by two men: Giovanni Giolitti, five-time prime minister, and Benito Mussolini, "Il Duce" of the Fascist state. Giolitti addressed Italy's profound problems with a series of progressive reforms in the era he dominated (1900–1914), but his reputation for cynical manipulation and his habit of stepping down in the face of conflict ultimately undermined his reputation. In the wake of post–World War I malaise and political strife, Mussolini offered himself as savior from Bolshevism and vanguard of a new era, and, once he was named prime minister, consolidated his power through a series of authoritarian measures. Because the Giolittian era ended in Fascist dictatorship, historians have long debated the merits of this period and the politician who dominated it: Was this as historian A. William Salomone argued, a period of "Italian democracy in the making"?

ECONOMIC GROWTH

After decades during which severe problems had dragged down the European economy, general prosperity ushered in the new century, fueled by a broad-based industrial boom. The expansion of markets and the advent of new technology enabled Italian industry to develop at a rapid pace, closing the gap with northern European economies. Particularly in the decade before World War I, the economy experienced broad expansion, especially in the industrial, commercial, and financial sectors. As the European and American economies recovered, demand for goods increased, expanding exports and accelerating Italian industrial production. Notable success in the textile, chemical, electrical, military arms, and automotive industries created jobs, drove up salaries and wages, and, in turn, increased domestic demand for goods. An industrial-commercial "triangle" developed among the northern cities of Milan, Turin, and Genoa. In automotives, for example, Giovanni Agnelli organized Fiat in 1899, then Alfa Romeo, Lancia, and Maserati followed suit. At the same time, investment capital became more readily available as Italy rationalized (modernized) banking by creating the Bank of Italy. An agricultural boom followed, particularly in the Po Valley, providing profits that in turn fed the supply of available capital. Government spending contributed to growth as well, notably in expanding the infrastructure through public works projects. As a result, Italy experienced an industrial boom of "revolutionary" proportions, virtually doubling production in the fifteen years preceding the outbreak of World War I in 1914.

As a product of industrial expansion, the standard of living in northern Italy began to approach European levels, distributing wealth among an expanding urban middle class and lifting the literacy rate to near 90 percent in some areas. However, per capita income was still just half that of France by 1914, and the South lagged sadly. Peasant farmers shared little in the economic growth, emigration from the South persisted at an ever-increasing rate, and well over half of Southerners remained illiterate. Giolitti's liberal organization (not a party, but a loosely knit group committed to the prime minister) relied heavily on southern deputies who represented the landlord class and thus opposed reform. And although Giolitti's electoral machine continued to deliver elections in the South, his inability to address the Southern Problem, evidenced by an ever-widening North-South gap, further tarnished Giolitti's record of reform. In fact, Italy's general economic growth created an opportunity for Giolitti to introduce a series of reforms to benefit Italian workers and to expand the political process, particularly in response to the growth of Italian socialism.

SOCIALIST GAINS

In its newspaper, *Avanti!*, the Italian Socialist Party pressured Giolitti for reforms, especially workers' insurance, universal suffrage (the right of all Italians to vote), and the right to organize and strike. Controlled by reformist socialists Turati, Anna Kuliscioff, Ivanoe Bonomi, Claudio Treves, and the paper's editor, Leonida Bissolati, the PSI took a gradual approach to socialism, adopting a strategy of pursuing change through the parliamentary process. At its Rome Congress of 1900, Turati's reformists were challenged by the revolutionary Marxists and a group of syndicalists, led by Arturo Labriola, who believed in violent action and the general strike. Although the reformist socialists continued to dominate the PSI through the first decade of the century, revolutionary socialism spread, especially in Milan and in the northern agricultural centers of Emilia, a sign that Turati's group would meet a serious challenge.

These divisions weakened the PSI and provided an opening into which the calculating Giolitti attempted to drive a wedge. He avoided applying forceful repression that would unify socialists while providing reforms to entice reformist socialists into his parliamentary majority, isolating the left wing of the movement. This was an important element in a broader strategy by which Giolitti hoped to forge a broad consensus among moderate political groups, both Left and Right, thereby bolstering his liberal machine.

GIOLITTI AND SOCIAL REFORM

Having first served as prime minister in 1892–1893, Giovanni Giolitti built a legendary political "machine" that enabled him to be named prime minister in 1903, 1906, 1911, and 1920. His presence so dominated this period that it has been called the Giolittian era. Because of his effective commitment to reform and his refusal to resort to the authoritarian methods of Crispi and De Rudinì, Giolitti presided over a decade of relative peace and prosperity. He made a decisive commitment to a program of reforms that would improve the standard of living of the Italian urban working class, believing that material progress would undermine socialism, alleviate violent confrontation in the workplace, and, for those reasons, win the political support of businessmen and moderate conservatives. To build the power base necessary to sustain his reforms, Giolitti mastered the system by which prefects could deliver victory in elections to Parliament.

Already an advocate of reform as a member of Parliament (where he served for forty-two years), Giolitti successfully supported the regulation of working conditions for women and children, the right of workers to organize and to strike, mandatory public holidays, and free quinine treatment for malaria. When economic setbacks spurred socialist protests and strikes in 1903, Giolitti invited PSI leader Turati into his cabinet. When Turati refused, Giolitti turned to more conservative elements to strengthen his government.

Confronted by left-wing socialist insurgency in the fall of 1904, Giolitti demonstrated his renowned political skills. When revolutionary socialists in Milan called Italy's first general strike, they virtually shut down much of the country. In contrast to his predecessors' use of force in the face of domestic dissent, Giolitti refused to intervene. Criticized by conservatives for inactivity, he then called for new elections to send a political lesson to the leftist socialists by reaching out to Catholic voters and moderates. The strategy—abetted by widespread manipulation and voter fraud—led to gains in the general election of 1904, increasing Giolitti's majority. The election is notable also for the re-entry of Catholics into active politics at the behest of the new pope, the politically moderate Pius X (pope 1903–1914). Governing by a shaky coalition, frustrated by labor problems in the railroads, and criticized by both extremes, Giolitti once again made a tactical withdrawal, stepping down in March 1905 in favor of the undistinguished Alessandro Fortis.

After a year during which he nationalized the railroads, Fortis saw his government fall in a crisis precipitated by a tariff favoring the import of Spanish wines. Giolitti's tenuous majority supported the formation of a new government by Baron Sidney Sonnino. Severe and conservative, the son of a Welsh mother and a wealthy Tuscan Jew, Sonnino had given up a career in the foreign service to enter politics. He was now destined to play a major role in Italian public life in the early years of the new century. Supported by a small parliamentary group, Sonnino was forced to reach out to the extreme Left to form a coalition cabinet that lasted only three months in the face of a damaging general strike in Turin.

Sensing that a return was timely, Giolitti formed his third cabinet and resumed the campaign of reform. Significantly, he adjusted downward the rates on government bonds, lowering interest rates, stabilizing the economy, and stimulating growth. However, in the general election of 1909 left-wing forces gained significantly. Failing to rally the Left to support a progressive tax program, and rebuffed by the Estrema, Giolitti stepped down once again. After brief governments assembled by Sonnino and Luigi Luzzatti, Giolitti organized a coalition around his demands for universal suffrage and won a vote of the Chamber of Deputies.

Returning to power in March 1911, Giolitti once again appealed to socialists, offering universal manhood suffrage (without a literacy standard) and, this time, offering a cabinet post in his fourth government to Bissolati.

Like fellow socialist Turati before him, Bissolati declined, maintaining the PSI's posture of independence. It was in the context of soliciting socialist support for his 1911 government that Giolitti created his greatest political legacy, the voting law of 1911–1912. In one stroke, the law expanded the eligible voters from three to eight million, enfranchising all men over age thirty and all military veterans. Support existed for extending the vote to women, but Giolitti suspected such a commitment would strengthen the influence of the Church. Likewise, he rejected Sonnino's bid for proportional representation, fearing that such a system, by rewarding small parties with seats in Parliament proportional to the percentages of votes won, would further fragment the party system and make parliamentary majorities—including his own—more difficult to assemble.

CULTURAL AND SOCIAL TRENDS

In the period that now bears Giolitti's name, Italian society showed signs not only of economic growth but of significant social change and cultural revival. In addition to the rise of socialism, nationalism, and futurism, a number of other intellectual currents surfaced. Within Catholicism, changes had begun as early as the 1890s when Pope Leo XIII (pope 1878–1903) had issued his famous encyclical *Rerum novarum*, acknowledging the difficulties the poor faced in modern society and approving labor unions. Later in the same decade, Catholics formed Christian democratic organizations, cooperatives, and agricultural unions; at the same time, doctrinal modernism (a reinterpretation in the light of modern scientific thought) challenged the Vatican's orthodoxy, whose leading defender was Pius X. Church leaders recognized that their opposition to the Italian state had failed and, in fact, that they had forfeited their advocacy of Catholic views in national debates over policy. Thus, when on a number of occasions Giolitti solicited support from Catholic voters, the Church softened its opposition against its parishioners' participation in politics.

In the arts and sciences, Italians made notable contributions in the pre-war era. Among the more prominent Italian scientists, Guglielmo Marconi won a share of the Nobel Prize in 1909 for his pioneering work in wireless transmission. In the formal arts, Italy's contributions rank as modest in comparison to the magnificence of its past traditions, but they were nonetheless vigorous. In music, Italian opera continued its tradition of excellence. Giuseppe Verdi's greatest operas (*Aida*, 1871; *Otello*, 1887) had come in the decades following the Risorgimento, although he composed *Falstaff* in 1893. The pre-war era also witnessed Pietro Mascagni's *Cavalleria*

Rusticana, Ruggero Leoncavallo's *Pagliacci*, and Giacomo Puccini's *La Boheme, Tosca,* and *Madame Butterfly.*

Italian writers wrote in a variety of interesting genres during the pre-war era. The Sicilian novelist and playwright Giovanni Verga developed the influential school known as *verismo,* or realism, in which he depicted the lives of Sicilian peasants in stark detail. Among his best-known works are *Cavalleria Rusticana* (1880), the source of Mascagni's opera, and *I malavoglia* (1881), from which Luchino Visconti would derive his 1948 movie *La Terra Trema.* Poetry thrived as well. The Tuscan Giosuè Carducci became the first Italian to win the Nobel Prize for literature (1906) based primarily on his earlier works, *New Rhymes* (1861–1887), *Pagan Odes* (1877–1889), and *Lyrics and Rhythms* (1899). Among Carducci's successors, Antonio Fogazzaro and Giovanni Pascoli stand out. Fogazzaro, novelist and poet from Vicenza, addressed the tension between the carnal and the religious, leading the Church to ban his later books. Pascoli's most notable collection of poems, *Songs of Castelvecchio* (1903), expresses the deep melancholy that inspired a school of Italian poets known as the *crepuscolari* ("twilight poets").

In philosophy, the historian and senator Pasquale Villari introduced scientific positivism (the belief that knowledge must be derived from empirical evidence) to Italy in the 1890s, where it flourished in the universities in the early century. Even more influential in the realm of thought was the Neapolitan philosopher Benedetto Croce, who rejected the materialism of positivists and socialists in favor of his own idealism, derived from the nineteenth-century German philosopher G. W. F. Hegel. In his journal, *La Critica,* and in several major works of philosophy and history, Croce relied on art and systematic logic to interpret the past and present, and thus he provided an appealing alternative to the popular materialistic philosophies. One who disagreed vehemently with Croce's philosophical method was the historian Gaetano Salvemini, a native of Bari province, a student of Villari, and a professor at the Universities of Messina, Pisa, and Florence. Drawn to positivism and then socialism, Salvemini employed "concrete" social and economic analysis in writing about medieval and modern history as well as contemporary politics. Salvemini's most searing criticism, *Il Ministro della malavita* (The Minister of the Underworld), was leveled at Giolitti. In particular, Salvemini attacked the prime minister's record of political corruption in the South. Salvemini's condemnation of Giolitti would eventually place him in conflict with Croce's more charitable postwar assessment of the politics of Liberal Italy.

Two writers of fiction mark Italy's transition to twentieth-century culture. Gabriele D'Annunzio, born in the Abruzzi and educated in Florence and Rome, wrote extravagant poetry and prose. In his lifestyle as well as his writing, D'Annunzio conducted a one-man assault on conventional mores and aesthetic standards. He worked in a wide variety of genres, including poetry (*New Song*, 1882), fiction (*Pleasure*, 1889; *Songs of Death and Glory*, 1911), and drama (*The Flame of Life*, 1900, an account of his affair with actress Eleanora Duse; *La nave*, 1908). By 1910 the poet had moved into politics, becoming first a socialist, then a member of Parliament, then an ardent nationalist. In many ways D'Annunzio's elaborate iconoclasm reflected, in exaggerated form, the new generation's excesses, its impatience with the status quo, and its inclination to seek extreme alternatives to the conventions of bourgeois life. Also representative of changing values at the advent of the new century was the Sicilian dramatist Luigi Pirandello, who introduced highly original elements into his plays, most notably *Six Characters in Search of an Author* (1921). In staging six unfinished characters, Pirandello raises questions of relativism (the belief that truth is subjective) and anticipates the pessimism and existentialism (the philosophy that humans must make choices without knowing what is right or wrong) that would influence much of modern literature.

Just as formal culture underwent significant changes in the early twentieth century, so did the everyday lives of Italians, although more slowly and with even greater adhesion to tradition. Italy remained in the period before World War I an overwhelmingly peasant society, characterized by isolated provincial towns—each speaking its own regional dialect, steeped in local traditions—and expansive rural areas where bucolic scenes often masked profound poverty. In spite of its critics, the Roman Catholic Church continued to dominate much of the peninsula, while the government had failed largely to create a sense of national identity among the small-town and rural populations, particularly in the South and in the islands. In spite of the expansion of the electorate, national governance remained in the hands of a small leadership class. And, ironically, in a nation with a high rate of illiteracy, the expansion of the university system had begun to create a problem sometimes referred to as an "overeducated" population. A middle class of "overeducated" bureaucrats and professional politicians dominated local governments. With very few exceptions, women remained in domestic roles, managing large extended families. Relegated to second-class citizenship, Italian women were denied the right to vote or own property in a legal system that shielded men, but not women, from being penalized for adultery.

Nonetheless, change came to Italian society in the early twentieth century, most obviously in the large cities of the Center and North. Major cities installed street lighting and electric trolleys, popularizing local travel; the development of a national railway system similarly encouraged longer trips, including vacations. At the same time, telephones and such appliances as electric irons and vacuum cleaners modernized domestic life. Although women remained largely tied to domestic roles, they began to marry later and practice birth control more widely, reducing the average size of families, particularly in urban areas, and freeing women for formal education and employment. Still, progress for women remained modest.

THE RISE OF NATIONALISM AND THE WAR IN LIBYA

In the midst of social and cultural change, a surge in Italian nationalism swept throughout the country in the first years of the new century, carrying the Italian government into war in Libya. The nationalist movement derived from arguments that Italy should dominate the Mediterranean Sea and claim its "unredeemed" territories of Trieste and the Trentino to complete the Risorgimento (an idea known as *irredentismo*). Italian nationalists were emboldened by a number of new intellectual currents circulating through Italian society at the turn of the century. Sociologists Vilfredo Pareto and Gaetano Mosca theorized that a political elite invariably dominates politics at the expense of ordinary citizens, and the flamboyant poet and playwright Gabriele D'Annunzio celebrated the heroic and irrational pursuit of action and power. At the same time, a group of artists known as "futurists" brazenly repudiated tradition while ritualizing the glory of war and power. In the Futurist Manifesto of 1909, the writer Filippo Marinetti exulted: "We sing the love of danger. Courage, rashness, and rebellion are the elements of our poetry."

As these audacious new ideas spread, they challenged both Giolitti's manipulation of Parliament and the socialists' commitment to pacifism and mass politics. Condemning the politics of the Giolittian era as corrupt and unimaginative, nationalists called for Italy to boldly pursue its national destiny. In Florence, Enrico Corradini, Giovanni Papini, and Giuseppe Prezzolini founded the magazine *Il Regno* (1903–1905) around which ardent nationalists gathered and in which they lashed out at Giolittian politics in favor of imperialism and the aggressive pursuit of power. In 1908, Prezzolini and Papini rejected the extremes of aggressive nationalism by launching the Florentine journal *La Voce*, drawing a number of notable writers in rejecting the status quo in pursuit of national renewal. Two years later, at a gathering at the Palazzo Vecchio in Florence, Corradini, Luigi Federzoni, and their followers established the Italian Nationalist Association, committed to Italy's pursuit of empire; the next year, they launched their journal, *L'Idea Nazionale*. At the Florence congress, Federzoni exhorted the Italian government to invade Libya. While industrialists began to funnel funds to the nationalists, the nationalist campaign appealed especially to a young generation of Italians, bored by the drabness of Giolittian politics.

The impact of nationalist ideas can be found in the rhetoric used in the Italian press, which, in turn, placed before the reading public highly emotional pleas for building an empire. Italians read of their historic burden to expand into Africa and the Balkans; of the need to recover national pride by reversing the embarrassments of Dogali and Adua; and of the need to "take back" the ancient Roman province of Libya as an outlet for overpopulation in the Italian South.

As the British and French moved to solidify their colonial holdings in North Africa, Italian nationalists raised the specter of permanent exclusion while the newspapers contributed to an imperialist frenzy. Giolitti responded to changing international and domestic politics with characteristic realism; a quick victory would fortify Italy's Mediterranean presence while simultaneously strengthening his political standing. After a perfunctory ultimatum to the Ottoman Turks (who claimed imperial possession of Libya), Giolitti's government declared war on the Ottoman Empire in September 1911 and in October began bombardment of the Libyan coastline. After military occupation of the coast, Giolitti decreed Italy's annexation of Libya in November.

The Libyan War proved more difficult than Giolitti's government had expected and provided marginal benefits at best. The Italian military encountered great difficulty in adapting to desert and guerilla warfare, and it found that the indigenous population refused to rally against the Turkish government as Italy had hoped. Eventually, Italy was given limited international approval by the Treaty of Lausanne for ruling both Libya and the Dodecanese Islands in return for paying the Turks a stipend. At the same time, the war proved very costly and provided Italy control of only limited areas of the Libyan coast, especially in the face of resistance from the indigenous Senussi. And although the military incursion boosted Giolitti's popularity, it also contributed to the general destabilization of Europe, most notably in the rapid decline of the Ottoman Empire.

In the wake of the annexation of Libya, Giolitti found his consensus politics challenged by the Socialist Party's move to the left. In their 1912 Congress at Reggio Emilia, left-wing Socialists prevailed behind the defiant campaign of a young revolutionary from the Romagna, Benito Mussolini. Already jailed for his opposition to Italy's war in Libya, Mussolini used an anti- war argument to drive Bonomi and Bissolati from the party. The Congress named Mussolini to the PSI executive, and in December he was appointed editor of the party paper, *Avanti!*

With the PSI moving markedly to the left, Giolitti turned toward the Right to bolster support. Anticipating that the new election law might attract Catholic votes, Giolitti made an agreement with Count Ottorino Gentiloni, head of the Catholic Union. The "Gentiloni Pact" of 1913 provided that all of Giolitti's supporters who opposed socialism and divorce, while favoring the priesthood and private education, would be given Catholic support in the elections. Gentiloni claimed to control over two hundred votes in the Chamber, enough to guarantee Giolitti a majority. In turn, the Gentiloni Pact drove the Left further from Giolitti. When the radicals withdrew their support from his government in February 1914, Giolitti once again resigned, expecting eventually to return. On his advice, the king appointed as prime minister Antonio Salandra.

THE "NEUTRALITY CRISIS" AND THE DECISION TO FIGHT

Giolitti's resignation marked the end of an era in which he had dominated Italian politics even when out of office, and it left in the hands of Salandra and his foreign minister, Sonnino, grave decisions that would guide Italy through a period of spiraling crisis and into war. Salandra inherited the unenviable task of presiding over a badly divided public and a contentious, politicized debate over the European conflict. After a long and divisive debate, and to the detriment of its political system, Italy would enter World War I with the support of only a minority of its population. Ultimately, in an attempt to acquire territory at the expense of Austria, the nation would suffer severe consequences.

Italy's 1911 invasion of Libya had contributed to growing attitudes of belligerency on the continent, as the Serbs and their Russian sponsors moved to take advantage of the crumbling Ottoman Empire. The escalating arms race and the alliance system, to which Italy was tied by its Triple Alliance commitment (Triplice, negotiated in 1882 and repeatedly renewed, finally in 1912) to Germany and Austria, threatened to convert what otherwise might have been a minor conflict to a much wider war. The powers had gone to the brink of war over imperial conflicts in North Africa but had stepped back as Britain and France moved closer in their cooperation against the bellicose bluster of German emperor Wilhelm II. But conflict in the Balkans touched more sensitive nerves.

As the European powers prepared for a war that seemed ever more likely, Britain, France, and Russia solidified their Triple Entente to counter the Triple Alliance. Germany's authoritarian political system and aggressive foreign policy, particularly Austria's tendency to ignore certain provisions in the treaty, raised doubts about the wisdom of the Triplice among a growing number of Italians. Furthermore, some nationalists viewed Austria as the likely adversary in a quest for the "unclaimed lands" of Trieste and the Trentino.

The Balkan Wars of 1912 and 1913 had strengthened Serbia in its drive to become a larger state, threatening its Austrian neighbor, and raising questions about Italy's obligations to support Austria under the Triplice. Both Giolitti and his foreign minister, Antonio di San Giuliano, maintained that the defensive nature of the alliance would not obligate Italy to follow Austria into an aggressive war against Serbia. Consequently, when, after the assassination of Archduke Franz Ferdinand, the Austrians declared war against Serbia in July 1914 (not informing its Italian ally, as the Triplice required), Italy remained neutral. At the same time, the British and French secretly extended offers to join their alliance, leading San Giuliano to negotiate quietly over future Italian prospects in Trieste and the Trentino.

The Italian government's decision to stay out of the war touched off a protracted and divisive debate known as the "neutrality crisis" (or "interventionist crisis"). When Salandra took over negotiations with the belligerents, he announced that Italy would be guided by her *sacro egoismo* ("sacred self-interest"). All the while, the Italian government quietly mobilized and built stockpiles in the event war should come.

A majority of Catholics and businessmen opposed the war, although many businessmen worried that remaining on the sidelines might limit Italy's opportunity to expand access to markets and raw materials. Most liberals likewise opposed war, following Giolitti's pragmatic advice that neutrality itself might provide the greatest leverage in negotiations. Among the political parties, the fractured PSI officially maintained its traditional position of neutrality; certain prominent members, of whom Benito Mussolini was the most vocal, advocated intervention. In a widely publicized incident, Mussolini published an editorial in *Avanti!* advocating war as a means to revolution. Expelled from the party shortly thereafter, he would in November launch his own newspaper, called *Il Popolo d'Italia*, to carry on the campaign for intervention. With the first issue of Mussolini's paper came charges, now substantiated, that *Il Popolo d'Italia* was subsidized by the French in an effort to encourage Italian intervention on the Allied side.

In addition to Mussolini's left-wing revolutionary socialist and syndicalist followers, a number of groups supported intervention, but with divergent aims. Futurists celebrated war as the manifestation of their bold campaign against the conventional life of the Liberal State—according to Marinetti, war alone presented "the only remedy for the world." In agreement, the poet D'Annunzio lent his bellicose rhetoric to the clamor for war.

And, often sharing with the futurists a shrillness of tone, Italian nationalists viewed the war in both ideological and pragmatic terms. Corradini, Federzoni, and their supporters saw an opportunity for Italy to pursue its greatness and to fulfill its territorial aspirations, especially at the expense of Austria, while ridding itself of the "bankrupt" Giolittian system.

Democratic interventionists came primarily from the ranks of intellectuals, newspapers (most prominently *Il Corriere della Sera*), reformist socialists, and the moderate Left, sharing the world view of U.S. president Woodrow Wilson that the defeat of Germany and Austria was essential to the future of democracy. Among the best known were Bissolati and Salvemini. Bissolati led reformist socialists in advocating Italy's intervention in order to strengthen democracy in England and France, as well as in Italy, and to ensure Italy's pro-democratic influence in a postwar settlement. Salvemini, a former PSI member and anti-Giolittian advocate for southern causes, had opposed Italy's partnership in the Triple Alliance in favor of improving relations with the Entente powers. In anticipation of war, the history professor pointed out in his journal, *L'Unità*, the strategic advantages of supporting the Entente: freeing France to move troops to its German border and forcing Austria to dispatch regiments to the Russian front, thereby serving the long-term interests of both Italy and the Allies. And in a mood of optimism reflective of the broadest expectations the democratic interventionists held for the war, Salvemini hoped that "1914 will signal the dawn of the new world of national and social justice. . . . Let us work together for the destruction of imperialism and the triumph of international democracy" (*Carteggio, 1914–1920*, 1984). Inflated expectations on all sides—democrats, revolutionaries, and nationalists—left many Italians vulnerable to profound disappointment at the war's end.

In the spring and summer of 1915, new signs of upheaval appeared. In what was labeled "Radiant May," nationalists, democratic interventionists, and socialist internationalists clashed. In Milan, Mussolini called for a popular uprising: "War or revolution!" In Rome, nearly 100,000 swarmed the train station to greet D'Annunzio, who, from his hotel balcony, harangued: "It is no longer time for speeches, but for action! . . . If it is a crime to incite people to violence, I boast of now committing that crime" (Denis Mack Smith, *Modern Italy, A Political History*, 1997, 264).

In the midst of disorder and rancorous debate, without the approval of Parliament, the advice of the military, or even complete consultation with the king, Salandra and Sonnino committed Italy to World War I on the Allied side. Sonnino signed the Pact of London in April 1915 by which the Entente powers agreed to reward Italy with territory in return for its entry into the war within three months. The British secretly guaranteed Italy the

Trentino, the Tyrol to the Brenner frontier, Trieste, Gorizia, most of Istria, northern Dalmatia, and the nucleus of Albania. Not once did Salandra reveal the terms of the Pact or lead a debate. In the major cities, interventionists' confrontations with anti-war forces brought violence back to the piazzas.

Under growing pressure, Salandra asked party leaders to endorse his policy. Finding support from Bissolati alone, and counting a mere sixty votes in Parliament, Salandra gave his resignation to the king, thus abandoning the stage at this critical moment and forfeiting this momentous decision to the king and forces outside the Parliament. When Giolitti and other candidates turned down requests to form a cabinet, the king, speaking in dire tones of abdicating the throne, refused Salandra's resignation and recalled him. On May 20, Salandra asked for and received parliamentary approval to go to war against Austria.

ITALY IN WORLD WAR I: CAPORETTO AND VITTORIO VENETO

Italy entered World War I unprepared in most respects for the great challenge that lay ahead. Like the other participants, Italy had anticipated a short war. Furthermore, the country had not recovered from the military campaign in Libya, which had left morale damaged, supplies short, and finances drained. Italy's strategic plans were based on the assumptions of fighting a defensive war alongside Austria and Germany as Triplice allies, leaving the general staff precious little time to adjust to the reality of fighting offensively *against* Austria in treacherous Alpine terrain. Furthermore, Salandra's government had failed to mobilize either the Parliament or the public behind the war, forcing the prime minister to execute the war largely by decree. Even the strategic assumptions on which Italian belligerency was based turned for the worse, as Russian losses and Serb inactivity against the Hapsburg Empire freed the Austrians to send more divisions to the Italian border.

In the final week of May 1915, Italy's commanding general, Luigi Cadorna, ordered an invasion of Austria. Committed to large-scale infantry assaults designed to break through the Austrian lines, Cadorna ultimately ordered a dozen such attacks that would win temporary control of no more than ten miles of turf—at the cost of 200,000 lives. Most of the fighting occurred along the River Isonzo and the Carso sector, where the terrain inhibited Cadorna's strategic plans. A year later Austria launched an offensive, the *strafexpedition* ("punitive campaign"), with the intention of winning the conflict. Although failing to end the war on their Italian front, Austrian forces broke through Italian lines to the plains around Venice.

Salandra's government fell victim to this campaign, replaced by the seventy-eight-year-old caretaker Paolo Boselli. Counterattacking, the Italian forces captured Gorizia, then bogged down in ferocious fighting for the most meager advances. In August, the Boselli government declared war on Germany, aligning itself with its allies. At home, criticism of the war effort intensified; at the front, morale among the troops deteriorated in the face of senseless slaughter, inadequate support, and Cadorna's severe personnel policies.

In October 1917 came the calamity at Caporetto, the lowest point in the war. Germany shifted troops to bolster a surprise Austrian attack that drove 700,000 Italian troops into panicked retreat, sending shock waves through the peninsula. Boselli fell from power, succeeded by V. E. Orlando, and General Armando Diaz took command from Cadorna, who blamed his own troops for the humiliating loss.

In the midst of recriminations, a number of Italian political leaders closed ranks, and the military recovered, regaining lost ground along the River Piave by June 1918. In the fall, as Allied forces pressed to win the war in France against the foundering Central Powers, General Enrico Caviglia's army crossed the River Piave, driving the Austrians into retreat while taking a multitude of prisoners, capturing the village of Vittorio Veneto and then much of the Trentino. With the Austrian Empire collapsing in disarray and spreading defeatism, Italians accepted an armistice. The victory at Vittorio Veneto helped restore the reputation of Italian armies and symbolized the resilience of the Italian people. It also raised expectations that a postwar settlement would reward Italy for its contribution to the Allied victory in compliance with the Treaty of London.

9

The Fascist Era and World War II, 1919–1945

THE HISTORICAL ROOTS OF ITALIAN FASCISM

World War I left over one-half million Italians dead and perhaps one million total Italian casualties. Compounding the losses was the profound disappointment that Italy's sacrifices had not been sufficiently rewarded. Furthermore, the war destabilized Italian politics and devastated the economy, just as it disrupted life throughout Europe. Economic suffering and unfulfilled expectations in turn fueled political instability, which tested the very roots of the constitutional system. In the midst of spreading malaise and violence, Italian revolutionary socialists entertained a Soviet-style revolution. In reaction, a new, militant movement appeared, dispensing intimidation and violent retribution primarily against socialists while employing symbolism and rhetoric that they called "Fascist."

Fascism's roots lie in a combination of historical influences, including extreme nationalism, syndicalism, imperialism, and socialism. But because Fascist ideology was fluid and contradictory, sources of political support may prove more useful than ideology as a means to understand the movement. As time passed, Italian Fascists won sympathy from an increasingly insecure middle class and financial backing from industrialists fearful of an Italian Bolshevist revolution. Just as revealing were conditions in postwar

Italy that drew many young Italians, especially veterans, to a movement that promised to take action against the moribund Liberal State.

THE PARIS PEACE CONFERENCE, "MUTILATED VICTORY," AND THE RED BIENNIUM

Prime Minister Vittorio Emanuele Orlando and the Italian delegation arrived at the Paris Peace Conference hoping to claim the spoils of victory in World War I. In addition to the territories promised in the Pact of London, they demanded the city of Fiume. When the "Big Three" powers (the United States, Britain, and France) disregarded Italy's claims to Fiume, Orlando and Sonnino led the Italians out of the conference in April 1919 to return to Rome. Arriving with nothing to show for their efforts, and inflaming public opinion for a variety of reasons, Orlando sealed his fate. In the language of Italian nationalist newspapers and politicians, the failure of the Paris Peace Conference to deliver territory to Italy rendered the war a "mutilated victory." In June, economist F. S. Nitti replaced Orlando as prime minister, establishing proportional representation in time for the November elections.

Buffeted by inflation, rising unemployment, and general deterioration of the economy, Italy fell prey to the so-called Red Biennium ("the red years") of 1919–1920. Food riots, lawlessness, industrial conflict, and spreading violence raised the specter of revolution. Strikes spread, taking over a million workers off the job in 1919 and periodically disabling major sectors of Italian industry. In the countryside, land-hungry peasants occupied large estates.

In September 1919 the poet, wounded veteran, and political provocateur Gabriele D'Annunzio contrived a bold, theatrical gesture. Marching at the head of several thousand students, veterans, syndicalists, and rabid nationalists, D'Annunzio occupied the contested city of Fiume. Welcomed by many Italian-speaking residents, he dramatically proclaimed himself head of a "Regency," talked of a "march on Rome," and began to employ a number of symbols, including black shirts, that Fascists would later adopt. In a disconcerting demonstration of weakness, Nitti failed in his efforts to expel D'Annunzio from Fiume. Although Giolitti would later oust him, some would term D'Annunzio's coup a "dress rehearsal" for Fascism.

In the midst of turmoil, the 1919 elections proved more crucial than could have been imagined. Under the new election laws, two mass parties won sweeping support. The new Catholic democratic party, the PPI, organized by Sicilian priest Don Luigi Sturzo, won 100 seats; the PSI's 156 seats made it the largest party in the Chamber of Deputies. Clearly, voters had opened the door to change. However, the PSI and PPI could not agree to co-operate, providing Giolitti the opportunity to resume power. In June 1920, at age seventy-seven, Giovanni Giolitti returned to form his fifth government and prepared to apply his considerable political skills to the spreading crisis.

Just prior to Giolitti's return, in the spring of 1920, Italian workers formed "Factory Councils," based loosely on the Soviet model. In the fall, anticipating lockouts, workers took control of plants in Milan and Turin. True to form, despite pressure from industrialists, Giolitti continued his policy of restraint in the face of the "occupation of the factories." Worker militancy rose to a feverish pitch by September 1920, then began to wane. The PSI revolutionary leaders, most notably G. M. Serrati, while employing Bolshevik symbolism and rhetoric, declined to pursue a revolution, convinced that the conditions for revolution did not exist. But because of the spreading violence, industrialists and landlords feared that a communist revolution threatened, ironically at the very time revolutionary action began to lose its steam. Soon these conservative groups would summon Fascist squads to counter the perceived threat of Bolshevism and to gain for themselves assurances that the government would protect their property and investments.

THE *SQUADRISTI* AND THE FASCIST MOVEMENT

The Fascist movement originated in the years immediately following World War I. At the Piazza San Sepolcro in Milan in March 1919, about one hundred socialists, syndicalists, futurists, and *arditi* (special forces) led by Mussolini formed the Fascio di Combattimento (Fighting Groups). Convinced that a socialist revolution was doomed to failure, Mussolini now attempted to build a new movement. The original Fascist program delivered a radical message, with heavy doses of anti-clerical and republican rhetoric, vaguely left-wing in its politics and economics, strongly appealing to its lower-middle-class, urban base.

At first negligible and politically isolated, the Fascist movement began to gain momentum as it spread from provincial capitals to small towns. By late 1921 it had burgeoned to include perhaps 250,000 members organized in more than 800 *fasci* (groups) throughout Emilia, Romagna, the Marches, Tuscany, and Umbria. In each case, Fascist paramilitary squads (*squadristi*, or Blackshirts) attacked Socialists and their institutions. These "punitive raids" destroyed the local offices of the Socialist Party, labor organizations, newspaper offices, and the peasant leagues (agrarian socialist groups organized in north central Italy since the 1890s). The squadrist battle cry, *Me ne frego* ("I don't give a damn") dramatically proclaimed their defiance of both legal authority and the conventions of middle-class morality. Many victims died as police widely ignored the violence, often in sympathy with Fascist attackers. Notorious among the early Fascist leaders (*ras*, named after Ethiopian tribal chiefs) of the *fasci* were Italo Balbo in Ferrara, Roberto Farinacci in Cremona, and Leandro Arpinati and Dino Grandi in Bologna. Farm laborers joined the movement, many under duress, but the bulk of the members came from the youthful ranks of the middle class. Conservative businessmen were drawn to Fascism as a counter to socialism while nervously observing the violence and anti-government flourishes of the *squadristi*.

In 1921 and 1922, Mussolini exploited the anxieties of landlords, industrialists, and the middle class in the hope that they would turn to Fascism out of fear of a Bolshevik revolution. In his drive for political power, he had to maintain the support of rabid nationalists, syndicalists, veterans, futurists, and followers of D'Annunzio—the extremist elements of the early movement—while courting the newly won conservative forces that could both diversify his constituency and bankroll his movement. All the while, he had to reconcile internal tensions between urban and rural Fascists and between the dominant lower-middle-class rank-and-file and the newly recruited elites.

THE 1921 ELECTIONS AND THE COLLAPSE OF LIBERAL ITALY

Back in power, Prime Minister Giolitti relied on his political skills to restore order, believing he could succeed in the risky game of playing off Fascists against Socialists. To do so, the old master politician called for new elections in April 1921, hoping to strengthen his government. He allied his Liberal group with Fascist candidates, hoping to co-opt the Fascists while at the same time keeping his distance from the *squadristi* as they attempted to beat the Socialists into submission. Giolitti's electoral strategy failed, as the Fascists won 36 seats out of 535 in the Chamber of Deputies, accounting for over one-quarter of the Liberal coalition's victories while outstripping Liberal candidates in a number of head-to-head races. Among the Fascists elected to the Chamber of Deputies was Mussolini, who immediately abandoned Giolitti's Liberal bloc in favor of the opposition. The Left (the Italian Communist Party, or PCI, had split from the Socialists in January 1921) generally held its ground at about 167 seats, whereas the PPI increased its representation to 107, leaving Giolitti with severely weakened, minority control of Parliament. Unable to forge a stable coalition, Giolitti once again stepped away from crisis, resigning in June 1921 to be replaced by moderate Socialist Ivanoe Bonomi.

THE CRISIS OF THE LIBERAL STATE AND THE "MARCH ON ROME"

Mussolini considered a "truce" with the Socialists, but when his support for Bonomi's "Pact of Pacification" was rebuffed by his own rank-and-file, he reneged. Then, sensing an opportunity to acquire power, Mussolini shrewdly abandoned the Fascist movement's early radicalism to create the Fascist Party (PNF). Recruiting landowners, industrialists, and the middle class, the PNF adopted a new, more conservative program that emphasized a pro-business, nationalist agenda, cutting taxes and diminishing the role of the government while boosting military spending and supporting the monarchy and the Catholic Church. However, at the very time Mussolini's new platform made him more appealing to moderates, black-shirted *squadristi* continued their punitive attacks, descending by the truckload on Socialist offices to dispense violence, virtually immune from justice despite mounting casualties.

In February 1922, Bonomi's resignation renewed the political crisis. When Catholics and Socialists could not agree on a government, the king turned to the indecisive Giolitti loyalist Luigi Facta to form an interim cabinet. During the summer and early autumn of 1922, while Facta reshuffled his government, backstage negotiations continued as former prime ministers—including Giolitti, who waited on the sidelines for the right time to return—conferred with Mussolini. In August, in what became a last, futile attempt to protest Fascist violence, the Socialists played into Mussolini's hands by calling a general strike. Mussolini now simply promised order in the face of what appeared to be a paralyzed government incapable of governing. Neither Liberals nor Socialists had proven able to summon the political will to stop him. While publicly pledging to avoid drastic economic changes, Mussolini carefully bolstered his support with the military, so that when the king consulted generals, they gave Mussolini their vote of confidence, as did leaders of the Catholic Church.

When the Fascist congress met in Naples in October 1922, party leaders drafted secret plans for their March on Rome, made all the more urgent by rumors that D'Annunzio planned a large demonstration in Rome during the first week of November. The march would be a bold seizure of power by which Fascist operatives would take control of rail lines and strategic public buildings in major cities, then converge on the capital, driving the government out of office. The plan involved serious risks, however, because superior numbers and firepower gave the military a significant advantage over the poorly armed Fascists—assuming King Vittorio Emanuele III would order the military to intervene.

Former prime minister Antonio Salandra hastened the final crisis of the Liberal State when he withdrew his support from Facta's government on October 27—at the very time the Fascist march was scheduled to begin. Over the next few days, the various parties engaged in frantic negotiations. Before taking the train to Milan, out of harm's way, Mussolini reassured military leaders while leading Facta to believe that the two could forge a coalition. When the king arrived in Rome, Facta's negotiations with Mussolini had broken down. Meanwhile, evidence of Fascist armed insurgency led Facta on the morning of October 28, with the unanimous support of his cabinet, to advise the king to invoke martial law. However, Vittorio Emanuele was unwilling to ask the military to use force against a party that most people believed should join the government. When the king refused to proclaim martial law, Facta resigned.

Although the king preferred Salandra, Mussolini held out and got his way, refusing to join any government he did not lead. The next day, the king turned to thirty-nine-year-old Benito Mussolini to head the government. Mussolini assembled a cabinet that exaggerated his party's strength: three Fascists, two Catholics, a Liberal, a Nationalist, and a handful of others. Safely in power, the Fascists completed the March on Rome, streaming into the capital as they claimed other cities, defiantly lashing out at their enemies in a wave of triumphant violence.

THE CONSOLIDATION OF FASCIST POWER

The March on Rome marked both an end to the Liberal State and the beginning of two decades of authoritarian Fascist rule. Technically, Mussolini's seizure of power occurred within the letter of the Italian constitution; at the same time, by employing systematic violence and wantonly ignoring Parliament, the Fascists destroyed what was left of traditional constitutional government.

When Mussolini called for a parliamentary vote of confidence in November 1922, many assumed that he would govern in the tradition of Italian prime ministers. Once again, this bold tactician had been underestimated. He would never be bound by the niceties of constitutional government. Announcing that the vote was a mere courtesy, he boasted that he could replace the coalition with a Fascist government at any time he wished. Over the next three years, Mussolini embarked on the process of consolidating his power while attempting to reconcile the disparate elements within his own Fascist movement. While paying lip service to existing law and cultivating an image of respectability to reassure his more conservative supporters, he defied many constitutional traditions by condoning—and encouraging—Blackshirt violence. But sooner or later Mussolini would have to reconcile these conflicting aims. One thing was certain: He would never voluntarily relinquish power.

Strengthening his hold on power, Mussolini established the Fascist Grand Council (1922) to set policy and a voluntary militia (1923) to bring the turbulent *squadristi* under control. At the same time, he used various tactics to co-opt the powerful and unruly *ras*, eventually transferring them from their provincial power bases. Among the other forces Mussolini brought under his influence were the Catholic Church, major industrialists, large landowners, the king, and the army.

The Acerbo Law of 1923 provided Mussolini the instrument to dominate the Chamber of Deputies. To get the law passed, he had to appeal directly to the Vatican to undercut PPI opposition while at the same time dropping the PPI from his government. Passage of the law awarded two-thirds of the seats in the Chamber to the party that won a plurality victory (provided that party won 25 percent of the votes), thus assuring the PNF control if it could reach the threshold. In the process of negotiating with the Vatican, Mussolini extended favors, including a guaranteed Catholic presence in the schools and a bailout of the Vatican-controlled Bank of Rome; the Church, in turn, abandoned the PPI and its leader, Sturzo.

Among Mussolini's earliest attempts to build a power base were the December 1923 Palazzo Chigi Accords, by which the Confindustria (the manufacturers' association) agreed to negotiate with the newly created Fascist unions in return for dropping plans to experiment with corporativism. This agreement represented only the first of a series of assurances that Mussolini gave the industrialists. In the Palazzo Vidoni Pact of 1925, the Confindustria solidified its agreement with the Fascist unions, opening the way for the banning of strikes, lockouts, and non-Fascist unions.

Although large landowners could forge no national organization as effective as the Confindustria, they both contributed to and benefited from the Fascist seizure of power. Most directly, the Fascists drove local socialist governments out of power while destroying the peasant leagues, thereby virtually ending agrarian militancy. In turn, Mussolini provided the landholders with tax breaks and brought them into his Fascist power base. Already part of that base were the king and the military leadership, who, along with the Senate and the bureaucracy, continued to provide Mussolini with important links to Italy's past.

THE 1924 ELECTIONS AND THE MATTEOTTI CRISIS

When Italian voters went to the polls in April 1924, the economy had recovered from the postwar crisis and Mussolini had established some degree of respectability as prime minister. Mussolini proceeded to recruit a national list of candidates that brought Liberals (including Orlando and Salandra) and former PPI conservatives into the fold alongside Fascists. While Mussolini controlled the voting apparatus, *squadristi* intimidated the badly divided opposition. In this atmosphere of fraud and violence, Mussolini's national list won a decisive victory, capturing 374 of the 535 seats in the Chamber of Deputies and placing him in position to solidify his power.

Vocal criticism of Fascist election abuses from Unitary Socialist (PSU) deputy Giacomo Matteotti provoked violent retaliation that, in turn, brought Mussolini's government to the brink of disaster. The Matteotti crisis arose in the summer of 1924 when Mussolini, angered by Matteotti's charges, let it be known that he expected retribution. On June 10, ten days after his speech from the floor of Parliament, Matteotti disappeared. For two months, Italians speculated that Matteotti had been a victim of foul play orchestrated by Mussolini. In August, Matteotti's body was discovered. In fact, evidence eventually linked two close aides of Mussolini directly to the murder and coverup.

The Matteotti crisis sent shock waves through Italian public life, polarizing politics, aggravating tensions within the Fascist movement, and making it difficult for Mussolini to continue building a constituency around "respectable" parliamentary government. In June, Giovanni Amendola led opposition members of Parliament in initiating a boycott known as the "Aventine Secession," telling the king that they would return to Parliament only when he removed Mussolini. At the same time, conservatives in Mussolini's cabinet, led by nationalist Luigi Federzoni, while convincing the prime minister to reshuffle his government, fell in line to support him. Emboldened by the closing of conservative ranks and, at the same time, aware of the need to reassure the *ras* and their squads, Mussolini delivered a defiant speech to Parliament on January 3, 1925: "I declare before all Italy that I assume full responsibility for what has happened." He then reminded the remaining members of Parliament of their constitutional right to impeach him. None took up the challenge.

THE FASCIST REGIME

Within two days of his bold speech, Mussolini dropped all pretense of democratic government and began to construct an authoritarian Fascist regime, still operating largely within the broad outlines of the traditional Italian state. A crackdown on the press marked the first step toward greater repression, followed by the expulsion of the deputies who had participated in the Aventine Secession. Then in December, in response to an assassination attempt against Mussolini by PSU deputy Tito Zaniboni, the Parliament fundamentally altered the constitution by surrendering to the king its traditional control over the prime minister and his cabinet. Mussolini now had to answer only to the king. Shortly thereafter, Mussolini outlawed organized political opposition and abolished local governments, each replaced by an appointee known as the *podestà*, responsible to the prefect, and thereby to the central government. In a move that signaled renewed violence against opponents, Mussolini appointed intransigent Blackshirt leader Roberto Farinacci head of the PNF.

In response to three successive assassination attempts in 1926, Mussolini cracked down even more decisively and created the legal framework for full repression of dissent. By taking over from Federzoni as Secretary of Interior, Mussolini gained control of the internal security apparatus and the ability to rein in the *ras* and local party leaders when necessary. The resourceful Arturo Bocchini, a non-Fascist professional, was appointed head of the national police. A new law gave the regime pervasive power to punish political crimes with confinement. Then, in December 1926, the "Law for the Defense of the State" established the secret police (the OVRA), a Special Tribunal to punish political crimes, and the death penalty for attempted murder of members of the government and the royal family.

With a system in place that rendered political opposition perilous, Mussolini proceeded to ensure Fascist control of the civil service, the professions (including the university faculty), and the press. In 1927, he replaced many career civil servants and diplomats with Fascists who brought into government their own political sentiments and style, but whose impact never fully shaped policy. Imposing Fascist conformity on the universities proved problematic as well. Professors who opposed Fascism, such as University of Florence historian Gaetano Salvemini, were subject to Blackshirt threats, arrest, and political confinement. To achieve conformity, Mussolini issued a decree in 1931 requiring university professors to swear their loyalty to Fascism. Although anti-Fascist sentiments ran high within the university community, only about twelve of twelve hundred refused, illustrative of the accommodation many Italians made to the regime's growing repression. Still, there was a passive, or "quiet," resistance to Fascism as exemplified in the journal *La Critica*, published throughout the Fascist era by the influential Neapolitan philosopher Benedetto Croce. Croce offered liberal, idealist interpretations of history and philosophy that Mussolini allowed to be published, fearing that censorship of Croce would bring international criticism of his regime. However, Mussolini did not extend such toleration to the press, on which the axe of Fascist repression fell decisively. By 1926 he had removed the managers of two of Italy's most esteemed newspapers, *Il Corriere della Sera* and *La Stampa*, and had shut down a number of opposition papers. In 1928, a decree required journalists to join the Fascist Journalists' Association. Although historians sometimes have referred to the Fascist regime as totalitarian, many would argue that the regime fell short in its attempt to penetrate civil society and private life.

FASCIST IDEOLOGY, PROPAGANDA, POPULAR CULTURE, AND THE CULT OF IL DUCE

Historians have long and passionately debated Fascism and its leader. Once seen as a mere opportunist whose pursuit of power led him to abandon socialism for Fascism, Mussolini is now viewed as a more complex figure—cruel, vain, and violent, but nonetheless a skilled tactician whose ideological views were shaped in part by an understanding of the dynamics of twentieth-century life. As historians reassess Mussolini, they continue to focus on such issues as the role of ideology, propaganda, and the personality cult in shaping life in Fascist Italy.

In the process of consolidating power, Mussolini made himself "Head of Government" in 1925 and took control of the bureaucracy and local and provincial governments in an unprecedented centralization of authority. He utilized both the traditional machinery of government—police, prefects, and the army—and the new forms of power—the PNF and the Fascist Grand Council—to control dissenters and keep dissident Fascists in check.

In reorganizing the apparatus of power to suit his affinity for personal dictatorship, Mussolini exhibited exceptional powers of manipulation; but his true gift lay in propaganda. To elevate the prestige of the regime and his own genius as dictator, Il Duce ("leader," from the Latin *dux*) launched a propaganda barrage exalting Fascism's themes. Typical was the "battle of grain," a campaign to provide Italy a self-sufficient food supply that enjoyed at least partial success. But did his countless "battles" add up to a coherent ideology? The Fascist creed derived from a number of sources, most notably syndicalism, nationalism, and futurism, which, when intermingled, often gave rise to incoherence and contradiction. Most notably, exclaiming heroic virtues that emphasized action, violence, and warfare, Fascism derisively dismissed "bourgeois" values such as equality and majoritarian democracy.

As the regime stabilized its control, Mussolini called on the philosopher Giovanni Gentile to formulate a coherent Fascist ideology. At the core of

Gentile's Fascist philosophy was the concept that all ethical value derived not from the individual, but from the nation-state; that by authoritarian methods, the state could resolve problems in the interest of all. Still, conflicting views within the movement prevented the development of a unified, comprehensive ideology, and the debates over abstract ideas never fully engaged the Italian people.

Fascism's symbolism did portray some sense of the ideological foundations, especially its emphasis on militarism and action. To instill Fascist values in the population, Mussolini established a number of organizations. Among the best known were three. The Balilla was created to train future generations of Fascists by organizing young Italians into uniformed, disciplined clubs. GUF ("Fascist University Youth") would prepare university students for leadership roles in the movement. And the Dopolavoro ("leisure time organization")—by far the most successful of the three—provided discounts for entertainment, sporting events, and vacations. In addition, the regime developed policies aimed at women, hoping to mobilize them as part of the work force while discouraging feminism. As Mussolini began to build an empire in the 1930s, the need for a larger population of soldiers and workers led the government to award medals to women who produced large families. Still, despite often conflicting government policies, women constituted more than one-fourth of the Italian work force by the mid-1930s.

By then, in spite of Mussolini's efforts, Fascist ideology had lapsed into little more than the "cult of Il Duce" and a propaganda offensive derived from a series of ritualized slogans. "Il Duce is always right" permeated public life, as Mussolini struck heroic poses before cameras. Influenced by Nazi Germany, Mussolini proceeded to create his own propaganda machine. He placed his son-in-law, Galeazzo Ciano, in charge of the Press Office, then created a Secretariat for Press and Propaganda along with offices of film, theater, and radio. The one occasion when Fascist propaganda seemed most effective came in Italy's 1935 invasion of Ethiopia, when Italians rallied in support of the war and the declaration of empire.

The regime also made an effort to utilize the formal arts to propagate Fascist doctrine, none more effectively than architecture. But, as was the case in a number of other instances, several different styles co-existed, representing the tastes of conflicting elite groups within the regime, each of which espoused different aesthetic visions of Fascism. Generally, the regime favored the stark, neoclassical buildings of Marcello Piacentini, who directed the building of EUR (Esposizione Universale di Roma), Mussolini's "new Rome." However, Mussolini also sponsored buildings in both traditional and modern "international" style, although, by the late 1930s, he had begun to favor architecture that invoked the glories of Italy's past. In painting and the other visual arts, as in architecture, overt censorship was minimal.

In 1937, Mussolini reorganized the various propaganda agencies under the authority of the Ministry of Popular Culture. Concerned with non-Italian influences, particularly Hollywood films, the Fascist government outlawed American movies in 1938, then dedicated more resources to producing its own newsreels, particularly through the LUCE (L'Unione Cinematografica Educativa) institute. At the same time the School Charter of 1939, developed by education minister Giuseppe Bottai, committed the educational system to reforms designed to create a new generation committed to Fascist values. For example, the ministry placed greater emphasis on technical training and on the value of labor, both to alleviate the oversupply of professionals and to underscore the Fascist ideological commitment to the concept of hard work. Although they ballyhooed the new educational discipline, the Fascist regime's impact on the education system appears minimal. In fact, the pervasiveness of propaganda led some critics to argue that Mussolini's primary role was as promoter of Fascism; that claims of progress in a new society were merely empty verbiage.

THE CORPORATE STATE

Despite its limitations and overblown rhetoric, Fascism was grounded in economics, especially the theory and practice of corporativism. Corporativism was a new state planning system under which capital and labor were integrated into self-governing units called corporations for the purpose of reorganizing the economy through a rational process of negotiation. Mussolini launched the "Corporate State" in 1926 by establishing a Ministry of Corporations to bring together labor and management into single associations in each sector of the economy. As an antidote to Marxist theories of class warfare, corporativism generated enthusiasm among Fascist intellectuals and some non-Fascists, especially after Bottai was named Minister of Corporations in 1929. In 1934, twenty-two corporations were created. Four years later the regime abolished the Chamber of Deputies in favor of a Chamber of Fasces and Corporations. What materialized was a vast military-bureaucratic-industrial complex that fell well short of theory. Although Fascist propagandists trumpeted this new model, public enthusiasm and concrete results lagged sadly.

One reason that Fascism's economic innovation failed to create a successful new economy was the devastating impact of the Great Depression. Such gauges of prosperity as the stock market, banking, industrial production, employment, exports, and wages all suffered severely. In 1933, the

Fascist government intervened by creating the IRI (Institute for Industrial Reconstruction) to bail out banks and private companies. As a result, before World War II the state controlled a number of industries, including steel, shipping, and communications, and organized cartels (combinations of producers designed to limit competition) in other industries. As a result, such companies as Pirelli, Fiat, and Montecatini set production limits, prices, and wages with limited competition.

THE LATERAN PACT

Although less significant than economic policy, church-state relations assumed a place of significance in the Fascist era. In the Lateran Accords of 1929, Mussolini reached an agreement with the Vatican, thereby normalizing the Fascist regime in the eyes of many Catholics in Italy and around the world. In return, the Roman Catholic Church won guarantees of the autonomy of the Vatican state, protection of Catholic schools, and the latitude to organize groups such as Catholic Action. By negotiating the treaty, Mussolini gained invaluable support in sustaining his government. He not only reversed the Church's longstanding boycott of Italian politics but at the same time won the Church's stamp of legitimacy for the Fascist regime.

FASCIST DIPLOMACY BETWEEN THE WARS

Because Mussolini had significantly less interest in foreign than domestic policy when he assumed office, he originally left Italy's international interests largely in the judicious control of the Foreign Ministry. However, as he consolidated his power, Il Duce began to utilize the diplomatic arena both to build popular support and to pursue his own aggressive drive to extend Italian influence in the Mediterranean and the Balkans, and ultimately to attain Italian imperial greatness.

As a comparatively weak European state, Italy had little choice but to define its interests in the larger context of Great Power diplomacy. But would Mussolini accept these constraints? The Fascist March on Rome occurred in a period when Germany was suffering severely from hyper-inflation and from the great burden of the Versailles Treaty, leaving France and Britain as the dominant European powers. As the German Weimar Republic began to normalize relations with its former adversaries in the mid-1920s, the Italian Foreign Ministry cautiously pursued Italy's interests behind the scenes while, in public, Mussolini made theatrical gestures.

Among Mussolini's first challenges were three incidents in the Balkans. In 1923, he aggressively ordered the Italian navy to take the Greek island of

Corfu in response to the assassination of two Italians there. After marching to the brink, he backed down and accepted Greek reparations. In 1924, in a typical carrot-and-stick charade, Mussolini prevailed on Yugoslavia to yield Fiume. Although relations with Yugoslavia temporarily improved as a result, they deteriorated as the two quarreled over Albania and later over central European diplomacy. Throughout the 1920s, Italy remained on relatively good terms with Britain while encountering tensions with France, particularly over Italian ambitions in North Africa and the Balkans. In an effort to shake up the Paris peace settlement in the Balkans and Danube, Mussolini promoted subversion against the governments in Vienna and Belgrade, and he sided with the losers of World War I—Bulgaria, Hungary, and Germany. But this destabilizing diplomacy came to an inglorious end in 1929. After a temporary interlude, during which Foreign Minister Dino Grandi postured as a proponent of League of Nations principles, Mussolini took back the Foreign Ministry in 1932 to infuse Fascist dynamism into a moribund diplomacy. This bolder approach reflected the influence of extreme nationalists and Mussolini's own effort to play the nationalist card in order to build popular support for his regime and to spread Fascism in Europe.

Suddenly Hitler arrived in power in January 1933. Mussolini was at once elated and fearful. Like Il Duce, the Fuehrer yearned to destroy the peace settlement of 1919. Still, Mussolini worried about runaway Nazi expansion that would steamroller Austria, the German-speaking South Tyrol, and Trieste, the latter two of which had been awarded to Italy at the Paris Peace Conference. Beguiled by Hitler's camaraderie and deference, but dubious of his ambitions, Il Duce walked the narrow line between the Franco-British pole and the ever more menacing Germans.

In this risky game, Austria assumed new importance. Formerly an adversary, Austria had become the linchpin of Italy's security in Europe. Il Duce hastened to befriend the authoritarian Austrian chancellor, Engelbert Dollfuss, and prop up his regime against the Nazi threat. But Hitler upstaged Il Duce by permitting the assassination of Dollfuss in July 1934. When Mussolini answered by sending Italian troops to the Austrian border, relations between the two dictators worsened. To gain some insurance against Nazi ambition, Mussolini turned to France and England.

THE ETHIOPIAN WAR AND THE SPANISH CIVIL WAR

The changing diplomatic climate in Europe provided Mussolini an opportunity to fulfill his imperialist ambitions by retaliating against Ethiopia for Italy's humiliating 1896 defeat at Adua. Hitler's move to rearm Germany threatened France, making it less likely that France would challenge Italy over East Africa. At the same time, with the Corporate State initiative having lost its initial excitement, Mussolini believed that an Italian drive for empire would rally public support behind the glory and heroism of war. Eying Ethiopia for its natural resources and potential for Italian settlement, Mussolini made his move, convinced that he would encounter no serious opposition from a Europe distracted by Hitler's rise to power.

As Il Duce brazenly plotted war, England orchestrated a League of Nations defense against aggression. Not to be denied, Mussolini launched an invasion of Ethiopia in October 1935. The League responded by imposing sanctions that, for several reasons, proved ineffective. Not only were petroleum products omitted from the list of embargoed items, but the United States, Germany, and Japan—not League members—refused to respect the boycott, while the British refrained from closing the Suez Canal to Italian ships. After initial difficulties, Italian troops under General Pietro Badoglio took Addis Ababa in May 1936 by virtue of superior firepower, a half-million troops, and the use of poison gas. On May 9, Mussolini declared the Italian Empire. The victory brought a surge of support for the regime, but at the cost of major debt. More damaging still were the over-confidence the victory engendered and the diplomatic estrangement of England and France produced by the war. In response, Mussolini veered toward Germany.

At the completion of the Ethiopian War, Mussolini turned over the Foreign Ministry to the pro-German Ciano. Within a year, Ciano faced a major crisis in Spain. He convinced Mussolini to support the rebel forces of Francisco Franco against the Spanish republican government, which he characterized as "leftist." When Germany joined Italy, they developed an ominous diplomatic understanding that Il Duce dubbed the "Axis." Intervention in Spain proved more costly than anticipated; a contingent of Blackshirts fighting as "volunteers" was routed by Italian anti-Fascists at Guadalajara (March 1937), requiring Mussolini to replace them with seventy-thousand regular troops and substantial equipment. Only in 1939 did Franco's pro-Fascist forces prevail.

THE "PACT OF STEEL," ANTI-SEMITISM, AND ITALY'S ENTRY INTO WORLD WAR II

Well before the conclusion of the Spanish Civil War, Hitler and Mussolini had begun the process of diplomatic and military alignment that would take Italy into World War II. When Mussolini visited Germany in 1937, he was swayed by an enthusiastic welcome and carried away by a dazzling display of German military might. Three months later, Italy withdrew from the League of Nations, further separating it from the western democracies.

One stunning consequence of the warming of Nazi-Fascist relations was Italy's introduction of anti-Semitic laws in the *Manifesto of Fascist Racism* of 1938. Although Italy had little history of persecuting Jews—a minuscule part of the population—an undercurrent of anti-Semitism that stirred within the Fascist movement and the Catholic Church had surfaced as early as 1936. After 1938, the regime issued decrees removing Jews from certain occupations, restricting property holdings, and prohibiting inter-marriage with Italians (who were proclaimed "Aryans"). Rather than aris-ing from direct Nazi pressure, the anti-Semitic campaign came as a result of efforts by certain Fascist fanatics to align the regime's policies more closely with those of Nazi Germany and from Il Duce's desire to break into the sphere of private life—something he had largely failed to do.

Reluctant at first to respond to Hitler's diplomatic overtures, Il Duce stood by as his "junior partner" absorbed Austria and the German-speak-ing Sudetanland of Czechoslovakia in the spring of 1938. After helping de-fuse the Czech crisis at the Munich Conference, Il Duce came away convinced that France and Britain lacked the will to stop Hitler. As Euro-pean diplomacy became more polarized, Mussolini ordered an Italian oc-cupation of Albania. The British countered by pledging to protect Greece against Italian aggression, leading Mussolini to engage Germany in discus-sions about a military alliance. The result was the "Pact of Steel." In May 1939, Mussolini committed Italy to fight beside Germany in war, even if provoked by German aggression. Hitler ignored Mussolini's attempt to tack on a proviso that Italy needed at least three years to prepare for war. Three months later German armed forces invaded Poland, leading Britain and France to declare war on Germany. World War II had begun.

Unprepared to fight, Mussolini mulled over the decision to honor the Pact of Steel. After consulting Italian interests, perhaps for the last time, he finally, if reluctantly, declared Italy's "non-belligerency." However, a rapid string of Nazi victories convinced Mussolini to enter the war. In April 1940, German naval and airborne forces invaded Denmark and Norway, and by the end of the month they had broken Norwegian resistance. Ten days later, with lightning speed and without warning, German armies invaded the Netherlands, Belgium, and Luxembourg. By mid-May, German mecha-nized divisions drove deeply into northern France, dividing British, Bel-gian, and French forces.

Believing the Nazi juggernaut to be unstoppable, Mussolini found it im-possible to remain on the sidelines. On June 10, from the famed balcony of the Palazzo Venezia, Il Duce declared war on France and Britain. The ill-prepared Italian troops labored across the Alps into southern France after the Germans had broken French defenses. No sooner had Italian troops crossed the border than France signed an armistice with Germany. Convinced that Hitler was about to invade England, Mussolini moved to capture the Suez Canal. But the British responded decisively in January 1941, driving Italian general Rodolfo Graziani and his ten divisions back into their Libyan colony, leaving behind over 300,000 prisoners.

Exasperated that Hitler was collecting all the laurels of victory and determined to fight his own "parallel war," Mussolini ordered the invasion of Greece on October 28, 1940. Within days, the Greeks drove the Italian forces into full retreat. Haunted by the specter of heightened British involvement in defense of Greece, Hitler rushed to rescue Italy's beleaguered forces bogged down in Albania. Thus ended Mussolini's "parallel war." At home, the loss undercut much of the Fascist regime's credibility, already suffering from commodities shortages and rising prices.

In the broader war, Italy's fortunes mimicked those of Nazi Germany, but they fell sooner and farther. In March 1941, Rommel's Afrika Korps struck quickly to take North Africa, while in June Hitler ordered his fateful invasion of Russia—which Mussolini supported with 200,000 Italian troops. When the Japanese struck at Pearl Harbor in December, Mussolini declared war on the United States. After initial setbacks, the British and American armies retaliated, gaining the upper hand in North Africa, while the Russians successfully held out at Stalingrad. Now seizing the initiative, the Allies decided to strike at the Axis through Italy.

THE ALLIED INVASION OF ITALY AND THE FALL OF THE FASCIST REGIME

By the time Allied forces invaded Sicily on July 10, 1943, Italian military resources had deteriorated badly, and formerly solid support for Mussolini among Fascist insiders was beginning to erode. Lack of fuel had paralyzed the fleet, and only five-hundred planes remained available. Il Duce's explanations for the Italian military failures sounded increasingly hollow as he shuffled and reshuffled his cabinet to ward off criticism and keep the opposition fractured. But with Italian military defeat imminent, several Fascist insiders and highly placed army officers were emboldened to contact the king in the hope of easing Mussolini from power and pursuing a separate peace with the Allies.

Allied bombing of Naples and Rome shocked Italians into recognizing the desperate situation they faced and encouraged Mussolini's Fascist opponents. On the night of July 24–25, the Fascist Grand Council, with Il Duce at the table, voted nineteen to seven to support Grandi's motion to remove Mussolini from power. The king appointed General Badoglio head of a military government. As the exhausted Mussolini left the king's residency, agents of the *carabinieri* (the domestic military force) arrested him without complications.

War-weary citizens greeted the news with enthusiastic demonstrations—to which the Badoglio government, fearing a coup, responded with force. Afraid also of German retribution, Badoglio announced plans to continue the war against the Allies while looking for a way out. A furious Hitler rushed troops to defend Italy and punish his "traitorous" ally. On September 8, amidst confusion in military ranks, the Italian government announced it had agreed to an armistice with the Allies. The king and Badoglio fled the ensuing German attack, ingloriously seeking shelter among the Allies in the South, thus abandoning Italian troops who were now left defending Rome without orders.

On September 12, German commandos rescued Mussolini from prison and transported him behind German lines to Lake Garda, in northern Italy, where they established the Salò Republic, a last attempt by Nazis and zealous Fascists to preserve a Fascist presence in the peninsula. As the remaining Fascist diehards captured and executed opponents and dissident Fascists, including Mussolini's son-in-law Ciano, a robust armed resistance movement surfaced, including a wide range of anti-Fascist groups under the direction of Committees of National Liberation (CLNs) in Rome and Milan. As the British and American armies moved northward, resistance fighters took the initiative in liberating cities from German and Fascist forces. Especially prominent in the liberation of Italy were Communist partisans who created for themselves a heroic legacy on which they would draw after the war.

In September 1943, Allied forces landed south of Rome and continued their fierce campaign to take the peninsula against determined German opposition, over mountainous terrain and in miserable weather. In October, Allied troops took Naples and, after setting up a military government in the South and advancing only at great cost, liberated Rome in June 1944. As promised, King Vittorio Emanuele abdicated in favor of his son, Umberto, who was named "lieutenant general of the realm." Five weeks later, after bitter fighting, Allied armies and anti-Fascist resistance fighters liberated Florence. Fighting continued, subjecting Italians to a brutal civil war as retreating Nazis and Fascists resorted to acts of desperate revenge against civilians. Partisan resistance fighters took control of cities as they were liberated, and when Germany collapsed in April and May 1945, partisans forced the surrender of the last German troops in Italy. On April 27, Mussolini and his mistress, captured by partisans as they attempted to flee, were executed, their bodies displayed as trophies in a public square in Milan. In this ignoble manner, with its "infallible" leader exposed to public ridicule, the Fascist era ended.

The Regions of Italy. Digital Wisdom®, Inc.

10

Postwar Italian Political and Economic Life

THE LEGACY OF THE RESISTANCE MOVEMENT AND THE EMERGENCE OF THE COLD WAR

The heroic contribution made by partisan fighters in liberating the Italian peninsula in 1944 and 1945 began to shape postwar culture even before the armistice was signed. One of the more powerful resistance movements in Europe, the Italian partisans—at the cost of perhaps forty thousand deaths—contributed to a sense of restored pride and heightened expectations. Seizing the opportunity, the Committees of National Liberation forced Socialist prime minister Ivanoe Bonomi out of power in favor of a cabinet headed by partisan commander Ferruccio Parri of the Action Party, a group of intellectuals in the radical democratic tradition. Although most parties contributed, Communists and Socialists dominated the northern partisan movement known as "the Wind from the North." Prominent in the new national government, as well as many municipal councils, left-wing forces pushed to purge Italy of Fascists and Fascist influences, pursuing an agenda of radical social and economic change.

The reality of Allied military occupation, American economic influence, and a powerful Catholic Church placed severe limits on the Left's ability to institute change. Catholics and Communists ousted Parri, replacing him with a government headed by Alcide De Gasperi of the new Christian

Democratic Party (DC). The conservatism of the Allied military government reflected a growing apprehension among British and American authorities that the PCI, with direct links to Moscow, might win a commanding position in the politics of the new Italy. As the Grand Alliance disintegrated into conflict over the shape of the postwar world, Cold War politics entangled Italian policy decisions. British and American authorities looked to the conservative influence of the Catholic Church to counter "the Wind from the North," while the United States disagreed with the British attempt to redeem the monarchy. Nonetheless, the heroic tradition of partisan resistance, embellished by Communist propaganda, buttressed a powerful Marxist influence that would shape many aspects of Italian culture and ensure the Left a durable presence in local and national politics.

THE INSTITUTIONAL REFERENDUM, THE REPUBLICAN CONSTITUTION, AND THE 1948 ELECTIONS

Facing the profound challenges of building new political and economic systems, Italians struggled to survive in the aftermath of sweeping wartime devastation. A breakdown of the industrial and agricultural sectors, housing shortages, and destruction of much of the electrical grid, roads, and railways created emergencies in employment and food supply. At the same time, the anti-Fascist political coalition unraveled, leaving a polarized political landscape of Communists and Catholics that directly reflected Cold War tensions.

The main beneficiary of the heroic legacy of the resistance, the Italian Communist Party emerged from the war a formidable force. Well organized and disciplined under the leadership of Palmiro Togliatti, the PCI plotted a course designed to win elections—leaving enough ambiguity in its message to keep the image of Stalinism alive. In the immediate postwar years, the resurrected PSI cooperated loosely with the PCI in hopes of maintaining a left-wing presence to block Catholic political ascendancy. While major constitutional decisions loomed, the Catholics resurfaced as the DC, grounded in a number of Catholic organizations, led by De Gasperi and supported by the substantial influence of the Vatican. The DC's strongest appeal was its opposition to communism, which enabled De Gasperi to reach well beyond traditional Catholic constituencies and to win ample backing from the United States.

On June 2, 1946, Italian voters went to the polls to vote on the future of the monarchy and to elect delegates to the Constituent Assembly that would write the new constitution. By a narrow margin of just 54 percent (out of almost 24 million voters), Italians abandoned the Savoy dynasty in favor of a republic. Large majorities of southern votes favoring the monarchy emphasized the continuing regional breach. Of the 556 delegates elected to the Constituent Assembly, the Christian Democrats won 207, the Socialists 115, the Communists 104. The assembly drafted a document that created a republic of regional governments; a bicameral legislature elected by universal suffrage, having seats allocated by proportional representation; a weak presidency; and an independent court system. Because of compromises necessary to win the support of opposing political factions, the constitution adopted language that proved often contradictory and merely rhetorical. For example, the republic, "founded on labor," protected individual rights. The constitution also secured private property, but with exceptions, providing a mixed economy that guaranteed both free enterprise and a social safety net. It incorporated the Lateran Accords when the Communists for tactical reasons supported the DC demand that the Vatican be extended this permanent, favored status.

The Left maintained a strong presence in Italian politics. Communists won municipal elections in Bologna and Florence and periodically governed Turin and Rome, while dominating regional governments in Emilia-Romagna, Tuscany, the Marches, and Umbria. However, the Socialist Party split of 1947 weakened the Left. The left-wing socialist Pietro Nenni then forged a Popular Front with the PCI, further polarizing politics. As the first parliamentary elections approached, after returning from Washington, D.C., De Gasperi dismissed Nenni and other Socialist and Communist members from his cabinet, fueling speculation that he had acted under pressure from the United States. The campaign attracted huge subsidies and various forms of clandestine interference from both Moscow and Washington. Also influential in the campaign was the fear that the Soviet Union might impose the kind of satellite state in Italy that it had forced on Eastern Europeans, most dramatically in Prague two months before the election.

The republic's first election of April 1948 proved decisive. The Christian Democrats, with the support of the Vatican and the United States, won a surprisingly convincing victory, taking in 48.5 percent of the votes and 375 of the 574 seats in the Chamber of Deputies. In contrast, the parties of the Left won a combined total of 31 percent, giving the PCI 140 seats in the Chamber, but leaving the PSI with a paltry 41. By winning an absolute majority, the DC established itself as Italy's ruling party, a position it would retain for more than forty years. Throughout the remaining years of the twentieth century—and beyond—no single party would again win an absolute majority in a national election. With the PSI reduced to minor party status, the PCI emerged as the dominant opposition party and remained so through the next generation. However, U.S. disapproval tied to massive economic assistance and Cold War fears of Moscow's influence blocked the Communist path to power and left the new republic a competitive democracy in name only. Consequently, in spite of averaging more than one change of government per year, Italy would remain, for better or worse, one of the most stable political systems in Europe, a fact that escaped many casual observers.

POSTWAR RECONSTRUCTION AND THE "ECONOMIC MIRACLE"

Frequent shuffling of cabinets did not prevent Italy's economic recovery, which proved by the mid-1960s to be so remarkable as to be termed the Economic Miracle. Political factors in part explain the success. The Italian political system remained grounded in DC dominance and thus was an ideal beneficiary of American Cold War economic assistance as a model of anti-communism; in turn, the implicit threat of PCI ascendency amplified the importance of DC rule. The DC governments continued to commit to free-market economics and integration with the broader European economy, largely the result of the influence of the liberal economist Luigi Einaudi. In turn, economic growth produced by this pro-Western, capitalistic orientation reflected enough credit on the Christian Democrats to buttress their power.

Italians faced acute economic crisis. Inflation reached an annual rate of 50 percent by 1947, severely eroding wages and living standards. The war's exhaustion of capital and foreign currency prevented Italy from rebuilding its infrastructure, resuming foreign trade, or even importing emergency food supplies to fend off widespread hunger. In response to the economic emergency, the Italian government adopted a series of policies that not only promoted reconstruction from the war's spoliation but contributed to remarkable long-term growth.

Reconstruction began with the deflationary currency program that by mid-1949 managed to stabilize the lira. Wages remained low, compressed during the Fascist era and kept low by wage limits, promoting immediate profits and capital accumulation. Strong outside assistance came from the United States, which worked to rebuild the Italian economy in an effort to fend off communism and encourage European integration. The United States contributed to currency stability by infusing the economy with $3.5 billion of capital before the expiration of Marshall Plan assistance in 1952.

The Marshall Plan (the U.S.-funded European Recovery Program, implemented 1948) placed fundamental emphasis on rebuilding infrastructure and industry—as opposed to agriculture—and thus contributed significantly to the recovery of Italy's manufacturing sector. Italian industrial growth reached nearly 50 percent in four years, exceeding U.S. targets. Re-industrialization favored heavy, mass production industry fashioned on the American model, and thus it faced constraints in an economic culture traditionally characterized by weak domestic demand and small producers. Nonetheless, progress proved striking, building on Italy's large supply of cheap but productive labor and substantial economic foundations that had survived Fascism. In fact, a number of the major leaders in Italy's postwar recovery had gained their experience during the Fascist era, and major corporations such as Pirelli and Fiat endured to lead postwar recovery, along with Fascist-era public corporations such as IRI, AGIP, and the Bank of Italy.

Another major factor in spurring recovery was the Italian government's policy of European integration, including the opening of import-export markets. On top of Marshall Plan stipulations, Einaudi's liberal program pushed Italy toward a European common market by lowering tariff barriers and participating in associations such as the Organization for European Economic Cooperation (1948) and the European Coal and Steel Community (1951). Consequently, Italy, without major deposits of iron or coal, emerged as Europe's second-ranking steel producer.

With the remarkable reconstruction of the industrial and transportation sectors, Italy embarked on its Economic Miracle in the early 1950s. Industrial output virtually doubled over the next decade, with the pace being set in the production of automobiles, airplanes, ships, railroad rolling stock, appliances, office machines, electricity, and chemicals. By the early 1960s, industry accounted for nearly one-half of national income—having accounted for only about one-third in the period before World War II. Over the period 1950–1958, the Italian economy expanded at an annual rate of 5.3 percent, outstripping that of Great Britain, France, and the United States. In the five following years, growth built to an annual average of 6.6 percent, surpassing the rate of all the industrialized economies except the Japanese, and catapulting Italy to the status of a major industrial power.

Although the economy was largely driven by exports of mass-produced industrial goods, the American assembly-line model only partly explains the expansion. Also significant in contributing to the Economic Miracle was notable growth in the small and medium-sized entrepreneurial economy, always a mainstay in Italy. Similarly, wage increases fueled domestic consumption, further stimulating growth.

The stunning success of Italy's postwar economic surge masked a range of problems. In the drive to industrialize, the government's efforts to introduce agricultural reforms proved only minimally successful. At the same time, many Southerners abandoned farms for industrial jobs in the North and in the tourist sector along the coasts, resulting in the need to import food—except for rice, wine, fruit, and vegetables—at great cost to Italy's balance of payments.

In a bold effort to strike a blow at the Southern Problem, the government launched the Cassa per il Mezzogiorno (Fund for the South) in 1950. A major investment in southern infrastructure and economic development, the Cassa poured substantial sums into the region, producing both visible results and widespread criticism of corruption and political influence peddling. One result was to increase southern demand for northern products by means of an infusion of cash into massive public works projects. Too often Cassa resources were controlled by such criminal organizations as the *mafia* (as well as the *camorra* and *'ndrangheta*), which, in turn, used the funds partly to strengthen alliances with the major political parties.

SOCIALISTS AND THE CENTER-LEFT COALITIONS OF THE 1960S

The Christian Democratic Party under De Gasperi's leadership could neither repeat its decisive victory of 1948 nor maintain its internal unity. De Gasperi's sponsorship of a new election law designed to exaggerate the margin of victory for any coalition that won a majority cost him not only his ministry but his career. In the 1953 election, the DC lost seats to the extreme Left and Right, leaving an unstable series of DC coalitions that now relied on shuffling cabinet positions in favor of an array of splintered factions, voting blocs, and personalities.

The DC prime ministers of the 1950s, including Amintore Fanfani, Mario Scelba, and Antonio Segni, all looked to broaden their coalitions in a quest for stability. Both the Vatican and the United States opposed a DC "opening to the left" to bring the PSI into its coalition. Eroding public support and internal disagreements within the DC in the late 1950s led the party to reshuffle its leadership, making conservative Fernando Tambroni prime minister in March 1960. Tambroni explored both a constitutional change to strengthen the executive and an "opening to the right." When the neo-Fascist (MSI) party voted to support his government, ten members of his cabinet resigned. The MSI Congress in Genoa touched off strikes and riots, persuading Tambroni to call on massive force. Critics warned of a return to Fascism, while, in his own party, DC secretary Aldo Moro eased Tambroni from power.

By 1960, the elections of liberals to the papacy and the U.S. presidency removed the most durable opposition to the DC's "opening to the left." In the Second Vatican Council of 1962 and in papal encyclicals he issued, John XXIII (pope 1958–1963) reversed the Church's course by embracing liberal democracy and progressive social thought. At the same time, some evidence exists—although it is disputed—that John F. Kennedy used his presidential influence to soften opposition to the Left within his own diplomatic and intelligence communities. Consequently, DC conservatives lost influence, and Fanfani offered a DC reform program that attracted PSI support. This DC program, including increased funding for education and social welfare, nationalization of power companies, and opposition to U.S. missile bases in Italy, marked a shift to the Left that prevailed in Italian politics throughout the 1960s.

The DC-PSI Center-Left coalition became a reality when Aldo Moro formed a government in 1963 with Socialist Pietro Nenni as deputy prime minister. The coalition encountered difficulty when it had to slow down inflation and then battle over divisive educational proposals, but it survived in one form or another through 1968, never satisfying its own left and right wings. By the time the 1968 elections occurred, the Center-Left had failed to meet expectations for reform of basic institutions—public education, the court system, taxes, or church-state relations—and had failed to establish itself as a viable, working coalition.

THE ADVENT OF RADICAL REVOLT, THE "HISTORIC COMPROMISE," AND THE "YEARS OF LEAD"

Italian voters dealt the PSI a setback in the May 1968 general elections, badly dividing the Socialists and driving the PSI away from the Center-Left coalition and toward the Communist Party. At the very time that Italian centrist politics dissolved, student-led revolutions swept through Europe, demanding reforms in higher education and broadening to oppose the Vietnam War and to embrace expansive left-wing causes. In Italy, the movement touched off a wave of militant strikes among northern workers known as the "Hot Autumn" of 1969.

Shortly thereafter began campaigns of terrorism known as the "years of lead," conducted by both extreme rightist and leftist groups that lasted through the 1970s. Although the violence revolved around ideological rhetoric, it seemed to take on a life of its own. Right-wing groups (including the mysterious "Black Order" with its shadowy ties to the Italian security forces) engaged in ongoing terrorist warfare, as did groups of the extreme Left—both aimed at the governing class in an attempt to disrupt order. The most notorious of the leftist groups, the Red Brigades formed out of alienation from the PCI. Their sense of estrangement heightened in 1973 when PCI leader Enrico Berlinguer announced his "historic compromise" with all progressive political groups. In committing to the democratic process and accepting NATO, Berlinguer took his party away from Moscow and down the path of "Eurocommunism," willing to work with other parties. Out of a sense of abandonment by Berlinguer, a number of left-wing splinter groups formed. The Red Brigades gave left-wing terrorism spectacular visibility through anti-capitalist propaganda and a series of abductions and executions of well-known public figures. Both right- and left-wing extremists seemed committed to destabilizing the government by creating a sense of emergency and outrage. By 1975, Italy had experienced thousands of terrorist acts (including kidnapings and "kneecappings"), most carried out in carefully targeted public places. The result was a growing sense that the Italian republic was unraveling in the face of emerging political warfare.

In the late 1970s, several developments further traumatized Italian society. In 1976 Berlinguer gave his implicit support to Giulio Andreotti's DC government as part of a coalition of "national solidarity" designed to combat instability and terrorism. In response, the DC, over U.S. opposition, cleared the path for Communist membership in the governing coalition. While high-level political negotiations ensued, the Red Brigades founder, Renato Curcio, faced trial in a highly charged atmosphere in Turin. At the same time the Red Brigades renewed their campaign of terrorism, which culminated in the daring daylight kidnapping of former prime minister Aldo Moro in March 1978. Holding Moro through the spring, his captors made a series of demands; when the government refused, the militant conspirators left Moro's corpse in the trunk of a car.

After failing to rein in the violence throughout the 1970s, Italian police began to succeed in turning terrorists into police informants, a strategy that ultimately undercut militants of both extremes. Relative calm was restored to Italian politics by the mid-1980s, although terrorist incidents have continued sporadically to the present. In the meantime, Berlinguer's "historic compromise" had proven a failure. Committed to the coalition of "national solidarity," the PCI shared the blame for a program that introduced unpopular belt-tightening initiatives while failing to correct fundamental economic problems. Blocked from power by the United States and aware of the political price being paid for association with an unpopular government—while deprived of any influence on policy—the PCI seceded from the coalition in January 1979.

DEFICITS, INFLATION, AND A RETURN TO PROSPERITY: THE ECONOMY IN THE 1970s AND 1980s

A spiral of strikes, wage increases, and inflation in the mid-1960s, sharpened after the "Hot Autumn" of 1969, ended the Economic Miracle, and set the stage for a series of crises that lasted through the 1970s. The *scala mobile* ("escalator clause," 1946, 1975) tied wages to inflation, and the Workers' Statute (1970) strengthened unions by providing them a legal presence in the workplace. A series of other laws benefited workers, including improved pensions and a comprehensive national health service (1978). The rate of annual wage increases surpassed 20 percent in the 1970s, outstripping productivity. Contributing to instability was OPEC's quadrupling of oil prices in 1973 that fed inflation and forced the government to devalue the lira, in turn aggravating inflation. At the same time, the costs of education and unemployment benefits soared. Although tax reform followed, it failed to produce adequate revenues, leaving Italy strapped with large budget deficits, the highest ratio of government spending to GDP (gross domestic product, the total value of goods and services) in Western Europe, and soaring inflation that reached an annual rate of over 21 percent by 1980. When the government took countermeasures—raising taxes and interest rates—recession and unemployment spread. Equally troubling was the bloated public sector, which accounted for virtually half of Italy's production. Included, for example, were such government-controlled industries as steel, shipbuilding, airlines, and some banks and automakers.

One serious limitation on economic reform was the "stable instability" of the 1970s. The coalition governments found an equilibrium based on satisfying various client groups by handing out favors. This clientelism was enormously expensive to sustain, and it prevented any party from sponsoring economic or political reforms that challenged the status quo. It also entailed widespread corruption that held important implications for the future.

In spite of lingering political problems, changes in the 1980s contributed to economic improvements, culminating in a return to economic growth that propelled Italy to a position alongside the world's major economies. The first sign of political change came when Republican Giovanni Spadolini took office in June 1981, the first non-DC prime minister in thirty-five years. Although Spadolini's government did not last, it paved the way for the popular Socialist Bettino Craxi to govern for nearly four years (1983–1987).

In an effort to reduce inflation, Craxi used his influence to keep wage and salary increases in check, partly by limiting the *scala mobile* in defiance of the unions and the PCI. In 1984 the inflation rate dropped from 15 percent to 10.6 percent, while the economy grew at a modest 2.8 percent. The number of strikes subsided and productivity improved, leading to greater profits and a boom in investment. Improvement was generated in part by lower oil prices and a general European recovery, to which Italy was more closely tied after the creation of the European Monetary System (EMS) in 1979, and by impressive growth in small and medium-sized enterprises, particularly those that exported. By the mid-1980s, large industries also made a robust recovery. Fueled by a surge in consumption, the Italian GDP (according to Italian calculations that counted the underground, or "black," economy) surpassed that of Great Britain, making Italy the fifth largest economy in the world.

Despite impressive growth, the economy had not fully stabilized, and by the general election of April 1992, the new government of Socialist Giuliano Amato faced grave problems. No government had been able to control public spending or debt, and inflation, down below 6 percent, hovered above the European average. Capital investment fled the country, and the balance of payments worsened. Unemployment held in excess of 10 percent (although the inability to count workers in the "black" economy may have caused that figure to be exaggerated). Speculation against the lira, brought on partly by inflation, dramatized the real possibility that Italy might fail to meet the Maastricht standards of fiscal discipline for entrance into the European Monetary System (government deficits of less than 3 percent and debt no more than 60 percent of gross domestic product; an inflation rate within 1.5 percent of the three lowest EU rates).

The Amato government moved decisively on many fronts, protecting the lira by means of devaluation, imposing emergency spending cuts, and moving to privatize IRI and the other state holding companies and to raise the retirement age for pensions. Over protests, Amato moved to restructure the Italian economy and, by doing so, to inspire public confidence in the republic. He managed to win approval for his budget before reaching agreement with unions and management to abandon the *scala mobile*. However, Amato's austerity measures, only partly successful, were upstaged by a vast and spreading scandal.

THE END OF THE COLD WAR, *TANGENTOPOLI*, AND THE 1993 REFERENDUM

The political circumstances that brought Amato to power heralded profound change in a system that had maintained DC supremacy for more than forty-five years. The collapse of the Soviet Union and the end of the Cold War drastically altered Italian politics, most directly in the dissolution of the PCI into a more moderate faction called the Democratic Party of the Left (PDS) and the hard-line Rifondazione Communista (Communist Refoundation, or RC). In turn, the DC, which had relied on anti-Communism to sustain its power, lost substantial support, part of which was picked up by the newly formed Lega Nord (Northern League). Behind its flamboyant leader, Umberto Bossi, the Lega condemned corruption and called for northern Italy to separate itself from the "parasitic" South by forming the northern state of "Padania." At the same time, allegations spread of a major scandal involving bribes paid by businessmen in Milan to party leaders, including Bettino Craxi, whose Socialist Party virtually disappeared during 1993.

The scandal, known as *tangentopoli* ("kickback city" or "bribesville"), shook the very foundations of the Italian republic, mobilizing a drive for fundamental change in the political and constitutional systems. Magistrates in Milan began a series of investigations dubbed *mani pulite* ("clean hands"). Soon the scandal encompassed other party leaders and former prime ministers, including Christian Democrats Andreotti and Arnaldo Forlani and Republican Giorgio La Malfa, as well as prominent businessmen such as Fiat's Cesare Romiti. Investigations revealed a long-standing web of bribes, required of businessmen simply to conduct business, by which the parties handed out favors and maintained themselves in power. This system of bribes was so encompassing that it clearly had contributed to mounting deficits and had blocked real political competition and fundamental change in policy. By the spring of 1993, many in Amato's cabinet were forced to resign under an investigation that also netted one-third of the members of Parliament. In 1994, Craxi fled to Tunisia to avoid arrest.

Publicity about the unfolding scandal aroused public opinion, creating a mandate for ending corruption and continuing economic reforms that would further divorce government from the private sector. As the public clamored for punishment, investigations expanded, at times recklessly, to envelop over three thousand businessmen and politicians, provoking rumors and suicides. Most important, the *tangentopoli* scandals revealed the enormously abusive power wielded by the political party leadership (especially the party's top executives, known as secretaries) and created momentum that would not only complete the destruction of the old parties but fundamentally alter the system by which they had flourished since the fall of Fascism.

The movement for constitutional reform focused on the proportional method of election that, while guaranteeing equitable representation of the small parties, had made majority government impossible, feeding the corrupt system wherein party leaders traded favors for power (*partitocrazia*). Over the opposition of much of the old party leadership, reformers, particularly DC renegade Mario Segni, called several referendums designed to move Italy away from proportional representation at all levels of government. Favored by more than 80 percent of the voters, the referendums of 1991 and 1993 replaced the proportional system by introducing winner-take-all elections in local government and in three-fourths of the elections for Parliament.

ITALIAN FOREIGN POLICY AND THE EUROPEAN UNION

In the period since 1945, Italy has pursued a foreign policy consistent in some respects with its pre-Fascist past, particularly in its attempt to integrate into European affairs. In his pursuit of empire, Mussolini had taken Italy down a more autonomous path—until coupling Italy's destiny to Germany's. In the postwar era, Italian diplomacy realigned with some of its earlier traditions while moving much more directly toward U.S. Cold War policy, NATO, and the emerging European Community.

Left powerless as the Cold War threat heightened, Italy had little choice but to attach itself to the United States, accepting massive American aid tied to American influence over its domestic politics. In the diplomacy of the postwar decades, Italy's membership in the NATO alliance (since 1949) enabled it to remain anchored to the one power, the United States, that dominated both the Atlantic and the Mediterranean. Although the United States loosened its hold on Italian politics in the 1960s—and in spite of periodic setbacks in Italo-American relations—the United States continues to exert great influence on Italian diplomacy.

The other major dimension of Italy's postwar foreign policy has been integration into the European Union, begun largely as a condition of accepting U.S. Marshall Plan aid and accelerated by the end of the Cold War. Although few Italians went so far as to embrace European integrationist Altiero Spinelli's vision of a federated Europe, most political parties supported a pragmatic movement that would take Italy into a common market as a means to achieving greater prosperity—without, at the same time, abandoning American security guarantees. Entry into the new European Economic Community (EEC) in 1957 brought remarkable benefits to Italy. Free movement of labor among the member states allowed Italian workers to move their families in pursuit of opportunities in France, Germany, and elsewhere. In the first ten years of its membership in the EEC, Italian exports doubled, its exports to Europe increased five-fold, and its GDP increased by nearly 60 percent.

After the mid-1960s, as the superpowers moved from confrontation toward détente, Italian foreign policy underwent serious scrutiny from the

DC and its PSI partners, particularly the governments of Craxi and Andreotti. While carefully moving to extricate itself from U.S. Middle East policy in order to protect its supply of OPEC oil imports, Italy managed to avoid serious damage to its U.S. relations. Putting aside public criticism of Italy's NATO membership, the Andreotti and Craxi governments accepted U.S. cruise missiles, thus repairing any damage that might have been done.

At the very time the Maastricht Treaty (which created the European Union, or EU) was signed in 1992, Italy faced serious crises that placed into question its ability to meet the EMS standards. The fall of the Berlin Wall and the collapse of the Soviet Union accompanied the spreading *tangentopoli* scandal and the subsequent dissolution of Italy's major political parties. Nonetheless, Andreotti restated his commitment to meet the Maastricht standards and fought off attempts to entrust Italy's future solely in European defense alignment, believing that its Atlantic commitment to the United States (through NATO) provided the most reliable security guarantee. By the time NATO used Italy as a base for staging its military operations in the Balkans in 1995, it had become clear that none of the strains on Italian-U.S. relations had proven fatal.

In the spring of 1998, overcoming grave doubts, Italy met the Maastricht standards and gained admission to the European Monetary Union. Considerable credit goes to Carlo Azeglio Ciampi (former head of the Bank of Italy), who, both as prime minister (1993–1994) and as treasury minister in the cabinet of Romano Prodi (1996–1998), held the nation to the austerity and fiscal discipline necessary to confront Italy's debt, deficit, and currency problems. While pushing Italy relentlessly into European integration, Prodi simultaneously shored up relations with the United States. Very little dissent surfaced to the postwar balance of pursuing both European and Atlantic interests while working simultaneously to stabilize the Middle East.

THE BICAMERALE PROPOSALS AND THE GENERAL ELECTION OF 2001: A "SECOND REPUBLIC?"

The election laws implemented in response to the 1993 referendum, on the heels of the *tangentopoli* prosecutions, so significantly altered Italy's political landscape that some heralded the advent of a "second republic." Two general elections have since reinforced the significance of the election laws while at the same time raising doubts about the likelihood of constitutional changes.

The 1990s produced significant change in the political system. The parties that had dominated the republic collapsed, and the Parliament passed new election laws designed permanently to reduce the importance of party machinery—in short, to dismantle the system of *partitocrazia*. Just as the Communist Party had dissolved, so did the Christian Democrats, with their left-wing reforming as the Partito Popolare (PPI) and much of their right wing gravitating to the Alleanza Nazionale (AN), which its leader, Gianfranco Fini, had attempted to distance from its Fascist past. Several new parties developed as well. However, the sharpest change in the new political landscape was the emergence of two coalitions, Center-Left and Center-Right, that provided the prospect of real choice and eventual alternation of government along American and British lines, something that had not happened in the life of the Italian republic.

In the much-anticipated March 1994 elections, two broad-based coalitions emerged. The Center-Left Progressisti ("Progressives") incorporated the PDS, the Socialists, the PPI, and some smaller parties. They faced a Center-Right coalition, Polo delle Libertà ("Liberty Pole"), assembled by media magnate Silvio Berlusconi, that included his Forza Italia ("Go Italy") Party, also home to many former Christian Democrats, the AN, and Bossi's Lega Nord. Running a campaign based on expanding the economy through privatization and reduced taxes, Berlusconi won a startling victory, taking a majority of the seats in the Chamber of Deputies and a near majority in the Senate. With some difficulty, Berlusconi assembled a government. He managed to preside for a scant seven months, fending off criticism of conflict-of-interest and scandal, until the troublesome Bossi withdrew his support. President Oscar Luigi Scalfaro then replaced Berlusconi in January 1995 with a government headed by former central banker Lamberto Dini that focused with some success on the nation's economic problems.

Behind the scenes, the two coalitions regrouped. The Center-Left reorganized as the Ulivo ("Olive Tree") coalition, led by Romano Prodi, economist and former Christian Democrat head of IRI, backed by the PDS and its new leader, Massimo D'Alema. In the April 1996 elections, Prodi and D'Alema led the Ulivo to victory, winning the Senate but relying on the hard-line RC for a majority in the Chamber of Deputies. Vulnerable to threats from RC leader Fausto Bertinotti, Prodi focused on meeting the EU standards for adopting the single currency (the Euro). Pushing to reduce deficits and rein in the welfare system, Prodi found himself confronting Bertinotti, who staunchly defended government benefits for workers and retirees. In October 1998, on a confidence vote of 313–312, Prodi's Ulivo government fell, primarily because Bertinotti opposed Prodi's austerity measures in the budget. President Scalfaro turned to D'Alema, who managed to assemble a cabinet without the RC and, with the thinnest majority, continue the pursuit of economic reform while treading carefully in support of NATO's offensive against Serbia. The first former Communist to head a Western

European government, D'Alema survived until April 2000, when a setback in mid-term local elections led to his resignation and replacement by treasury minister Giuliano Amato.

Before serving as prime minister, D'Alema headed the parliamentary reform commission (Bicamerale) that had proposed fundamental constitutional reforms designed to create a "bipolar" political system to overcome party fragmentation in the interest of greater stability. Among the commission's proposals, adopted in June 1997, was a presidential model providing for direct election of a president with enhanced foreign policy powers while leaving domestic policy-making power in the hands of the prime minister. The 1993 election law would be modified by adding a second ballot designed to strengthen the majority. Changes would be made in the justice system. Finally, Italy would move toward a federal model. However, referendums to implement the changes by converting the remaining parliamentary seats to winner-take-all elections failed in both April 1999 and May 2000 because of poor voter turnout encouraged by opponents of reform.

In March 2001, Prime Minister Amato dissolved Parliament at the conclusion of its five-year term. The campaign for the May general election paired two distinct coalitions resembling those that survived the 1996 election. The candidate of Ulivo, Francesco Rutelli, former mayor of Rome, faced the media tycoon and former prime minister Berlusconi, whose Center-Right coalition was renamed Casa delle Libertà ("House of Freedoms"). Rutelli criticized his opponent's conflict of interest—Berlusconi's Fininvest empire includes all three of Italy's private televison networks—and solicitation of support from separatists (Bossi's Lega Nord) and former Fascists (Fini's AN and Pino Rauti's Fiamma Tricolore), all part of the Casa delle Libertà coalition. A flamboyant campaigner, Berlusconi—Italy's richest and the world's fourteenth-richest man—promised tax cuts, pension reform, privatization, economic growth, decentralization of government, and tougher laws on immigration and crime. Rutelli countered with his own proposals to get tough on crime and to target tax relief for poor Italians. The acrimonious campaign attracted considerable interest in Europe, most of it critical of Berlusconi, whose rhetoric took on an anti-EU and anti-immigrant tone and whose tax cut proposals prompted warnings that his victory might swell Italy's deficit and endanger its standing in the EMS.

As the campaign drew to a close in May, it appeared that the criticism of Berlusconi by Rutelli and the European press was proving ineffectual. Instead, Berlusconi, a charismatic former lounge singer, seemed to gain support in response to resentment against interference from Europe and because he convinced many voters that the charges against him were politically motivated. Most fundamentally, Italians seemed to want a change from the Center-Left that had governed for five years. On May 15, 2001, Italian voters handed Silvio Berlusconi and his coalition a resounding victory. The final count gave the Casa delle Libertà coalition a majority in both houses of Parliament, providing the new prime minister the likelihood of some longevity and the political system the possibility of unaccustomed stability. This being the case, attention will focus on Berlusconi's ability to deliver on his promises: cutting taxes and government expenditures while at the same time reforming pensions and expanding public works projects without increasing public debt and jeopardizing Italy's standing in the European Union. The January 2002 acrimonious resignation of pro-European foreign affairs minister Renato Ruggiero indicated a hardening of the anti-EU stance of the Burlusconi government.

Predictions abound about Italy's future. Some see Berlusconi's victory as a turning point in Italian relations with the European Union. Unabashedly pro-American, Burlusconi endorses the United States withdrawal from the ABM treaty, stands alone among European heads of government in supporting the Bush administration's missile defense program, and warns of excessive European influence in Italy. The prime minister's comments in the wake of the September 11, 2001, terrorist attacks against the United States—lauding the superiority of Western, Christian civilization over Islamic—brought public criticism from the archbishop of Milan for holding an entire culture responsible and assured that Berlusconi would remain controversial.

The most immediate questions facing Italy seem to revolve around major issues that have dominated recent politics: economic rehabilitation, European integration, and reform of both elections and the constitutional system. If the coalitions of 2001 remain intact and present Italian voters with legitimate choices at the polls, then many will applaud the latest elections as a confirmation of a more competitive political system and the death of the smothering influence of political parties. A few danger signs provide sobering reminders of the durability of lingering problems. The Left may be too fractured to lend meaningful opposition to Berlusconi at the very time his continuing refusal to divest his control of his media holdings creates a monopoly over national televison news. Even more foreboding are indications that the *mafia* may be rebounding to assert even greater influence than it had before the spectacular maxi-trials of the 1980s.

11

Postwar Italian Society and Culture

THE WEIGHT OF TRADITIONAL CULTURE AND SOCIETY

In many ways, Italy has changed more since World War II than in the century preceding it. Terrible hunger and poverty have given way to unprecedented material prosperity, which in turn has produced a secular, commercialized culture in place of the predominantly agricultural, Catholic one of the first half of the twentieth century. A culture traditionally dominated by large extended families now claims the lowest birth rate in the industrialized world. Italy's newly elected prime minister owns a media empire that has made him the world's fourteenth richest man, and he leads the state that boasts world's sixth largest economy.

And yet, in many other ways, little has changed. In spite of the widespread publicity given the trials of political party leaders, prominent businessmen, and *mafia* bosses, millions of cases are still pending, few of the accused have served jail time, corruption remains a problem, and organized crime seems to be on the rebound. Although successive governments have imposed stringent fiscal and economic reforms, the deficit and public debt remain high, and businessmen continue to complain that bureaucracy stifles innovation. A large "black" (underground) economy and extensive tax evasion persist. Although election laws have changed and party bosses have been removed in a "bloodless revolution," two-party competition is far from certain, and constitutional reform has stalled. Consumer capitalism, mass media, and social change have altered the face of Italy, yet the influences of Church, family, and localism remain powerful and the Southern Problem lingers. Many observers believe that in spite of change, the weight of Italian culture will continue to smother further reforms and leave the political system to struggle with the same basic issues it has faced since the origins of the Italian state. Although the study of history can provide only intimations of the twenty-first century, most historians would point to society and culture not only as keys to understanding Italy's past, but as strong indicators of its future.

THE LEFTIST TRADITION IN POSTWAR CULTURE

Italian culture in the immediate postwar era reflected the pervasive impact of the war and the widespread sense of relief from two decades of Fascist repression and wartime sacrifices. A burst of creative energy, most notable in Italian cinema, marked the daybreak of an era of freedom. Filmmakers, many of whom had gained valuable technical experience in the Fascist era, portrayed themes of individual acts of courage in the face of tyranny and the spiritual regeneration that accompanied liberation. The "Wind from the North" that established a powerful left-wing presence in Italian politics similarly gave Marxists substantial influence throughout much of Italian culture—in literature, the visual arts, the universities, and the writing of Italy's history. Most remarkable was the movement known as neo-realism, which captured the experiences Italians shared in breaking the bonds of Fascism and Nazi occupation. In cinema, the most innovative neo-realists were Vittorio De Sica (*Sciuscà; Bicycle Thieves*), Lucchino Visconti (*La Terra Trema*), and Roberto Rossellini (*Paisà; Rome Open City*). Each portrayed humanistic, socialist sympathies for poor Italians caught in tragic circumstances while capturing their images in stark tones with little technological embellishment. In spite of being overwhelmed by the mass release of Hollywood films that Mussolini had banned in 1938, neo-realist filmmakers implanted the spirit of the resistance movement in the public conscience.

The literary equivalent of neo-realist cinema proved less focused and, on the whole, less influential. Among the novelists who wrote of the war and the redemptive powers of the resistance were Carlo Levi (*Christ Stopped at Eboli*), Cesare Pavese (*Il compagno; La casa in collina*), Italo Calvino (*Il sentiero dei nidi di ragno*), and Elio Vittorini (*Uomini e no*). This last work, a sparse and agonizing account of partisans battling Nazis in Milan, conformed most closely to the style and subject matter of the neo-realist genre. Neo-realism reached its artistic zenith by 1950 and by 1960 had run its course. The expansion of public education, literacy, and prosperity—accompanied by the proliferation of movie houses and television—brought new, youthful audiences to embrace commercialized culture. As spreading popular culture forced Marxist writers and artists into a more extreme posture of alienation, new forms of film and literature emerged.

ITALIAN CULTURE IN THE COLD WAR ERA

At the height of the Cold War the dominant Italian political parties, Communist and Catholic, vied for the support of the masses by sponsoring myriad sporting events, music festivals, and other celebrations. Emblematic of this propaganda campaign was a remarkable series of bicycle races between perennial Giro d'Italia (Tour of Italy) rivals Fausto Coppi (Communist) and Gino Bartali (Christian Democrat). In the postwar years before soccer surpassed cycling as the favorite Italian sport, the respective newspapers built the rivalry to superhuman proportions, describing the younger Coppi as the "wave of the future" when he challenged "God's cyclist" Bartali, whom the Catholic press called "the perfect Christian athlete," virtuous and prayerful. Among the most memorable events in Italian sporting history were Bartali's 1948 and Coppi's 1949 victories in the Tour de France.

Although the Communists derived certain advantages from the legacy of partisan resistance fighters, particularly songs such as "Bella Ciao" and styles that appealed to Italian youth, their condemnation of American culture fell flat as images of American affluence aroused the collective imagination of Italians. The impact of American movies, television, music, clothing, and other influences from popular culture reshaped Italian tastes in the years of the Economic Miracle and beyond. Influenced by the surge of private development and the papacy's encouragement to return to "traditional" values, Italian mass culture in the late 1950s and 1960s embraced the symbols of commercial capitalism while maintaining at least the trappings of the leftist heroism of the partisan movement. The synthesis of materialistic values and Catholic dogma was theoretically an uncomfortable fit, but one that the DC deftly managed in its propaganda.

By the late 1960s, Italian television—in addition to programming a seemingly endless stream of American situation comedies and B-movies—began to produce more of its own entertainment, typified by game shows, quiz shows, and talk shows. Similarly in cinema, commercial influences and changing tastes spelled the end of neo-realist primacy and opened the medium not only to comedies but to an array of experimentation. Among the notable innovators were several young filmmakers who moved beyond neo-realism, Federico Fellini (*I vitelloni; La Strada; Nights of Cabiria*) and Bernardo Bertolucci (*Before the Revolution; The Conformist*), the writer Leonardo Sciascia (*Il giorno della civetta*), and the poet-novelist-filmmaker Pier Paolo Pasolini (*Accatone; Mamma Roma; The Gospel According to St. Matthew*).

Blocked from political power, Italian Marxists ironically managed to retain a vigorous influence on postwar "high" culture, particularly in academic scholarship and literary circles. Notable were the journals *Politecnico* and *Rinascita* and the publication of Antonio Gramsci's prison letters and notebooks. Marxist cultural hegemony showed a few cracks as early as the 1950s, with the publication of Ignazio Silone's anti-Communist essay in *The God That Failed* (1950) and Giuseppe de Lampedusa's *The Leopard* (1958). Whereas Lampedusa's style and treatment of nineteenth-century Sicily merely fell outside the bounds of socialist realism, attacks on Silone for his heresy took on a fiercer tone. A former founder of the PCI and leader of the underground resistance during the Fascist era, Silone became a living symbol of courage in the 1950s, taking on an aura of spirituality as a champion of individual freedom in defiance of godless forces.

The iconoclastic work of Pasolini in particular pointed the way toward abandoning the Marxist paradigm in favor of less ideological avant-garde trends that grew to dominate Italian formal culture by the end of the 1960s. Highly experimental, this eclectic avant-garde movement explored new psychological and perceptual dimensions while rejecting the spreading commercialism believed to be suffocating artistic creativity. The most notable exponent of the movement was the filmmaker Michelangelo Antonioni (*L'Avventura; La Notte; Eclipse; Blowup*). At the same time, this avant-garde undercurrent attracted a growing array of poets and writers, including Umberto Eco, contributors to the journal *Il Verri*, and those who collaborated in the Gruppo '63 movement (a circle of experimental writers searching for a language suitable to the post-industrial era). Implicit in the work of each was a culturally subversive tone of social criticism apparent in Fellini's film *La dolce vita* and the plays of Dario Fo (1997 Nobel laureate in literature). Fo's break with commercial theater in 1968 and his movement to revolutionary drama (*Mistero Buffo; Accidental Death of an Anarchist*) marked a more militant turn in Italian formal culture. Revolutionary drama paralleled the emerging student movement of 1968, "Hot Autumn" of 1969, and the era of polarized militancy known as the "years of lead" that persisted through the 1970s. Also significant in the 1970s was the emergence of an array of women writers, including novelist Natalia Ginzburg (*Small Virtues; You Never Must Ask Me*), who described in powerful and elegant prose the lives of Italian women and children, and journalist-memoirist Oriana Fallaci (*Interview with History*; *A Man*). Most notable was the work of Elsa Morante, whose celebrated novel, *History*, captures in mythical terms the war's impact on a poor Roman family.

THE SOCIAL IMPACT OF ECONOMIC DEVELOPMENT

Just as the Economic Miracle and subsequent expansion transformed Italian culture, so they unleashed forces that changed Italian society in fundamental ways. Italy's economic history, which parallels that of the European continent in some general respects, is otherwise unique. Italy industrialized late, with its large factory production peaking in the 1960s in response to Marshall Plan incentives and a burgeoning market. By 1970, over 40 percent of Italians worked in industry and only about 17 percent in agriculture, meaning that the tertiary sector (mostly services) accounted for well under half of Italian jobs. Very quickly, Italy moved to a post-industrial economy, with industrial workers dropping to around 30 percent by the late 1990s and farmers to under 8 percent, while the tertiary sector rapidly expanded. Uniquely Italian is the large segment of production that occurs in small and medium-sized shops, highly productive niche industries that have propelled economic success and maintained the family social structure.

Amid the vast changes Italians have experienced since World War II, emigration, internal migration, and urbanization stand out. In the half-century after unification approximately thirteen million Italians left the country, most to the Americas. After World War II, emigration once again exploded as Italians left for Switzerland, France, and Germany. At the same time, young southern men migrated to northern Italian cities. Often illiterate, they faced hostility and deprivation when they arrived, but largely through the efforts of unions and political parties these internal migrants quickly became acculturated and summoned their families. This massive influx of population overwhelmed northern cities (as well as Rome), creating squalid suburbs with wholly inadequate services. Abandoned by their young men, many southern villages languished.

A major agent of change in the 1950s was the spread of commercial culture, expedited by the burgeoning presence of television sets and automobiles. Nationwide television broadcasts transmitted a vernacular (as opposed to literary) language accompanied by images of modern conveniences and fashions. The availability of small, inexpensive cars, mostly Fiats, opened new possibilities to ordinary Italians, further contributing to internal migration and the development of a national popular culture. By the mid-1990s, more than half of Italian workers held jobs outside agriculture and industry, most in the service sector. Not surprisingly, trends toward urbanization and modernization altered Italy's class structure. In step with other post-industrial societies, a growing middle class, featuring many newly empowered women, surpassed the working class in importance.

SOCIAL CLASS, FAMILY, AND THE WOMEN'S MOVEMENT

The massive population shift to urban areas that accompanied industrialization brought about significant changes in social class and family life. Southerners tended to leave agriculture for white-collar jobs and an entree into the middle class in DC-created government employment, whereas Northerners more frequently located middle-class jobs in industrial management and in the burgeoning niche economies.

Postwar economic development profoundly affected not only social class but family—and particularly the roles of women, who began to enter the labor market in larger numbers. At first, prosperity produced by the Economic Miracle tended simply to reinforce traditional gender roles; the earnings of male "breadwinners" left women largely as "homemakers." When women did enter the work force they were usually relegated to lower-paying jobs, often in the "black" economy. By 1980, however, women had grown to about one-third of the work force, and increases in formal education had enabled them to break into the better-paid professions, as had women in the rest of Europe. At the same time, a decrease in the size of the Italian family prompted women to seek jobs to supplement family incomes.

Changing roles of women in the workplace have been accompanied by changes in the Italian family. The average family size dropped from about four persons at the end of the war to fewer than three persons in 1990, while the number of two-person households increased markedly. The number of marriages per thousand has dropped, whereas the rates of divorce (10 percent vs. 31 percent in France), out-of-wedlock births (7 percent vs. 25 percent in France), and common-law marriage climbed. In general, these rates have leveled off to approximate European norms, but divorce rates remain well below average. The most significant changes in all categories have come in northern Italy; the traditional family remains stronger in the South. Despite these changes, the family persists as the dominant element of social life throughout the peninsula.

Two trends set Italians apart from other European families. One is a precipitous drop in fertility rates, leaving the average at a little over one child per woman, one of the lowest in the world. Birth rates for Italian women age twenty are one-tenth those in the United States. The other striking trend among Italian families is the extended period during which Italian youth continue to live with their parents. At age thirty, roughly one-half of Italian men and one-quarter of Italian women reside at home. Scholars attribute this exceptional tendency to the lack of good jobs and housing available to young people and the subsequent inclination to delay marriage.

The ability of many Italian women to make substantial gains in education and employment, delay marriage, and limit family size can be seen as both a cause and an effect of a growing Italian women's movement. Subjugated to traditional, domestic status by Fascist policy and Roman Catholic doctrine, Italian women began to experience marked success in the resistance movement and in the immediate postwar period. As organized components of the political parties of the Left, most notably the UDI (the Union of Italian Women), women acquired power and influence. Modernization in the 1950s triggered forces that would forever transform the role and status of women in Italy.

By the 1960s, women gained inspiration and experience from two new sources: the American women's movement, and the student movement of 1968. Male dominance of the student movement drove Italian women to develop new slogans (*Donna é bello*, "womanhood is beautiful") and forms of organization, such as the American model of decentralized, informal groups that used personal issues to leverage political gains. At the same time, attitudes toward sexuality became more open. Italian women demanded full access to contraception and abortion, as well as gender equality in education, law, and the workplace. Political gains were noteworthy, including the legalization of divorce in 1970; the Family Law of 1975, establishing gender equality; a workplace anti-discrimination law in 1977; and a law legalizing abortion in 1978. In electoral politics Italian women have made similar gains, although results remain modest. The number of women in the Chamber of Deputies remains under 10 percent, well below the European average, although it temporarily surpassed 16 percent in 1994. Among Italian women who have risen to positions of political influence, Nilde Jotti chaired the Chamber from 1979 to 1992, and Susanna Agnelli served as foreign secretary in Lamberto Dini's cabinet. More important in the long run are fundamental changes in cultural attitudes toward gender equality. Still, much of popular culture, including Italian television and weekly news magazines, retains obvious traces of traditional sexist attitudes. Economic and political power remain largely in the hands of men.

THE INFLUENCE OF THE CHURCH

In the face of profound modernizing and secularizing influences that have transformed postwar Italy, the Catholic Church continues to serve as the great bastion of tradition. From the founding of the kingdom until the signing of the Lateran Accords of 1929, the Church maintained its opposition to the government. Mindful of the presence of the Vatican and its storied history, the 85 percent of Italians who profess themselves to be Catholics—and many of the 35 percent who attend mass—have maintained a uniquely skeptical attitude toward the organized Church.

In the postwar era, Pius XII (pope 1939–1958) attempted to assert greater power over the state through a political party, the DC, which could directly influence Italian policy on a number of issues such as contraception, abortion, and divorce and, on a wider scale, impede the spread of communism in Europe. Pius remained conservative on doctrinal issues as well. As noted (see Chapter 10), Pope John XXIII altered the Vatican's course, speaking out on behalf of the working class, articulating a social democratic view, and softening Vatican Cold War policy. When Paul VI (pope 1963–1978) restated the Church's opposition to contraception and campaigned for repeal of the divorce law, he further distanced the Vatican from the Italian population. Polish-born Karol Wojtyla, elected in 1978 as Pope John-Paul II, the first non-Italian in 455 years, held the course on social policy, particularly Vatican opposition to contraception and abortion. Still, fewer than one-third of voters supported John-Paul's 1981 attempt to repeal the abortion law, and most Italians continue to ignore Church stands on sexual matters. On other issues, John-Paul inspires greater support in his moral opposition to war, including NATO bombing of Serbia; to separatism, by which the Lega Nord would abandon the economically weaker South; and to the *mafia*.

THE SOUTHERN PROBLEM AND THE *MAFIA*

In some respects the South has remained largely immune from the transforming social and cultural changes that have accompanied postwar modernization. In spite of billions of dollars in expenditures, an assortment of government programs, the Economic Miracle, and the transition of the economy through industrialization to a post-industrial phase, the persistent Southern Problem—the economic discrepancy between North and South—remains as serious as any issue. In the immediate postwar period, the Italian government launched a land reform program and a series of infrastructure projects that together boosted the national economy while building political support in the South for the DC. The migration of Southerners to work in northern industry also contributed to national economic development. In the 1960s, northern industrialists agreed to develop large production plants in the South that, in spite of some marked failures, eventually began to correct the regional imbalance in the standard of living. However, when the economic crises of the mid-1970s threw the national economy into recession, the government abandoned its attempt to industrialize the South in favor of supports for the ailing northern economy. As part of that plan, the DC government substituted a program of income subsidies and public works projects in the South to boost consumer demand for northern products, leaving Southerners with the consumer habits of an advanced, industrialized region but without the industrial base. Consequently, the South became a major client of the DC governments, heavily dependent on political favors.

During the economic boom of the 1980s, northern businesses expanded markets throughout the world. Notable was the fashion industry, which vaulted to first place among export businesses in the world. While the South became relatively less important, many northern politicians, most notably Umberto Bossi's Lega Nord, began to criticize the South as a drain on the national economy. A major part of Bossi's criticism focused on organized crime. He alleged that the *mafia* (including the *camorra* and *'ndrangheta*) was so entwined with political parties in the South that it had developed a stranglehold on the dispersal of public funds. Thus, the Southern Problem now bore the stain of organized crime.

Adjusting to changing politics in the postwar era, the *mafia* had cast its lot with the Christian Democratic Party and entrenched itself in government agencies through which the DC funneled development funds to the South. As the *mafia* shifted from traditional, land- and rent-based, rural power in central Sicily to enterprises connected to the new urban and suburban development, many observers predicted its extinction. But the *mafia* thrived by controlling construction and labor contracts. By the 1950s it had begun worldwide trafficking in narcotics. No longer could critics write it off as a nebulous cultural phenomenon without organization or influence. By the mid-1970s, the *mafia* bore little resemblance to its parochial Sicilian past, having moved into international finance and money laundering in a labyrinth of legal and illegal operations.

By the mid-1980s, the same enthusiasm that mobilized the campaign for political reform energized Italians to confront the endemic problem of organized crime, estimated to account for more than 12 percent of GDP. At the same time, the *mafia* seemed more vulnerable in the wake of the decline of the DC and the breakup of the Cold War–era equilibrium that had kept the DC and its clients in power—particularly in the light of *tangentopoli* investigations that had revealed the *mafia* as a DC-PSI client. Defending itself from aggressive investigations and distancing itself from politics, the *mafia* in 1982 committed the shocking murder of General Alberto Dalla Chiesa, former nemesis of terrorists and newly appointed anti-*mafia* commissioner. Public outrage supported an intensified campaign to prosecute, led by judges Giovanni Falcone and Paolo Borsellino, whose efforts culminated in the celebrated 1987 maxi-trial of nearly five hundred alleged *mafiosi* in Palermo. Highly publicized trials succeeded in turning *mafiosi* against some of their most notorious bosses. The capture of a number of them led the press again to predict the demise of the *mafia*. Most of those sentenced, however, were later released. The 1992 murders of both Falcone and Borsellino by massive bombs sent a clear, dramatic signal that the *mafia* was far from dead.

When authorities stepped up pressure in response to the Falcone and Borsellino murders in late 1992, attention once again turned to connections between the *mafia* and political parties. As a result, magistrates forced the trial of Giulio Andreotti, Italy's longest serving prime minister, who was accused—then later acquitted—of extensive *mafia* ties. Among Andreotti's alleged connections was a *mafia don*, Salvatore "Totò" Riina, who was implicated in the murders of Falcone and Borsellino. Riina's spectacular arrest in January 1993 ended almost a quarter-century of "hiding." In convicting Riina, investigators described a murderous and highly structured *mafia* enterprise that had established a comprehensive "cohabitation" with government at all levels throughout the postwar era. Although some see a weakening of *mafia* influence, others note that particularly in Sicilian cities, businesses are still forced to pay protection money. Nonetheless signs of progress exist, notably in politics, where local leaders such as former Palermo mayor Leoluca Orlando have attempted reforms, and in business, where the Etna Valley has attracted hundreds of high-tech companies, including Nokia, Canon, and Ericsson.

CONCLUSION

The rise of Silvio Berlusconi in the 1990s marked a distinctive convergence of three aspects of modern Italian culture: media, sports, and politics. It was in fact Berlusconi's masterful manipulation of the three that brought him to prominence. At the same time he controlled all three of Italy's private television networks, *Il cavaliere* ("the knight") owned AC Milan, one of Italy's most successful soccer clubs, whose fans he used to build a political base. In the process he adopted the imagery of Italian soccer, a great unifying cultural force. He took as his party's name Forza Italia! ("Go Italy!"), the cheer Italians chant for the national team; and as his party's informal name, the Azzurri ("Blues"), the nickname of the national team. Carrying on the politicized tradition of Cold War–era sports, supporters of the rival Roman clubs still divide along ideological lines, with the Lazio team boasting right-wing supporters hailed by neo-Fascist leader Gianfranco Fini as "the sons of Mussolini."

For some of his critics, one of whom accuses Berlusconi of haranguing the Italian people from an "electronic balcony," this blending of physical prowess and politics smacks too much of Mussolini. Furthermore, criminal proceedings involving a range of bribery and tax-related charges against *Il cavaliere* remain open. His defenders contend that if true, the charges merely indicate that he was conducting "business as usual" and that the judicial system holds a bias against him.

In the face of criticism, Berlusconi's popularity remains strong. Many believe that his political future—and to an extent Italy's future—rests on his ability to address lingering problems, particularly economic reforms. With an aging population that counts one child for every person over age sixty-five (the ratio was 5.65 children per sixty-five-year-old in 1900) and more pensioners than employed persons, reforming the pension system will provide a major challenge. Yet the familial tradition will continue to soften the problems related to aging, just as grandparents continue to nurture children of families with two working parents. Here as elsewhere, for better or worse, social and cultural influences impede rapid change.

The fundamental question remains whether Italians will be able to overcome parochial loyalties, regional hostilities, conventional politics, and a bloated public sector—in short, their past—in favor of political and economic reforms. Skeptics again point to the smothering influences of history and traditional culture and the continuing dominance of an elite, political class, more interested in protecting its power than in creating a "second republic." In the case of two of Italy's chronic problems—vast regional imbalance, and the numbing effect of organized crime—signs of economic development in the South provide hope that they may be alleviated. Evidence exists of progress in opening up the economy to greater competition, reforming the welfare system, and introducing structural changes that will infuse greater competition in Italian politics. Most would agree that Italy is more competitive and less corrupt in both business and politics than it was in 1980—and that its ability to compete economically and provide progress for its inhabitants rests largely on its success in continuing to pursue reform, even in the face of weighty tradition.

Notable People in the History of Italy

Dante Alighieri (1265–1321). Born in Florence to a family of the lower nobility, Dante studied at Santa Croce, Santa Maria Novella, and with the poet and rhetorician Brunetto Latini before becoming the most influential writer of the Italian Renaissance. Growing up amid political turmoil in Florence, Dante became enamored of a young woman whom he idealized in his poetry as "Beatrice." Among his first works is *Vita nuova* (New Life, 1292–1294), a collection of poems inspired by Beatrice. Active in politics, Dante served variously as a cavalryman, a councilman, and a member of the city council of Florence. While he was visiting Rome on a diplomatic mission in 1301, an opposition faction seized power in Florence and banished Dante. He never succeeded in returning to the city of his birth. While in exile in Paris and several Italian cities, Dante wrote extensively on language, philosophy, and politics and completed his epic masterpiece, *Commedia* (The Divine Comedy), an allegorical narrative depicting the poet's sojourn through hell, purgatory, and heaven.

Thomas Aquinas (1225–1274) was a preeminent Roman Catholic theologian and philosopher. Born to an aristocratic family near Aquino, Aquinas studied at the Benedictine monastery of Monte Cassino and at the universities of Naples and Paris. In 1258 he returned at the pope's request to teach in

Italy. Through his many writings he influenced Catholic thought, particularly in reconciling Aristotle's rationalism with Church doctrines of faith and revelation. The most important of his books are *Summa Contra Gentiles* (1261–64; trans. *On the Truth of the Catholic Faith*, 1956) and *Summa Theologica* (Summary Treatise of Theology, 1265–1273). Aquinas was canonized by Pope John XXII in 1323.

Michelangelo Buonarroti (1475–1564). A Florentine, Michelangelo became a dominant force in the Italian Renaissance and one of the most influential artists in history. Apprenticed to the painter Domenico Ghirlandaio at age thirteen and patronized by Lorenzo de' Medici at age fourteen, Michelangelo incorporated classical influences in his earliest sculpture. With the fall of the Medici he fled Florence for Bologna, then Rome, where he sculpted a *Bacchus* and his famous *Pietà*, now at St. Peter's. After a return to Florence, where he produced his *David*, he was called to Rome in 1505 by Pope Julius II to design his tomb and then to paint the ceiling of the Sistine Chapel at the Vatican, completed in 1512. In 1520 Michelangelo returned to Florence to execute the Medici Chapel at San Lorenzo. In 1534, with the Medici project complete, he went to Rome, where he painted his *Last Judgment* and designed the Piazza del Campidoglio for Pope Paul III. After the death of the brilliant architect Antonio da Sangallo the Younger, Michelangelo completed the Farnese palace and took over the construction of St. Peter's. While sculpting a *Pietà* in February 1564, Michelangelo died. He is buried at Santa Croce in Florence.

Enrico Caruso (1873–1921) was recognized as the greatest tenor of his age. Born in Naples, he first gained notice in Milan in 1898, then performed widely before his 1903 debut in Verdi's *Rigoletto* at the Metropolitan Opera House in New York. Among his many roles, Canio in Leoncavallo's *Pagliacci* became his most famous. A fixture in New York, renowned for his voice of rare beauty and strength, Caruso won worldwide fame as one of the first recording artists.

Camillo di Cavour (1810–1861). Camillo Benso, Count of Cavour, was a Piedmontese businessman and political leader who made himself the major architect of Italian unification. Cavour founded the nationalist newspaper *Il Risorgimento* in 1847 and campaigned successfully for the Piedmontese parliament in 1848. He joined the cabinet of Massimo d'Azeglio before becoming prime minister of Piedmont in 1852. As prime minister Cavour modernized Piedmont, making it a model of progressive agriculture and commerce. In 1854, he took Italy into the Crimean War as an ally of Britain and France to win their diplomatic support for the expansion of Piedmont. In 1859, Cavour made a secret alliance with Napoleon III against Austria after which he maneuvered Austria into war. Supported by French troops, Piedmont defeated the Austrian armies, only to find that Napoleon withdrew his support at a critical moment. In the peace treaty, Piedmont added Lombardy but failed to add Venetia. After resigning in protest, Cavour returned in 1860 to preside over the declaration of the Kingdom of Italy before dying in Turin in 1861.

Christopher Columbus (Cristoforo Colombo, 1451–1506). Born in Genoa, Columbus navigated the Atlantic Ocean on four voyages to claim a number of Caribbean islands for Ferdinand and Isabella of Castile. The colony he established in what is today the Dominican Republic was the first European claim in the New World. Celebrated as a hero throughout much of modern history, Columbus is now a more controversial figure as modern students of history focus on his record of brutality and enslavement of the aboriginal inhabitants.

Francis of Assisi (1182–1226). Born Giovanni Francesco Bernardone, the son of a wealthy merchant, Francis gave up his worldly possessions and began preaching in 1208 after suffering a serious illness. He gathered around him a band of disciples that became the Franciscan Order, dedicated to caring for the poor. By 1219, the Franciscans numbered five thousand members and Francis had begun preaching throughout Europe and in the Holy Land. In 1224, he returned to Italy and the marks (stigmata) of the crucifixion of Christ are said to have appeared on his body. He lived in pain until his death, after which he was canonized (1228).

Galileo Galilei (1564–1642), renowned physicist and astronomer, achieved momentous breakthroughs by discovering the laws of bodies in motion and developing the first astronomical telescope to observe the lunar surface, planets, and sunspots. Born in Pisa, Galileo fundamentally challenged existing dogma by arguing the importance of scientific inquiry in his publications on the theories of Ptolemy and Copernicus. As a result, the Inquisition sentenced Galileo to life imprisonment—commuted to house arrest—in 1633.

Giuseppe Garibaldi (1807–1882), a sailor born in Nice, became a key leader of the Risorgimento and a revered patriot. He joined Mazzini's Young Italy movement in 1833, then escaped after being sentenced to death for his part in a failed nationalist insurrection. In exile in South America for twelve years, Garibaldi led patriotic revolts in Brazil and Uruguay before returning to his homeland to join the revolutions of 1848–1949, in which he led nationalist troops against the Austrians and in defense of Mazzini's Roman Republic. After a stay in the United States, Garibaldi returned to Italy to live on the island of Caprera (north of Sardinia) before returning to the drive for independence. In 1860, he led his "Thousand" red-shirted volunteers in a successful invasion of Sicily. The "Red Shirts" then crossed the straits and defeated the troops of the king of Naples at the River Volturno. When King Victor Emmanuel of Piedmont arrived with his troops, Garibaldi turned over Naples and Sicily to the king. In 1862, leading a volunteer force in a campaign to seize Rome, Garibaldi was stopped at Aspromonte by Victor Emmanuel's forces. Wounded at Aspromonte, Garibaldi was subsequently pardoned and returned to Caprera, only to be called to duty again in an 1866 campaign against Austria. Eventually defeated at Mentana in 1867, he returned to Caprera. In 1870, he fought his final campaign on the side of France in the Franco-Prussian War. In 1874, he was elected to the Italian Parliament.

Giovanni Giolitti (1842–1928) was five-time prime minister of Italy and one of the most influential political leaders of the modern era. Born in Mondovì in Piedmont and trained as a lawyer, Giolitti began a career in the civil service before being elected to Parliament in 1882. During his first term as prime minister (1892–1893), Giolitti was forced out of office by a banking scandal. He returned to power in 1903, and as head of his own coalition governments he manipulated Parliament through the political process and produced significant reforms, including a national insurance act and a law creating universal male suffrage. His decision to invade Libya led to Italy's annexation of Libya, Rhodes, and the Dodecanese Islands. Retreating from power during World War I, he failed in his attempt to maintain Italy's neutrality. Back in office in the critical postwar years, Giolitti finally lost his parliamentary majority in 1921 and retired from politics. He is remembered not only for his reforms but for his tainted political methods and—as Italy's most powerful leader—for being the one man who might have stopped the Fascists from seizing power.

Giotto (c. 1266–1337) di Bondone was the most influential painter in fourteenth-century Italy, particularly because of his three-dimensional depiction of the human form. Born in Colle di Vespignano near Florence, Giotto is regarded as founder of the Florentine School of painting. His most important work was the fresco cycle called "The Lives of Christ and the Virgin" in the Arena Chapel in Padua. After painting in a number of Italian cities, Giotto was appointed in 1334 Master of Works of the cathedral and city of Florence, where he designed the cathedral's bell tower.

Pope Innocent III (c. 1160–1216, pope 1198–1216). Born to a noble family in Gravignano, Lotario de'Conti di Segni studied at the universities of Paris and Bologna. Elected at age thirty-seven, Innocent III became the most successful of the medieval popes, particularly in foreign affairs, by establishing Church control over the Papal States and English Catholicism. Less successful were the two crusades he proclaimed in the south of France and in Constantinople. In 1215, he summoned the historic Fourth Lateran Council to address matters of doctrine and politics.

Niccolò Machiavelli (1469–1527) was a statesman, historian, and political philosopher and one of the most influential writers of the Renaissance. Born to an aristocratic family in Florence, Machiavelli served his city in a number of positions, including many diplomatic missions. After the Medici returned to power in 1512, they arrested, imprisoned, and tortured him for suspected treason. When released, Machiavelli retired to his estate near Florence, where he produced an impressive volume of work, the most influential of which was *Il principe* (The Prince, 1532). In *The Prince* he argued that politicians are guided not by ethical constraints but by the pursuit of power.

Guglielmo Marconi (1874–1937), born and educated in Bologna, was the electrical engineer and Nobel laureate celebrated as the inventor of the first successful radio-signaling system. After sending his first signals in 1895, Marconi patented his system and organized Marconi's Wireless Telegraph Company, Ltd., in London in 1897. In 1899 he communicated across the English Channel and in 1901 across the Atlantic Ocean. Marconi won a share of the Nobel Prize for Physics in 1909.

Giuseppe Mazzini (1805–1872), Italian republican patriot and political thinker, is recognized as one of the indispensable contributors to Italian unification. Born to a middle-class family, Mazzini studied law in his hometown at the University of Genoa. Increasingly opposed to the expansion of Piedmont-Sardinia, which annexed Genoa in 1815, he joined the clandestine patriotic group known as the *carbonari* in 1827. Arrested, imprisoned, and exiled, he founded his own group, Giovine Italia (Young Italy), in Marseille in 1831, arguing in his writings and speeches that the Italian people could drive their princes and their main oppressors, the Austrians, out of the peninsula. On a number of occasions Mazzini supported nationalist uprisings throughout much of Europe, which forced him to flee from France to Switzerland and eventually to England, where he spent much of the remainder of his life. During the revolutions of 1848, Mazzini returned to Italy to organize the Roman Republic. The French army overturned the

Republic in 1849, driving Mazzini once again into exile. He returned to participate in the wars of the Risorgimento in 1859 and again in 1870, after which ill health forced his retirement in Pisa. Regarded as a mystic and a prophet, Mazzini kept alive the drive for an Italian republic until the Piedmontese prevailed, just before his death, to impose their own monarchy on the new Italian state.

Lorenzo de' Medici (1449–1492). "Lorenzo the Magnificent" was a statesman and banker who made significant contributions to the Renaissance by patronizing artists and scholars, including Michelangelo, Botticelli, and Giovanni Pico della Mirandola. Born in Florence to a family of bankers, Lorenzo eventually gained control of both the Medici bank and the Florentine republic, which he governed well. After members of the Pazzi family failed in an attempt to assassinate him in 1478, he struck back at the conspirators, including supporters of Pope Sixtus IV, who in turn declared war on Florence. Lorenzo resolved the conflict through diplomatic skill, increasing his popularity, power, and reputation.

Benito Mussolini (1883–1945) was the founder of Fascism and the prime minister and dictator (Il Duce) of Italy. The son of a socialist blacksmith from the Romagna, Mussolini became a schoolteacher and a socialist journalist, then was named in 1912 editor of *Avanti!*, the Socialist Party organ. He first denounced World War I, then reversed himself and endorsed Italy's intervention. Forced to resign as editor, he launched his own newspaper, *Il Popolo d'Italia*. At the war's end, Mussolini founded the Fascio di Combattimento, the first Fascist organization. As Blackshirt violence spread and the Fascist movement grew, Mussolini organized the "March on Rome," a threat of insurrection, which led the king to invite him to form a coalition government. By 1926, Mussolini had consolidated his power in a regime that outlawed political opposition. He created the Corporate State to reorganize the economy, then embarked on an aggressive foreign policy that led him to invade Ethiopia (1935), to send troops into the Spanish Civil War (1936), to invade Albania (1939) and then France and Greece (1940). After a number of military setbacks as an ally of Germany in World War II, Mussolini was removed from power by the Fascist Grand Council in 1943. Rescued by Germans, he set up a puppet regime at Salò on Lake Garda. While attempting to escape in April 1945, Mussolini was captured and shot by Italian partisans.

Andrea Palladio (1508–1580). Born Andrea di Pietro dalla Gondola in Padua, he became one of the great European architects. He studied classical architecture in Rome, where he wrote *Antiquities of Rome* (1554), an important guide to Roman ruins, and several influential scholarly treatises on architecture. Palladio is known for his homes and public buildings around Vicenza and his Venetian churches, particularly San Francesco della Vigna, San Giorgio Maggiore, and Il Redentore. In each instance Palladio incorporated striking architectural features, including Roman porticos and carefully planned internal spaces.

Petrarch (1304–1374). Born in Arezzo, Francesco Petrarca became a poet and humanist of great influence. At age eight he moved with his family from Tuscany to Avignon, France, and subsequently traveled through France, the Low Countries, Germany, and Italy, usually in the diplomatic service of the Church and the Visconti family. His most famous work is the collection of Italian verses known as *Canzoniere* (Songbook), sonnets and other love poems inspired by a young woman named Laura whom he had met in 1327. Petrarch became a model for generations of European writers and in 1341 was named poet laureate by the Senate in Rome.

Marco Polo (c. 1254-1324). The renowned Venetian traveler and writer provided Europeans with their most definitive accounts of life in the Far East. As a teen, Polo traveled with his father and uncle to present-day Israel and Iran and across the Gobi Desert into China, where he entered the diplomatic corps of Kublai Khan. Two decades after leaving Venice he returned by way of India, the Persian Gulf, the Black Sea, and Constantinople. *The Travels of Marco Polo* became the most famous travel account ever written, providing a source of information, mapping, and inspiration for explorers such as Columbus to find new routes to the East.

Raphael (1483–1520), born Raffaelo Sanzio in Urbino, became one of the most important of the Renaissance painters. Raphael studied painting under Giovanni Santi and (probably) Timoteo Viti until 1499, when he joined the studio of Perugino, whose style his early painting reflects. After arriving in Florence in 1504, Raphael was influenced by the work of Michelangelo and Leonardo, particularly notable in *La Belle Jardinière* and the *Madonna of the Goldfinch*. In 1508, Raphael moved to Rome, where he benefited from papal patronage until his death. Notable in his Roman period are the frescoes in the Vatican in the room called the Stanza della Segnatura—including the renowned *School of Athens*—and his work as chief architect of St. Peter's (after 1514) and director of antiquities in the environs of Rome.

Giuseppe Verdi (1813–1901), one of the great composers in the history of opera, was born in Roncole in the duchy of Parma. After studying in

Busseto, Verdi returned to conduct for the Busseto Philharmonic Society in 1833. After five years he went to Milan, where he enjoyed some success at La Scala. His first important work was *Nabucco* (1842), which generated patriotic enthusiasm as a symbol of the oppression of the Italian people by the Austrians. In the 1850s, Verdi composed three operas that earned him lasting fame: *Rigoletto, Il Trovatore,* and *La Traviata.*

Leonardo da Vinci (1452–1519). An inventor, painter, sculptor, architect, and engineer, Leonardo is revered as one of the great artists of the Renaissance. Apprenticed to the Florentine Andrea del Verrocchio at age fifteen, Leonardo opened his own studio in 1478. He applied to his painting principles of scientific perspective, light, line, and color. In 1482, he accepted from the duke of Milan the position as court artist. There he developed military machinery, painted his renowned *Last Supper,* and experimented with equestrian sculpture. When the French invaded Milan in 1499 he traveled to Venice, where he completed his portrait of Isabella d'Este. He then returned to Florence, where his prolific work included the *Mona Lisa.* In his later life in Milan, in Rome, and at the court of the French king Francis I, Leonardo focused on scientific observations with which he filled the numerous notebooks that have fascinated observers throughout the centuries.

Glossary of Selected Terms

Aventine secession. In the midst of the Matteotti crisis of 1924, about 150 anti-Fascists walked out of Parliament in protest, modeling their tactic after the demonstration of Gaius Gracchus and his supporters during the era of the ancient Roman Republic.

Carbonari. This nineteenth-century secret society probably took its name ("charcoal burners") from the practice of meeting in caves by firelight. The *carbonari* organized in opposition to the various powers that governed Italy and are regarded as founders of the Risorgimento. Giuseppe Mazzini was a member until he left to organize Young Italy.

Committees of National Liberation. The CLNs provided the political direction for the armed resistance movement from the fall of 1943 through mid-1946. The CLNs conducted a full range of resistance actions, including sabotage and economic warfare, both in the liberated South and in the occupied regions of the Center and North, where the CLN of northern Italy conducted an insurrection against Germans and Mussolini's Salò Republic.

Corporate State. Based on a theory of corporativism whereby the state reorganized capital and labor in a new system of institutions, the Corporate State was shaped by the Fascist regime from 1926 to 1934. Although its achievements were marginal, the Corporate State provided ideological focus and a structure for experimentation that generated significant interest among Western governments during the Great Depression.

Etruscans. Inhabitants of the region of Etruria (modern Tuscany) who formed a confederation of cities extending from north of Florence to Rome. The Etruscans achieved their greatest influence between the seventh and fifth centuries B.C., shaping the emerging Roman culture of central Italy.

Historic compromise. In 1973, Italian Communist Party (PCI) leader Enrico Berlinguer announced that the party would cooperate with all "progressive" groups, thus moving the PCI away from revolutionary ideology toward parliamentary "Eurocommunism."

Illuministi. The Italian *philosophes*, or advocates of the philosophy of the eighteenth-century Enlightenment, challenged the traditional assumptions on which the prevailing political power, social structure, and religious authority were based. Among the prominent *Illuministi* was the Neapolitan philosopher Giambattista Vico.

Interventionist crisis. The onset of World War I in August 1914 provoked divisive political campaigning over Italy's neutrality. The interventionists, diverse advocates of Italy's participation, prevailed when Italy declared war on Austria-Hungary in May 1915, but they failed to mobilize Parliament or unify public support.

Irredentismo. The idea advocated by Italian nationalists in the late nineteenth and early twentieth centuries that Italy should claim its "unredeemed" territories, including Trieste and the Trentino, to complete the Risorgimento.

Matteotti crisis. A turning point in Mussolini's consolidation of power, the crisis began when Fascists kidnapped and beat to death reformist Socialist deputy Giacomo Matteotti in June 1924 after Matteotti denounced Fascist election violence. When Matteotti's body was found in August, pressure mounted on Mussolini. In January 1925, Mussolini delivered a defiant speech, after which a second wave of Fascist violence silenced all opposition.

Papal States. The Papal States were territories in Central Italy (from the southern border of Venezia to the south of Rome), controlled through much of medieval and modern history by the Roman Catholic Church until incorporated into the newly unified Kingdom of Italy in 1870. Originally granted to the papacy in 754 by the Frankish king Pepin the Short, the Papal States continued to expand into the modern era. Napoleon Bonaparte seized most of the papal territory by military force and kept it until the Congress of Vienna restored it to the papacy (protected by the Habsburg Empire) in 1815. Throughout much of the nineteenth century, the Papal States developed a reputation as being badly governed and underdeveloped. When the Piedmontese unified Italy, the papacy was forced to give up all territory except the Vatican.

Red Brigades. An extreme left-wing group that appeared in Italy in 1970, one of many extremist groups of both Left and Right that contributed to the violent terrorism of the "Years of Lead." Their most infamous deed occurred in the spring of 1978 when they kidnapped and executed former prime minister Aldo Moro.

Red Shirts. The volunteer campaigners who fought under Giuseppe Garibaldi in the patriot's 1860 invasion to liberate Sicily and southern Italy from Bourbon control included Garibaldi's "Thousand" volunteers. Mostly Northerners, they landed at Marsala and took Sicily from the Neapolitan Bourbon troops before crossing the straits to the Italian mainland and defeating the papal army at Castelfidardo in September. Red Shirt ranks had grown twenty-fold when they defeated the Bourbon forces in the decisive engagement on the River Volturno in October.

Risorgimento. The nineteenth-century movement for Italian unification (literally, "resurgence"or "rebirth") that culminated in the acquisition of Rome in 1870. Italy unified through military and diplomatic means primarily at the expense of Austria, the Neapolitan Bourbons, and the papacy.

Roman Question. The Roman Question involves the historic relationship between the Roman Catholic Church and the Italian state, in particular Italy's acquisition of the Papal States and the decision to make Rome the capital city of the new Italian Kingdom. The Vatican protested, as Pope Pius IX proclaimed himself a "prisoner in the Vatican." The papacy boycotted Italian politics, issued the *Non Expedit* (prohibiting Italian Catholics from voting), and aggravated an openly hostile relationship with the new state. Benito Mussolini mended church-state relations by negotiating the Lateran Accords in 1929.

Sacro egoismo. The term ("sacred egoism"), used by Prime Minister Antonio Salandra in a speech of October 1914, became a slogan for nationalists and irredentists to advocate Italy's "sacred duty" to enter World War I against the Austrian Empire in order to acquire its "unredeemed" territories.

Southern Question. The Southern Question, a reference to the discrepancies between North and South, has dominated Italian history since the period before unification. Although the major disparity has been the relative poverty and economic underdevelopment of the South, the Southern Question connotes social, cultural, and political differences as well.

Squadristi. The *squadristi* were the para-military arm of the Fascist movement, notoriously active in the years immediately following World War I. Derived from the *arditi* (Italy's assault troops), drawn largely from the ranks of restless middle-class youth, financed by property owners, and aided by local police, the *squadristi* carried out punitive attacks against socialist and labor supporters. Although the terrorism of the *squadristi* aided Mussolini's seizure of power, their undisciplined violence created problems for Il Duce by 1923 as he appealed to conservative interests to consolidate his power.

Tangentopoli. The major scandal known as "kickback city," originally uncovered in Milan in 1992, that eventually led to the indictment of hundreds of major politicians, civil servants, and businessmen in a web of corruption and bribes (*tangenti*). *Tangentopoli* contributed to the dissolution of major political parties and the initiation of electoral reforms that launched what some have termed the "second republic."

Trasformismo. The system of "transformism" was announced by Prime Minister Agostino Depretis in October 1876 when he built a coalition of parties to achieve a majority. Although *trasformismo* simply formalized a traditional practice of Italian politics, to the extent that it led members of Parliament to abandon party loyalty it blurred policy distinctions.

Triple Alliance. Italy was a partner with Germany and Austria-Hungary in the Triple Alliance (or Triplice), formed in 1882. Strained relations with Austria-Hungary over the Balkans and the Adriatic Sea left Italy alienated from its partners until the outbreak of World War I, when Italy refused to honor its commitment to enter the war. Secretly offered substantial territorial promises by the British, Italy signed the London Pact in 1915, joining the Entente powers against its former allies.

Young Italy (Giovane Italia) was established in July 1831 in Marseille, France by the patriot Giuseppe Mazzini as a nationalist organization dedicated to winning the unification of an Italian republic. Mazzinians organized Young Italy cells in a number of Italian cities, inspired by the idealistic call of their prophet that Italians would win their independence through spontaneous popular uprisings. Much to the dismay of the Mazzinians, the armies of the King of Piedmont unified Italy through military campaigns. However, Young Italy is credited with keeping alive the movement for a democratic republic that eventually materialized after World War II.

Bibliographic Essay

This bibliography provides an organized list of English-language books for further reading in Italian history. It emphasizes recent works and is not complete. However, readers will find more comprehensive bibliographies in print, some of which are incorporated into these volumes. In addition to these books, a rich collection of periodical literature exists in historical journals.

GENERAL AND REFERENCE WORKS

There are a number of good general works and reference sources available for the study of Italian history. Among the bibliographies, in addition to those provided by the historical surveys listed below, are the following, each limited to a historical period: Frank J. Coppa and William Roberts, *Modern Italian History: An Annotated Bibliography* (New York, 1990); Charles F. Delzell, *Italy in the Twentieth Century* (Washington, D.C., 1980); Clara Lovett, *Contemporary Italy: A Selective Bibliography* (Washington, D.C., 1985); Peter Lange, *Studies on Italy* (Turin, 1977); and Borden W. Painter Jr., ed., *Perspectives on Italy* (Hartford, 1992). Two historical dictionaries have been published, again limited to historical era: Frank J. Coppa, editor-in-chief, *Dictionary of Modern Italian History* (Westport, 1985), and Philip V.

Cannistraro, editor-in-chief, *Historical Dictionary of Fascist Italy* (Westport, 1982).

A number of surveys of Italian history exist, most beginning in some phase of the modern era. Included are Spencer M. Di Scala, *Italy from Revolution to Republic: 1700 to the Present* (Boulder, 1998); Denis Mack Smith, *Modern Italy: A Political History* (Ann Arbor, 1997); Christopher Duggan, *A Concise History of Italy* (Cambridge, 1994); Martin Clark, *Modern Italy, 1871–1995* (New York, 1996); and Stuart Woolf, *A History of Italy* (London, 1979).

Numerous specialized studies follow particular topics or issues over long periods. Among them are Michael P. Carroll's analyses of popular religious practices, *Madonnas That Maim: Popular Catholicism in Italy since the Fifteenth Century* (Baltimore, 1992) and *Veiled Threats: The Logic of Popular Catholicism in Italy* (Baltimore, 1996); Jane Schneider, ed., *Italy's "Southern Question": Orientalism in One Country* (Oxford, 1988); Vera Zamagni, *The Economic History of Italy, 1860–1990* (New York, 1993); Richard J. G. Bosworth's diplomatic history, *Italy and the Wider World, 1860–1960* (London, 1996). A useful survey of literary works is Christopher Cairns, *Italian Literature* (London, 1977). For a survey of women writers, see Sharon Wood, *Italian Women's Writing, 1860–1994* (London, 1995).

CHAPTER 2

There are number of good studies of Italy in the ancient and classical ages, most limited by chronological or topical scope, and a number of original sources have been translated. For sources, see Naphtali Lewis and Meyer Reinhold, eds., *Roman Civilization: Selected Readings*, 2 vols. (New York, 1990); Robert K. Sherk, ed., *The Roman Empire: Augustus to Hadrian* (Cambridge, 1988); David Braund, ed., *Augustus to Nero: A Sourcebook on Roman History, 31 B.C. to A.D. 68* (London, 1985); Barbara Levick, *The Government of the Roman Empire: A Sourcebook* (London, 1985). John Wacher, ed., presents a survey of extant archaeological evidence in *The Roman World*, 2 vols. (London, 1987). The recently republished classic comprehensive study is Theodor Mommsen, Barbara Wiedemann, and Alexander Demandt, eds, Clare Krojzl, trans., *The History of Rome*, 4 vols. (London, 1999).

Books about the period from Bronze Age Italy through the Roman Republic and the transition to Empire abound. Among the relatively recent titles are David Ridgway and Francesca R. Ridgway, eds., *Italy before the Romans* (Edinburgh, 1979); A. M. Bietti Sestieri, *The Iron-Age Community of Osteria dell'Osa* (Cambridge, 1992); Peter Garnsey, *Famine and Food Supply in*

Graeco-Roman Antiquity (Cambridge, 1988); and Christopher J. Smith, *Early Rome and Latium: Economy and Society, c. 100 to 500 B.C.* (Oxford, 1995).

On the Etruscans, see R. M. Ogilvie, *Early Rome and the Etruscans* (London, 1976); Michael Grant, *The Etruscans* (London, 1980); and N. Spivey and Simon Stoddart, *Etruscan Italy: An Archaeological History* (London, 1990).

Studies of the Republic include Michael Crawford, *The Roman Republic* (London, 1992); Tim J. Cornell, *The Beginning of Rome* (London, 1995); Kathryn Lomas, *Rome and the Western Greeks, 350 B.C.–A.D. 200* (London, 1993); T. P. Wiseman, ed., *Roman Political Life, 90 B.C.–A.D. 69* (Exeter, 1985); Peter Brunt, *The Fall of the Roman Republic and Related Essays* (Oxford, 1988); Kurt A. Raaflaub, ed., *Social Struggles in Archaic Rome: New Perspectives on the Conflict of the Orders* (Berkeley, 1986); Richard E. Mitchell, *Patricians and Plebeians* (Ithaca, 1992); Ronald Syme, *The Roman Revolution* (Oxford, 1939); Claude Nicolet, *The World of the Citizen in Republican Rome* (London, 1980); Alan E. Astin, *Cato the Censor* (Oxford, 1978); Elizabeth Rawson, *Intellectual Life in the Late Roman Republic* (London, 1985); and Erich S. Gruen, *Culture and National Identity in Republican Rome* (Ithaca, 1992).

Of the works on the early Roman Empire, see S. M. Wells, *The Roman Empire* (London, 1992); Fergus G. B. Millar, *The Roman Empire and Its Neighbors* (London, 1981); Martin Goodman, *The Roman World, 44 B.C.–A.D. 180* (London, 1997); Howard H. Scullard, *A History of the Roman World 753 to 146 B.C.* (London, 1991); Ronald Syme, *The Augustan Aristocracy* (Oxford, 1986); Fergus G. B. Millar and E. Segal, eds., *Caesar Augustus: Seven Aspects* (Oxford, 1984).

Among the studies of Roman politics and government, see Benjamin H. Isaac, *The Limits of Empire: The Roman Army in the East* (Oxford, 1992); Andrew W. Lintott, *Imperium Romanum: Politics and Administration* (London, 1993); Peter Garnsey and Richard Saller, *The Roman Empire: Economy, Society and Culture* (London, 1987).

The classic social history of the Empire is Mikhail I. Rostovtzeff, rev. P. M. Fraser, *The Social and Economic History of the Roman Empire* (Oxford, 1957). See also Peter Garnsey and Richard Saller, *The Roman Empire: Economy, Society and Culture* (London, 1987); Richard Duncan-Jones, *The Economy of the Roman Empire: Quantitative Studies* (Cambridge, 1982) and *Structure and Scale in the Roman Economy* (Cambridge, 1990). Useful specialized social histories include Jane F. Gardner, *Women in Roman Law and Society* (London, 1986); Thomas Wiedemann, *Greek and Roman Slavery* (London, 1981); and Jane F. Gardner and Thomas Weidemann, *The Roman Household: A Sourcebook* (London, 1991).

Religious studies abound. On the ancient religions that survived in the Roman Empire, see Mary Beard and John A. North, eds., *Pagan Priests* (London, 1990); Robin Lane Fox, *Pagans and Christians in the Mediterranean World of the Second Century A.D. to the Conversion of Constantine* (Harmondsworth, 1986); Ramsay MacMullen, *Paganism in the Roman Empire* (New Haven, 1981); H. S. Versnel, *Tre Unus: Isis, Dionysus, Hermes: Three Studies in Henotheism* (Leiden, 1990).

Modern studies on Judaism include E. P. Sanders, *Paul and Palestinian Judaism: A Comparison of Patterns of Religion* (London, 1977) and *Judaism: Practice and Belief, 63 B.C.E.–66 C.E.* (London, 1992); Shaye J. D. Cohen, *From the Maccabees to the Mishnah* (Philadelphia, 1987); Lawrence H. Schiffman, *From Text to Tradition: A History of Second Temple and Rabbinic Judaism* (Hoboken, 1991).

On Christianity in the Roman Empire, see John Dominic Crossan, *The Historical Jesus: The Life of a Mediterranean Jewish Peasant* (Edinburgh, 1993); E. P. Sanders, *Jesus and Judaism* (London, 1987); Henry Chadwick, *The Early Church* (London, 1993); W. H. C. Frend, *The Rise of Christianity* (London, 1984); Wayne A. Meeks, *The First Urban Christians: The Social World of the Apostle Paul* (New Haven, 1983).

Historians have assessed various aspects of the Empire as a political unit. Among them are Guy MacLean Rogers, *The Sacred Identity of Ephesos: Foundation Myths of a Roman City* (London, 1991), and A. N. Sherwin-White, *The Roman Citizenship* (Oxford, 1973).

A number of historians have examined the Roman army, including R. MacMullen, *Soldier and Civilian in the Later Roman Empire* (Cambridge, Mass., 1963); George Ronald Watson, *The Roman Soldier* (London, 1969); Graham Webster, *The Roman Imperial Army of the First and Second Centuries A.D.* (London, 1985); and Lawrence J. Keppie, *The Making of the Roman Army: From Republic to Empire* (London, 1984).

CHAPTER 3

A few important original sources from the Medieval era have been translated. Among them are Paul the Deacon, trans. W. D. Foulke, *History of the Langobards* (Philadelphia, 1907); Katherine Fischer Drew, trans., *The Lombard Laws* (Philadelphia, 1973). Capitularies (decrees) and court cases are translated in H. R. Loyn and J. C. Percival, *The Reign of Charlemagne* (London, 1975); Liutprand of Cremona, trans. F. A. Wright, *Works* (London, 1930). Commercial documents are translated in Robert S. Lopez and I. W. Raymond, *Medieval Trade in the Mediterranean World* (London, 1955).

Of the general studies of Medieval Italy, the best are Donald A. Bullough, *The Age of Charlemagne* (London, 1965) and *Italy and Her Invaders* (Nottingham, 1968); David Herlihy, Robert S. Lopez, and Vsevolod.

Slessarev, eds., *Economy, Society and Government in Medieval Italy* (Kent, Ohio, 1969); Arnold Hugh Jones, *The Decline of the Ancient World* (London, 1966) and *The Later Roman Empire, 284–602* (Oxford, 1964); J. K. Hyde, *Society and Politics in Medieval Italy* (London, 1973); Giovanni Tabacco, *The Struggle for Power in Medieval Italy: Structures of Political Power* (Cambridge, 1989); Chris Wickham, *Early Medieval Italy: Central Power and Local Society, 400–1000* (London, 1981); and *The New Cambridge Medieval History,* 7 vols. (Cambridge, 1995–2000).

Scholars have produced a number of good works on Medieval politics in Italy. On the late Roman and Ostrogothic periods, see John B. Bury, *History of the Later Roman Empire,* 2 vols. (London, 1923). The Lombard and Byzantine period is treated in D. Talbot Rice, ed., *The Dark Ages* (London, 1965); J. M. Wallace-Hadrill, *The Barbarian West* (London, 1966); and T. S. Brown, *Social Structure and the Hierarchy of Officialdom in Byzantine Italy* (London, 1981). For the Carolingian era, Italy is addressed in the general histories, including Heinrich Fichtenau, *The Carolingian Empire* (Oxford, 1977); and Donald A. Bullough, *The Age of Charlemagne* (London, 1965). Very few studies exist on Italy in the period of the German Empire except in the relevant chapters of general works such as Geoffrey Barraclough, *Origins of Modern Germany* (Oxford, 1947) and *The Crucible of Europe* (London, 1976).

On the major figures of Medieval Italy, see David Abulafia, *Frederick II: A Medieval Emperor* (London, 1988); Louis Halphen, *Charlemagne and the Carolingian Empire,* trans. G. de Nie (Amsterdam, 1977); John Moorhead, *Theoderic in Italy* (Oxford, 1993).

A number of studies of particular Italian communes exist. Among them are William M. Bowsky, *A Medieval Italian Commune: Siena under the Nine, 1287–1355* (Berkeley, 1981); John J. Norwich, *Venice: The Rise to Empire* (London, 1977); Daniel Philip Waley, *The Italian City-Republics* (London, 1988).

Medieval Sicily has generated substantial scholarly interest. See Denis Mack Smith, *Medieval Sicily, 800–1713* (London, 1968); Donald Matthew, *The Norman Kingdom of Sicily* (Cambridge, 1992); Stephan Epstein, *An Island for Itself: Economic Development and Social Change in Late Medieval Sicily* (Cambridge, 1992).

On the Medieval Roman Church, see Jeffrey Richards, *The Popes and the Papacy in the Early Middle Ages, 476–752* (1979); Peter Llewellyn, *Rome in the Dark Ages* (London, 1971); Peter Partner, *The Lands of St. Peter* (London, 1972).

CHAPTER 4

A number of English-language sources and historical surveys of the Renaissance exist. A good reference is John R. Hale, ed., *A Concise Encyclopedia of the Italian Renaissance* (London, 1981). Among the better historical surveys are Jacob Burckhardt's classic *The Civilization of the Renaissance in Italy*, trans. S. G. C. Middlemore (Harmondsworth, 1990); Wallace K. Ferguson, *The Renaissance in Historical Thought* (New York, 1982); Eugenio Garin, ed., trans. L. G. Cochrane, *Renaissance Characters* (Chicago, 1991); John N. Stephens, *The Italian Renaissance: The Origins of Intellectual and Artistic Change before the Reformation* (London, 1990); Denys Hay and John Law, *Italy in the Age of the Renaissance, 1380–1530* (London, 1989); Trevor Dean and Chris Wickham, eds., *City and Countryside in Late Medieval and Renaissance Italy* (London, 1990); Benjamin G. Kohl and Allison Andrews Smith, *Major Problems in the History of the Italian Renaissance* (Lexington, Mass., 1995).

Renaissance Florence has generated numerous scholarly inquiries. Among them are Gene Adam Brucker, *The Civic World of Early Renaissance Florence* (Princeton, 1987); Peter Denley and C. Elam, eds., *Florence and Italy: Renaissance Studies in Honour of Nicolai Rubinstein* (London, 1988); Hans Baron, *In Search of Florentine Civic Humanism* (Princeton, 1988); David Herlihy and C. Klapisch-Zuber, *Tuscans and Their Families* (New Haven, 1985) and *Florence, Rome and the Origins of the Renaissance* (Oxford, 1986); Ann G. Carmichael, *Plague and the Poor in Early Renaissance Florence* (Cambridge, 1986).

On other Renaissance cities, see Lauro Martines, *Power and Imagination: City-States in Renaissance Italy* (London, 1980); Jerry H. Bentley, *Politics and Culture in Renaissance Naples* (Princeton, 1987); Trevor Dean, *Land and Power in Late Medieval Ferrara: The Rule of the Este, 1350–1450* (Cambridge, 1987); John J. Norwich, *Venice: The Greatness and the Fall* (London, 1981); David Chambers and Brian Pullen, eds., *Venice: A Documentary History, 1450–1630* (Oxford, 1992).

On the history of the visual arts, see Frederick Hartt, *A History of Italian Renaissance Art: Painting, Sculpture, and Architecture* (London, 1970); Michael Baxandall, *Painting and Experience in Fifteenth-Century Italy* (Oxford, 1972); John White, *Art and Architecture in Italy, 1250–1400* (New Haven, 1993); Ernest Hans Gombrich, *Symbolic Images: Studies in the Art of the Renaissance* (Oxford, 1985); F. W. Kent and Patricia Simons, eds., *Patronage, Art and Society in Renaissance Italy* (Oxford, 1987).

Among the cultural and intellectual interpretations of Renaissance Italy are Donald R. Kelley, *Renaissance Humanism* (Boston, 1991); Jill Kraye, ed., *The Cambridge Companion to Renaissance Humanism* (Cambridge, 1996); Paul

F. Grendler, *Schooling in Renaissance Italy: Literacy and Learning, 1300–1600* (Princeton, 1988); D. Hay, *The Church in Italy in the Fifteenth Century* (Cambridge, 1977); Michael Baxandall, *Giotto and the Orators* (Oxford, 1996); Timothy Verdon and John Henderson, eds., *Christianity and the Renaissance* (Syracuse, 1990); Diana Norman, ed., *Siena, Florence and Padua: Art, Society and Religion, 1280–1400*, 2 vols. (New Haven, 1995).

Among the better social histories are Martin Wackernagel, *The World of the Florentine Renaissance Artist* (Princeton, 1981); Bruce Cole, *Italian Art, 1250–1550: The Relation of Renaissance Art to Life and Society* (New York, 1987); Mary Hollingsworth, *Patronage in Renaissance Italy: From 1400 to the Early Sixteenth Century* (London, 1994); Evelyn Welch, *Art and Society in Italy, 1350–1500* (Oxford, 1997); Richard A. Goldthwaite, *Wealth and the Demand for Art in Italy, 1300–1600* (Baltimore, 1993); Alison Brown, ed., *Language and Images of Renaissance Italy* (Oxford, 1995); Lisa Jardine, *Worldly Goods: A New History of the Renaissance* (London, 1996); Daniel Williman, ed., *The Black Death* (New York, 1982). A number of new studies of women in Renaissance Italy have appeared in the past decade or so. See Margaret L. King, *Women of the Renaissance* (Chicago, 1991); Samuel K. Cohn, *Women in the Streets: Sex and Power in the Italian Renaissance* (Baltimore, 1996); Thomas Kuehn, *Law, Family, and Women: Towards a Legal Anthropology in Renaissance Italy* (Chicago, 1991); Letizia Panizza, ed., *Culture, Society and Women in Renaissance Italy* (Manchester, 1997).

Studies of the artists of the Italian Renaissance include the classic Giorgio Vasari, G. Bull, trans., *Lives of the Artists*, 2 vols. (Harmondsworth, 1965, 1987), which can be usefully accompanied by Patricia Lee Rubin, *Giorgio Vasari: Art and History* (New Haven, 1995); Quentin Skinner, *Machiavelli* (Oxford, 1981); Antonio Manetti and Howard Saalman, eds., *The Life of Brunelleschi* (University Park, 1970); Bruce Cole, *The Renaissance Artist at Work from Pisano to Titian* (London, 1983); A. Thomas, *The Painter's Practice in Renaissance Tuscany* (Cambridge, 1995).

CHAPTER 5

Two important interpretations of the post-Renaissance are Eric Cochrane, *Italy, 1530–1630*, Jules Kirschner, ed. (London and New York, 1988) and *Florence in the Forgotten Centuries* (Chicago, 1973). Another useful study of Florence in this period is R. Burr Litchfield's *Emergence of a Bureaucracy: The Florentine Patricians, 1530–1790* (Princeton, 1986). Several studies on Venice have contributed to the English-language literature of this period. A relatively recent work is Robert C. Davis, *Shipbuilders of the Venetian Arsenal: Workers and Workplace in the Preindustrial City* (Baltimore, 1991).

Antonio Calabria, *The Cost of Empire: The Finances of the Kingdom of Naples in the Time of Spanish Rule* (New York, 1991), examines the deterioration of that city.

Although much of the best literature on the Italian Enlightenment remains untranslated, several important works are available. Among the best are Dino Carpanetto and Giuseppe Ricuperati, *Italy in the Age of Reason, 1685–1789* (London, 1987); and Franco Venturi, *Italy and the Enlightenment* (London, 1972). Additionally, there are a number of excellent studies focused more narrowly, including Eric Cochrane, *Tradition and Enlightenment in the Tuscan Academies, 1690–1800* (Chicago, 1961); Benedetto Croce, *History of the Kingdom of Naples* (Chicago, 1970); Harold Acton, *The Bourbons of Naples* (London, 1956); and Denis Mack Smith, *A History of Sicily* (London, 1968). The Enlightenment era is examined in the context of broader histories of Venice by William H. McNeill, *Venice: The Hinge of Europe* (Chicago, 1974); and Frederic C. Lane, *Venice: A Maritime Republic* (Baltimore, 1973). Among the various social and economic studies of the Enlightenment era are Daniel Klang, *Tax Reform in Eighteenth-Century Lombardy* (New York, 1977); Stuart Woolf, *The Poor in Western Europe in the Eighteenth and Nineteenth Centuries* (London, 1986); Maurice Vaussard, *Daily Life in Eighteenth-Century Italy* (New York, 1963). See also Maeve Edith Albano, *Vico and Providence* (New York, 1986). Some of Vico's major works have been translated: Giambattista Vico, *On the Most Ancient Wisdom of the Italians*, trans. L. M. Palmer (Ithaca, 1987) and *Selected Writings*, ed. and trans. Leon Pomba (Cambridge, 1982). See also Michael Collins, *Opera and Vivaldi* (Austin, 1984).

Travelers' reflections provide a rich source of literature to frame this period. Among the most interesting are Arthur Young, *Travels during the Years 1787, 1788 and 1789* (London, 1794); Johann Wolfgang von Goethe, *Italian Journey* (New York, 1989); and Frank Brady and Frederick A. Pottle, eds., *Boswell on the Grand Tour: Italy, Corsica and France* (London, 1955).

CHAPTER 6

English-language studies of the French Revolution and Napoleonic eras in Italy are surprisingly limited. An excellent overview is Stuart Woolf, *A History of Italy, 1700–1860* (London, 1988). See also Frederick C. Schneid and Arthur Ferrill, eds., *Soldiers of Napoleon's Kingdom of Italy: Army, State, and Society, 1800–1815* (Boulder, 1995). John A. Davis has provided an excellent investigation of the brigands' war in *Conflict and Control: Law and Order in Nineteenth-Century Italy* (Atlantic Highlands, 1988). Milton Findley analyzes resistance to French rule in *The Most Monstrous of Wars* (Columbia,

S.C., 1996). Renato Pasta assesses the career of a Tuscan reformer in *The Making of a Notable: Giovanni Fabroni between Enlightened Absolutism and Napoleonic Administration* (Princeton, 1985). See also Michael Broers, *Napoleonic Imperialism and the Savoyard Monarchy, 1733–1821: State Building in Piedmont* (Lewiston, N.Y., 1997). A very useful new anthology is John A. Davis, ed., *Italy in the Nineteenth Century* (Oxford, 2000).

Standard works on Restoration era diplomacy are René Albrecht Carrié, *A Diplomatic History of Europe since the Congress of Vienna* (New York, 1973); Alan Reinerman, *Austria and the Papacy in the Age of Metternich I: Between Conflict and Cooperation, 1809–1830* (Washington, D.C., 1979) and *II: Revolution and Reaction, 1830–1838* (Washington, D.C., 1989); John Martin Robinson, *Cardinal Consalvi, 1757–1824* (New York, 1987); E. E. Y. Hales, *Revolution and the Papacy 1769–1846* (London, 1960); and A. C. Jemolo, *Church and State in Italy, 1850–1950* (Oxford, 1960).

On the revolutions that occurred from the 1820s through 1848 and the political and cultural conditions of that period, there are a number of good works. Included are George T. Romani, *The Neapolitan Revolution of 1820–1821* (Evanston, 1950); Elizabeth Eisenstein, *The First Professional Revolutionary: Filippo Michele Buonarotti* (Cambridge, 1959); George Fitz-Hardinge Berkeley, *Italy in the Making, Vol. I: 1815 to 1846; Vol. II: June 1846 to 1 January 1848; Vol. III: January 1, 1848 to November 16, 1868* (Cambridge, 1968).

CHAPTER 7

The era of Italian unification has produced a rich legacy of scholarship. Among the general works are Harry Hearder, *Italy in the Age of the Risorgimento, 1790–1870* (New York, 1983); Derek Beales, *The Risorgimento and the Unification of Italy,* Vol. 2 (New York, 1971); Edgar Holt, *Risorgimento: The Making of Italy, 1815–1879* (New York, 1970); Bolton King, *History of Italian Unity* (New York, 1967); John A. Davis and Paul Ginsborg, *Society and Politics in the Age of the Risorgimento: Essays in Honour of Denis Mack Smith* (Cambridge, 1991); Lucy Riall, *The Italian Risorgimento: State, Society and National Unification* (London, 1994).

Compilations of Giuseppe Mazzini's writings include *Life and Writings of Joseph Mazzini* (London, 1890–91), 6 vols.; Nagendranath Gangulee, ed., *Giuseppe Mazzini, Selected Writings* (London, 1945); Bolton King, ed., *Mazzini's Letters* (London, 1930); T. Okey, ed., *Essays by Joseph Mazzini* (London, 1894); Ignazio Silone, *The Living Thoughts of Mazzini* (New York, 1939); and Giuseppe Mazzini, *Letters to an English Family* (London, 1920–22), 3 vols.

Among the works on Mazzini are Roland Sarti, *Mazzini: A Life for the Religion of Politics* (Westport, 1997); Gaetano Salvemini, *Mazzini* (London, 1956); Denis Mack Smith, *Mazzini* (New Haven, 1994).

Historians have produced numerous good works in English on Camillo di Cavour. Included are the classic Cavour biography by William R. Thayer, *The Life and Times of Cavour,* 2 vols. (New York, 1971); Denis Mack Smith, *Cavour and Garibaldi: A Study in Political Conflict* (Cambridge, 1985); Harry Hearder, *Cavour* (London and New York, 1994).

The standard work on Giuseppe Garibaldi is George MacCaulay Trevelyan's trilogy: *Garibaldi's Defense of the Roman Republic* (London, 1907); *Garibaldi and the Thousand* (London, 1909); and *Garibaldi and the Making of Italy* (London, 1919). More recent studies of Garibaldi include Jasper Ridley, *Garibaldi* (New York, 1974); Denis Mack Smith, *Garibaldi: A Great Life in Brief* (New York, 1956); David Larg, *Giuseppe Garibaldi* (New York, 1970). See also Clara Lovett, *Giuseppe Garibaldi, 1807–1882: A Biographical Essay and a Selective List of Reading Materials* (Washington, D.C., 1983).

Monographs and topical studies have illuminated the history of this period as well. Among the more important are C. J. Lowe and F. Marzari, *Italian Foreign Policy, 1870–1940* (London, 1975); Raymond Grew, *A Sterner Plan for Italian Unity: The Italian National Society in the Risorgimento* (Princeton, 1963); Clara Lovett, *The Democratic Movement in Italy, 1830–1876* (Cambridge, Mass., 1982); Steven C. Hughes, *Crime, Disorder and the Risorgimento* (New York, 1994); John A. Davis, *Merchants, Monopolists and Contractors: A Study of Economic Activity and Society in Bourbon Naples, 1815–60* (New York, 1981); Paul M. Howell, *Capitalism in the Risorgimento* (Berkeley, 1983); Lucy Riall, *Sicily and the Unification of Italy* (Oxford, 1998).

The post-Risorgimento era has attracted wide-ranging scholarly interest. The classic interpretation is Benedetto Croce's *A History of Italy, 1871–1915* (Oxford, 1929). An excellent general treatment is found in Christopher Seton-Watson, *Italy from Liberalism to Fascism, 1870–1925* (London, 1967). Two military histories are John Whittam, *The Politics of the Italian Army, 1861–1918* (London, 1977); and John Gooch, *Army, State and Society in Italy, 1870–1915* (New York, 1989). Several historians have examined the Vatican in the nineteenth century, including Frank Coppa, *Cardinal Giacomo Antonelli and Papal Politics in European Affairs* (Albany, 1990); and E. E. Y. Hales, *Italy and the Vatican at War* (New York, 1968). An excellent economic history that includes the pre-Fascist era as well is Gianni Toniolo, *An Economic History of Liberal Italy, 1850–1918* (London, 1990). Roland Sarti's *Long Live the Strong* (Amherst, 1985) analyzes change in rural Apennine mountain villages, and David Kertzer examines social issues in *Family Life in Central Italy, 1880–1910* (New Brunswick, N.J., 1984), *Sacrifices for Honor*

(Boston, 1993), and *The Kidnapping of Edgardo Mortara* (New York, 1997). On women writers of this era, see Lucienne Kroha, *The Woman Writer in Late-Nineteenth-Century Italy* (Lewiston, N.Y., 1992).

Several good studies of the Southern Problem exist, including Robert Lumley and Jonathon Morris, eds., *The New History of the Italian South: The Mezzogiorno Revisited* (Exeter, 1997); Richard Drake, *Byzantium for Rome: The Politics of Nostalgia in Umbertian Italy, 1878–1900* (Chapel Hill, 1980). Two other social histories with a southern focus are Frank Snowden, *Naples in the Time of Cholera* (Cambridge, 1995); and Dino Cinel, *The National Integration of Italian Return Migration, 1870–1929* (Cambridge, 1991).

Three histories of the *mafia* are Eric Hobsbawm, *Primitive Rebels* (Manchester, 1959); Anton Blok, *The Mafia of a Sicilian Village* (New York, 1975); and Henner Hess, *Mafia and Mafiosi: The Structure of Power* (Lexington, Mass., 1973).

Left-wing politics in the post-Risorgimento era has generated a substantial amount of literature. Included are Nunzio Pernicone, *Italian Anarchism, 1864–1892* (Princeton, 1993); Richard Hostetter, *The Italian Socialist Movement, Vol. I: Origins (1860–1882)* (New York, 1958); T. R. Ravindranathan, *Bakunin and the Italians* (Montreal, 1988); Manuel Gonzales, *Andrea Costa and the Rise of Socialism in the Romagna* (Washington, D.C., 1980).

CHAPTER 8

The historical debates centering around Giovanni Giolitti and Italy's role in World War I have produced a wealth of literature. Although much of the work is in Italian, there are numerous English-language histories. Alexander De Grand's new biography, *Giovanni Giolitti and Liberal Italy from the Challenge of Mass Politics to the Rise of Fascism, 1882–1922* (Westport, 2001), contributes to the reassessment of Giolitti begun by A. William Salomone in *Italy in the Giolittian Era: Italian Democracy in the Making, 1900–1914,* 2nd. ed. (Philadelphia, 1960). An important primary source in English is Giovanni Giolitti, *Memoirs of My Life* (London, 1923).

Italian leftist movements have produced an abundant literature in English. Socialist politics are the topic of James E. Miller, *From Elite to Mass Politics: Italian Socialism in the Giolittian Era* (Kent, Ohio, 1990), Spencer Di Scala, *Dilemmas of Italian Socialism: The Politics of Filippo Turati* (Amherst, 1980); and Alexander De Grand, *The Italian Left in the Twentieth Century* (Bloomington, 1989). David D. Roberts investigates left-wing origins of Fascism in *The Syndicalist Tradition and Italian Fascism* (Chapel Hill, 1979). See also Elda Gentili Sappi, *If Eight Houses Seem Too Few: Mobilization of Women Workers in the Italian Rice Fields* (Albany, 1991).

An excellent assortment of studies of pre-Fascist culture exists in English. Among the best are Walter Adamson, *Avant-Garde Florence: From Modernism to Fascism* (Cambridge, 1993); James Thrall Soby and Alfred H. Barr, *Twentieth-Century Italian Art*, 2 vols. (New York, 1949), and Emily Braun, ed., *Italian Art in the 20th Century* (Munich and London, 1989) both include sections on pre-Fascist artistic production, while Richard A. Etlin explores *Modernism in Italian Architecture, 1890–1940* (Cambridge, Mass., 1991). Closely related to formal culture are studies of Italian nationalism in the pre-war period, including Alexander De Grand, *The Italian Nationalist Association and the Rise of Fascism in Italy* (Lincoln, 1978); and Ronald S. Cunsolo, *Italian Nationalism from its Origins to World War II* (Malabar, Fla., 1990).

On the major figures of the pre-Fascist era, see Denis Mack Smith, *Italy and Its Monarchy* (New Haven, 1979); Geoffrey Haywood, *Failure of a Dream: Sidney Sonnino and the Rise and Fall of Liberal Italy 1847–1922* (Florence, 1999); Charles Killinger, *Gaetano Salvemini: A Biography* (Westport, 2002); Ester Coen, *Umberto Boccioni* (New York, 1988); Philippe Jullian, *d'Annunzio* (London, 1972); Tom Antongini, *D'Annunzio* (New York, 1971); Ettore Albertoni, *Mosca and the Theory of Elitism* (Oxford, 1985); Joseph Lopreato, *Vilfredo Pareto* (New York, 1965); David D. Roberts, *Benedetto Croce and the Uses of Historicism* (Berkeley, 1987).

A number of other important topical histories exist, including many social and economic histories. Franklin Hugh Adler, *Italian Industrialists from Liberalism to Fascism: The Political Development of the Industrial Bourgeoisie, 1906–1934* (Cambridge, 1995), and Douglas J. Forsyth, *The Crisis of Liberal Italy: Monetary and Financial Policy, 1914–1922* (Cambridge, 1993) assess the economics of the period. Social histories include Mary Gibson, *Prostitution and the State in Italy, 1860–1915* (New Brunswick, N.J., 1986); Edward Muir and Guido Ruggiero, *Sex and Gender in Historical Perspective* (Baltimore, 1990).

The era of the Great War has been exhaustively studied. William A. Renzi's *In the Shadow of the Sword: Italy's Neutrality and Entrance into the Great War, 1914–1915* (New York, 1987) assesses the interventionist crisis, while a number of good books evaluate the diplomatic dimensions: H. James Burgwyn, *The Legend of the Mutilated Victory: Italy, the Great War, and the Paris Peace Conference, 1915–1919* (Westport, 1993); Richard J. B. Bosworth, *Italy, the Least of the Great Powers: Italian Foreign Policy before the First World War* (Cambridge, 1979) and *Italy and the Approach to the First World War* (London, 1983). The standard treatment of Italy's role at Versailles is René Albrecht-Carrié, *Italy at the Paris Peace Conference* (New York, 1938).

CHAPTER 9

Historians have focused great attention on the varied dimensions of the period between 1919 and 1945, most of them framed in controversy. General works on Fascist history include Alan Cassels, *Fascist Italy* (Arlington Heights, Ill., 1985); Alexander De Grand, *Italian Fascism: Its Origins and Development* (Lincoln, 1989); David Forgacs, ed., *Rethinking Italian Fascism: Capitalism, Populism, and Culture* (London, 1986). In *Fascism: An Informal Introduction to Its Theory and Practice* (New Brunswick, N.J., 1976), Renzo De Felice provides a summary of his influential views on Mussolini and Fascism. Very useful reference tools are Philip V. Cannistraro, editor-in-chief, *Historical Dictionary of Fascist Italy* (Westport, 1982); a number of collections of documents, including Roland Sarti, ed., *The Ax Within: Italian Fascism in Action* (New York, 1974); Charles Delzell, ed., *Mediterranean Fascism, 1919–1945* (New York, 1971); and Roger Griffin, ed., *Fascism* (Oxford, 1995). Emil Ludwig, *Talks with Mussolini* (Boston, 1933), also serves as a good documentary source.

Studies of left-wing influences in this period include an array of works on Antonio Gramsci, including John Cammett, *Antonio Gramsci and the Origins of Italian Communism* (Stanford, 1967), and, more recently, Richard Bellamy and Darrow Schecter, *Gramsci and the Italian State* (Manchester, 1993), and Dante Germino, *Antonio Gramsci: Architect of a New Politics* (Baton Rouge, 1990). Also important is Alexander De Grand's biography of Angelo Tasca, *In Stalin's Shadow* (DeKalb, 1986).

On the rise of Fascism and its connection with World War I, contemporaries produced some notable early interpretations: Gaetano Salvemini, *The Origins of Fascism in Italy* (New York, 1973); Ivanoe Bonomi, *From Socialism to Fascism* (London, 1924); G. A. Borgese, *Goliath: The March of Fascism* (New York, 1937); and Luigi Sturzo, *Italy and Fascism* (New York, 1967); all examine the roots of Fascism and the events leading up to and following Mussolini's seizure of power. More recent interpretations include Michael Ledeen, *The First Duce: D'Annunzio at Fiume* (Baltimore, 1977); James A. Gregor, *Young Mussolini and the Intellectual Origins of Fascism* (Berkeley, 1979); Adrian Lyttleton, *The Seizure of Power: Fascism in Italy, 1919–1929* (New York, 1973). Historians who have investigated the growth and influence of agrarian Fascism include Frank Snowden, *Violence and Great Estates in the South of Italy* (Cambridge, 1986); Alice Kelikian, *Town and Country under Fascism: The Transformation of Brescia, 1915–1926* (Oxford, 1986); Anthony Cardoza, *Agrarian Elites and Italian Fascism* (Princeton, 1982).

Among the early works on Mussolini's regime are Gaudens Megaro, *Mussolini in the Making* (Boston, 1938); Gaetano Salvemini, *The Fascist Dicta-*

torship in Italy (London, 1928) and *Under the Axe of Fascism* (New York, 1936); Carl T. Schmidt, *The Plough and the Sword* (New York, 1938) and *Italy under Fascism* (New York, 1939). In the postwar era, studies of Mussolini and the Fascist era proliferated. Among them is Giampiero Carocci, trans. Isabel Quigly, *Italian Fascism* (Harmondsworth, 1974). A number of historians have examined Fascist economic policy and the corporate state. Included is Roland Sarti, *Fascism and the Industrial Leadership in Italy, 1919–1940* (Berkeley, 1971).

Recent biographical studies include Richard Lyttle, *Il Duce* (New York, 1987). R. J. B. Bosworth has reexamined Mussolini and his regime in *The Italian Dictatorship: Problems and Perspectives in the Interpretations of Mussolini and Fascism* (London, 1998). In addition to Lyttleton's *The Seizure of Power,* a number of other authors have studied Mussolini's consolidation of power. Included is Doug Thompson, *State Control in Fascist Italy: Culture and Conformity* (Manchester, 1991). Other notable biographical studies of the Fascist era include Claudio Segrè, *Italo Balbo: A Fascist Life* (Berkeley, 1987); Harry Fornari, *Mussolini's Gadfly: Roberto Farinacci* (Nashville, 1971); and the study of Margherita Sarfatti by Philip V. Cannistraro and Brian Sullivan, *Il Duce's Other Woman* (New York, 1993).

Among the works on Fascist culture, including ideology, propaganda, and formal and mass culture, are the following: Zeev Sternhell, Mario Sznajder, and Maia Asheri, *The Birth of Fascist Ideology: From Cultural Rebellion to Political Revolution* (Princeton, 1994); Victoria De Grazia, *The Culture of Consent* (New York, 1981); Tracy Koon, *Believe, Obey, Fight: Political Socialization of Youth in Fascist Italy, 1922–1943* (Chapel Hill, 1985). Specialized topics in the cultural history of Fascism include Luisa Passerini, *Fascism in Popular Memory: The Cultural Experience of the Turin Working Class* (Cambridge, 1987); Victoria De Grazia, *How Fascism Ruled Women* (Berkeley, 1992); Perry R. Willson, *The Clockwork Factory: Women and Work in Fascist Italy* (New York, 1994); Marcia Landy, *Fascism on Film* (Princeton, 1986); James Hay, *Popular Film Culture in Fascist Italy* (Bloomington, 1987); Diane Yvonne Ghirardo, *Architecture and the State: Fascist Italy and New Deal America* (Stanford, 1983); Ellen R. Shapiro, *Building under Mussolini* (New Haven, 1985).

On Fascist diplomacy, Alan Cassels, ed., *Italian Foreign Policy, 1918–1945: A Guide to Research and Research Materials* (Wilmington, 1981), provides not only a guide to archives but an annotated bibliography.

A number of scholars have studied the lives of Italian Jews during the Fascist era. Among them are H. Stuart Hughes, *Prisoners of Hope: The Silver Age of Italian Jews, 1924–1974* (Cambridge, 1983); Susan Zuccotti, *The Italians and the Holocaust: Persecution, Rescue and Survival* (Lincoln, 1987); Ivo

Herzer, *The Italian Refuge* (Washington, D.C., 1989); Meir Michaelis, *Mussolini and the Jews: German-Italian Relations and the Jewish Question in Italy* (Oxford, 1978); Alexander Stille, *Benevolence and Betrayal: Five Italian Jewish Families under Fascism* (New York, 1991); Daniel Carpi, *Between Mussolini and Hitler* (Hanover, 1994).

On the relationship between the Roman Catholic Church and the Fascist state, see John F. Pollard, *The Vatican and Italian Fascism, 1929–1932* (Cambridge, 1985); Peter Kent, *The Pope and the Duce: The International Impact of the Lateran Agreements* (New York, 1981); Richard Webster, *The Cross and the Fasces* (Stanford, 1960); Anthony Rhodes, *The Vatican in the Age of Dictators* (London, 1973).

Sources on World War II and the wartime era in Italy include a number of memoirs, most in Italian. In English, see Pietro Badoglio, *Italy in the Second World War* (London, 1948). Among the best studies of the war is MacGregor Knox, *Mussolini Unleashed, 1939–1941* (Cambridge, 1980). On Mussolini's relationship with Hitler, see F. W. Deakin, *The Brutal Friendship: Mussolini, Hitler and the Fall of Italian Fascism* (London, 1962); Dino Alfieri, *Dictators Face to Face* (New York, 1955); Friedrich-Karl von Plehwe, *The End of an Alliance: Rome's Defection from the Axis in 1943* (London, 1971). Other histories of the period include Norman Kogan, *Italy and the Allies* (Cambridge, 1956); Alexander S. Cochran, *Spectre of Defeat: Anglo-American Planning for the Invasion of Italy in 1943* (Lawrence, 1985); John Ellis, *Cassino, The Hollow Victory* (New York, 1984).

On the various events relating to the resistance movement and the fall of the Fascist regime, see David Ellwood, *Italy, 1943–1945* (Leicester, 1985); Stuart Woolf, *The Rebirth of Italy, 1943–1950* (London, 1972); Charles Delzell, *Mussolini's Enemies: The Italian Anti-Fascist Resistance* (New York, 1974); Frank Rosengarten, *Silvio Trentin* (Milan, 1980); Stanislao Pugliese, *Carlo Rosselli: Socialist Heretic & Antifascist Exile* (Cambridge, Mass., 1999); Charles Killinger, *Gaetano Salvemini: A Biography* (Westport, 2002).

CHAPTER 10

The history of the postwar era is understandably incomplete, but historians have offered a number of useful books in English. Bibliographies include Roland Sarti, *A Select Bibliography of English-Language Books on Modern Italian History* (Amherst, 1989), and Peter Lange, *Studies on Italy, 1943–1975* (Turin, 1977). An excellent recent anthology is Patrick McCarthy, ed., *Italy since 1945* (Oxford, 2000.)

A number of good political histories exist. Douglas Day, *The Shaping of Postwar Italian Politics: Italy 1945–1948* (Chicago, 1982), assesses the formative years of the Republic, as does Frank Coppa and Margherita Repetto-Alaia, *The Formation of the Italian Republic* (New York, 1993). Among the more broadly based studies are Frederic Spotts and Theodor Wieser, *Italy: A Difficult Democracy: A Survey of Italian Politics* (Cambridge, 1986); Donald Sassoon, *Contemporary Italy: Politics, Economy, and Society since 1945* (London, 1986); Joseph La Palombara, *Democracy Italian Style* (New Haven, 1987); Robert Leonardi and Raffaella Nanetti, *Italian Politics: A Review, Vol. I* (London, 1986); Stephen Hellman and Gianfranco Pasquino, eds., *Italian Politics: A Review* (Kent, 1992); Robert D. Putnam, *Making Democracy Work: Civic Traditions in Modern Italy* (Princeton, 1993).

Among the more recent works examining the phenomenon of the "second republic" are Patrick McCarthy, *The Crisis of the Italian State* (New York, 1995); Carol Mershon and Gianfranco Pasquino, eds., *Italian Politics: Ending the First Republic* (Boulder, 1994); P. Furlong, *Modern Italy: Representation and Reform* (London, 1994); Mark Gilbert, *The Italian Revolution: The End of Politics, Italian Style?* (Boulder, 1995); Stephen Gundle and Simon Parker, eds., *The New Italian Republic: From the Fall of the Berlin Wall to Berlusconi* (London, 1996); Vittorio Bufacchi and Simon Burgess, *Italy since 1989: Events and Interpretations* (New York, 2001).

A number of books focus on Italian political parties. See Spencer M. Di Scala, *Renewing Italian Socialism: Nenni to Craxi* (New York, 1988) and *Italian Socialism: Between Politics and History* (Amherst, 1996); Leonard Swindler and Edward James Grace, eds., *Catholic-Communist Collaboration in Italy* (Lanham, 1988); Rosanna Mulazzi Giammanco, *The Communist-Catholic Dialogue in Italy* (New York, 1989).

Several historians have assessed political disorder in Italy. Included are Sidney Tarrow, *Democracy and Disorder: Protest and Politics in Italy, 1965–1975* (New York, 1989); Richard Drake, *The Revolutionary Mystique and Terrorism in Contemporary Italy* (Bloomington, 1989); Robert C. Meade, *Red Brigades: The Story of Italian Terrorism* (New York, 1990) and *The Aldo Moro Murder Case* (Cambridge, Mass., 1995); Robert Lumley, *States of Emergency: Cultures in Revolt in Italy, 1968–1977* (London, 1990); P. Willan, *Puppet Masters: The Political Use of Terrorism in Italy* (London, 1991).

An array of books have addressed Italy's postwar foreign policy. On U.S. policy toward Italy, the best sources are James E. Miller, *The United States and Italy, 1940–1950* (Chapel Hill, 1986); Emory Timothy Smith, *The United States, Italy, and NATO: American Policy Towards Italy, 1948–1952* (Kent, Ohio, 1982); and John L. Harper, *America and the Reconstruction of Italy* (Cambridge, 1986).

Among the histories of economic issues, see the following: Muriel Grindrod, *The Rebuilding of Italy* (London, 1955); Joseph La Palombara, *It-*

aly: The Politics of Planning (Syracuse, 1966) and *The Italian Labor Movement* (Ithaca, 1957). On the economy for the thirty years after World War II, see Chiarella Esposito, *America's Feeble Weapon: Funding the Marshall Plan in France and Italy, 1948–1950* (Westport, 1994); Raffaella Nanetti, *Growth and Territorial Politics: The Italian Model of Social Capitalism* (London, 1988).

CHAPTER 11

Still the best work on recent Italian society is Paul Ginsborg, *A History of Contemporary Italy, 1943–1988* (London, 1990). A number of histories have addressed women's issues. See, for example, Lucia Chiavola Birnbaum, *Liberazione della donna: Feminism in Italy* (Middletown, 1986); Maria Cicioni and Nicolle Prunster, *Visions and Revisions: Women and Italian Culture* (Providence and Oxford, 1993); Judith Adler Hellman, *Journeys among Women: Feminism in Five Italian Cities* (New York, 1988); Giuliana Bruno and Maria Nadotti, eds., *Off Screen: Women and Film in Italy* (London, 1988). See also Norberto Bobbio's classic *Ideological Profile of Twentieth-Century Italy* (Munich, 1989); Christopher Duggan and Christopher Wagstaff, eds., *Italy in the Cold War: Politics, Culture, and Society, 1948–1958* (Oxford, 1995); and David Forgacs, *Italian Culture in the Postwar Era: 1910–1980* (Manchester, 1990).

Historical studies of the postwar South include Judith Chubb, *Patronage, Power and Poverty in Southern Italy* (Cambridge, 1982). On the *mafia,* see Pino Arlacchi, *Men of Dishonor: Inside the Sicilian Mafia* (New York, 1993); Diego Gambetta, *The Sicilian Mafia: The Business of Private Protection* (Cambridge, Mass., 1993); M. Padovani, *Men of Honour: The Truth about the Mafia* (London, 1992).

Much of the literature on postwar Italian popular culture remains untranslated. In English, see Zygmunt Baranski and Robert Lumley, eds., *Culture and Conflict in Postwar Italy* (London, 1990). Among other works on popular culture with Italian references, see John M. Hoberman, *Sport and Political Ideology* (Austin, 1984); Ian Chambers, *Popular Culture: The Metropolitan Experience* (London, 1986); David Ellwood, *Rebuilding Europe* (London, 1992).

Works on the formal arts in the postwar era are more abundant in Italian than English. Among the English-language works on the rich Italian postwar cinema, see Peter Bondanella, *Italian Cinema from Neorealism to the Present* (New York, 1983); Millicent Marcus, *Italian Film in the Light of Neorealism* (Princeton, 1986); Mira Liehm, *Passion and Defiance: Film in Italy from 1942 to the Present* (Berkeley, 1984); Angela Dalle Vacche, *The Body in the Mirror: Shapes of History in Italian Cinema* (Princeton, 1992); John J. Michalczyk, *The*

Italian Political Filmmakers (London, 1986); Pierre Sorlin, *Italian National Cinema* (London, 1996).

Michael Caesar and Peter Hainsworth, eds., *Writers and Society in Contemporary Italy: A Collection of Essays* (New York, 1984), examines Italian literature in general, while Zygmunt Baranski and Linor Pertile have edited *The New Italian Novel* (Edinburgh, 1996). See also Lauren Mueller, *Semiotics in Italy: Cesare Segre, Gianfranco Bettetini, Pier Paolo Pasolini, Emilio Garroni* (Lafayette, 1982). Thomas Peterson assesses Pasolini's life and works in *The Poetics and Poetry of Pier Pasolini* (Providence, 1986). A recent study of women writers is Santo Aricò, *Contemporary Women Writers in Italy: A Modern Renaissance* (Amherst, 1990). Biographies of poets include Frederic J. Jones, *Giuseppe Ungaretti: Poet and Critic* (Edinburgh, 1977); Rebecca J. West, *Eugenio Montale: Poet on the Edge* (Cambridge, 1981).

Index

About the Author

CHARLES L. KILLINGER is Professor of History at Valencia Community College and Adjunct Professor at the University of Central Florida where he teaches Italian history. He is the author of *Rebel in Two Worlds: Gaetano Salvemini in Italy and America* (Praeger, 2002).

**Other Titles in the
Greenwood Histories of the Modern Nations**

Frank W. Thackeray and John E. Findling, Series Editors

The History of Argentina
Daniel K. Lewis

The History of Australia
Frank G. Clarke

The History of Brazil
Robert M. Levine

The History of Canada
Scott W. See

The History of China
David C. Wright

The History of France
W. Scott Haine

The History of Germany
Eleanor L. Turk

The History of Holland
Mark T. Hooker

The History of India
John McLeod

The History of Iran
Elton L. Daniel

The History of Ireland
Daniel Webster Hollis III

The History of Israel
Arnold Blumberg

The History of Japan
Louis G. Perez

The History of Mexico
Burton Kirkwood

The History of Nigeria
Toyin Falola

The History of Poland
M.B. Biskupski

The History of Portugal
James M. Anderson

The History of Russia
Charles E. Ziegler

The History of Serbia
John K. Cox

The History of South Africa
Roger B. Beck

The History of Spain
Peter Pierson

The History of Sweden
Byron J. Nordstrom

The History of Turkey
Douglas A. Howard